History, Historians and the Immigration Debate

"People have been on the move, voluntarily and involuntarily, permanently and temporarily, successfully and less successfully, continuously in the modern era. Their stories and experiences make up modern migration as we know it. But this phenomenon is hard to understand without using a robust historic lens—which is what the authors in this excellent volume have done. The result is an impressive array of studies that serve to focus that lens on many key ideas and debates in migration studies. It is an authoritative and timely volume that expands inter-disciplinary knowledge about migration in a way that benefits all researchers and interested readers."
> —Shamit Saggar, Professor of Political Science and Public Policy, University of Essex, UK, and former Senior Advisor, UK Prime Minister's Strategy Unit

"This wide-ranging volume shows how vital it is to contextualise contemporary debates about migration through an historical lens. The research shared within these diverse chapters informs our work presenting migration heritage to the public."
> —Sophie Henderson, Director of the Migration Museum Project, UK

"This important collection asks academics to urgently address the major questions of our time, using history as a 'martial art' in which to fight the social and political battles inherent in immigration debates."
> —Jayne Persian, Lecturer in History, University of Southern Queensland, Australia, and Author of *Beautiful Balts: From Displaced Persons to New Australians* (2017)

"This timely and provocative collection of essays illustrates how historians are uniquely placed to contribute in a meaningful and informed way to the polarizing debate over immigration and migration. Migrant peoples, as this book demonstrates, are far from anomalous or marginal; rather, they have long enriched and formed an essential part of the creative dynamic in their adopted communities."
> —David Wright, Professor of History, McGill University, Montreal, Canada, and co-editor of *Doctors Beyond Borders: The Transnational Migration of Physicians in the Twentieth Century* (2016)

Eureka Henrich · Julian M. Simpson
Editors

History, Historians and the Immigration Debate

Going Back to Where We Came From

Editors
Eureka Henrich
School of Humanities
University of Hertfordshire
Hatfield, Hertfordshire, UK

Julian M. Simpson
Independent Scholar
Lancaster, Lancashire, UK

ISBN 978-3-319-97122-3 ISBN 978-3-319-97123-0 (eBook)
https://doi.org/10.1007/978-3-319-97123-0

Library of Congress Control Number: 2018949696

This Palgrave Macmillan imprint is published by the registered company Springer Nature Switzerland AG
The registered company address is: Gewerbestrasse 11, 6330 Cham, Switzerland

ACKNOWLEDGEMENTS

This volume originated in a symposium at King's College London in June 2014, called 'Immigration, Nation and Public History'. The event was made possible by the Menzies Centre for Australian Studies through the Rydon Fellowship in Australian Politics and Political History, which Eureka Henrich held that year. Eureka would like to thank the staff of the Arts and Humanities Research Institute for making the day a success, and her colleagues at the Menzies Centre for their ongoing intellectual camaraderie and support. She is grateful to the historians, museum workers, sociologists and geographers who came together to share their work and kick-start a conversation about how immigration history is represented outside the academy, and particularly to Julian M. Simpson for agreeing to come on board and work together as editors on this volume.

Together we would like to thank our editorial team at Palgrave Macmillan, especially Jade Moulds, Peter Carey, Oliver Dyer and Molly Beck, for their enthusiasm for the ideas behind the volume and their professionalism during the publication process.

The chapter by Gérard Noiriel was first published in German as 'Die Rolle der Einwanderung bei der De-/Konstruktion der Arbeiterklasse in Frankreich (19.-20. Jahrhundert),' in Alexander Mejstrik, Thomas Hübel, Sigrid Wadauer, eds., *Die Krise des Sozialstaats und die Intellektuellen* (Frankfurt: Campus, 2012). It appears here in Julian M. Simpson's translation of Noiriel's original French text. We are very grateful to Florence Tamagne and Béatrice Murail who made the time to comment on the first draft of the English version.

Last, but certainly not least, we would like to heartily thank all of the contributors who agreed to write for this volume and work with us to bring a historical perspective into the global migration debate. From recent Ph.D. graduates to leaders in the field of migration history, they have worked hard to deliver chapters which reveal historical understandings and speak to contemporary concerns. Their work demonstrates that lively, complex histories of human mobility warrant a wide readership.

CONTENTS

NOTES ON CONTRIBUTORS

Lyndon Fraser is a professional historian who works at the University of Canterbury in Christchurch, New Zealand, and as a Research Fellow in Human History at the Canterbury Museum. His most recent books include *Rushing for Gold: Life and Commerce on the Goldfields of New Zealand and Australia* (Otago University Press, 2016, co-edited with Lloyd Carpenter) and *History Making a Difference: New Approaches from Aotearoa* (Cambridge Scholars, 2017, co-edited with Katie Pickles, Marguerite Hill, Sarah Murray and Greg Ryan).

Donna Gabaccia is Professor of History at the University of Toronto and past Director of the Immigration History Research Center at the University of Minnesota. She is the author of 14 books and dozens of articles on immigrant class, gender and food studies in the United States, on Italian migration around the world, and on migration in world history. Her 2015 book *Gender and International Migration*, co-authored with sociologist and demographer Katharine Donato, was awarded an Honourable Mention from the American Sociological Association's Znaniecki Prize.

Eureka Henrich is a Research Fellow in Conflict, Memory and Legacy at the University of Hertfordshire and an Honorary Associate of the Menzies Centre for Australian Studies, King's College London. Her work explores histories of migration, health, heritage and memory in Australian and transnational contexts. Her publications include 'Museums, History and Migration in Australia', *History Compass* 11/10

(2013): 783–800, and 'Mobility, Migration and Modern Memory' in *The Past in the Present: History, Memory and Public Life* (Routledge, 2018).

Leo Lucassen is Director of Research of the International Institute of Social History in Amsterdam and Professor of Global Labour and Migration History at the University of Leiden. He has published extensively on migration, integration, social policies and urban history.

Klaus Neumann is a senior research fellow with the Hamburger Stiftung zur Förderung von Wissenschaft und Kultur. He is the author of articles and books about public and policy responses to asylum seekers and refugees, including the award-winning *Refuge Australia* (2004) and *Across the Seas* (2015).

Gérard Noiriel is Director of Studies at the EHESS in Paris, France. His research interests are focused on the socio-history of the nation-state and immigration. He is the author of numerous works on the history of migration including *The French Melting Pot: Immigration, Citizenship and National Identity* (Minneapolis: University of Minnesota Press, 1996).

Anindya Raychaudhuri is a Lecturer in English at the University of St Andrews. His primary research interest is in the cultural representation and collective memory of war and conflict. He is also interested in postcolonial and diasporic identities and cultures. He edited *The Spanish Civil War: Exhuming a Buried Past* (University of Wales Press, 2013), and is the author of two forthcoming monographs: *Narrating Partition: Agency, Memory, Representation* (Oxford University Press) and *Homemaking: Postcolonial Nostalgia and the Construction of a South Asian Diaspora* (Rowman & Littlefield). In 2016, he was named one of the BBC Radio 3/AHRC New Generation Thinkers.

Mina Roces is a Professor of History in the School of Humanities and Languages, University of New South Wales, Sydney, Australia. She is the author of three major monographs: *Women, Power and Kinship Politics: Female Power in Post-War Philippines* (Praeger, 1998), *Kinship Politics in Post-War Philippines: The Lopez Family, 1946–2000* (de la Salle University Press, 2001) and *Women's Movements and the Filipina, 1986–2008* (University of Hawaii Press, 2012). In addition, she has co-edited five volumes on the topic of women in Asia and one on Asian women and migration. She is currently completing a book tentatively entitled *The Filipino Migration Experience, 1906–2015*.

Julian M. Simpson is an Independent Researcher and writer based in the North of England. He has published widely on the history of migration and the relationship between history and policy. He is the author of *Migrant Architects of the NHS: South Asian Doctors and the Reinvention of British General Practice (1940s–1980s)* (Manchester: Manchester University Press, 2018).

John Solomon is an Assistant Professor of History at the National University of Singapore, with research interests in diaspora and migration studies, nationalism, transnational identities, and race and identity in South and South East Asia. He received his Ph.D. from the University of New South Wales, Sydney, Australia.

Margaretha A. van Es is a social historian and religious studies scholar. Having obtained her Ph.D. from the University of Oslo, Norway, she currently works as a postdoctoral researcher at the Department of Philosophy and Religious Studies at Utrecht University, the Netherlands. Her book *Stereotypes and Self-Representations of Women with a Muslim Background: The Stigma of Being Oppressed* was published in December 2016 with Palgrave Macmillan.

LIST OF TABLES

CHAPTER 1

Introduction: History as a 'Martial Art'

Eureka Henrich and Julian M. Simpson

The global 'immigration debate' that has become so central to political life largely involves rehearsing false dichotomies:

Are you 'for' or 'against' immigration?
Do immigrants represent a threat to national identity or a welcome addition to the cultural mix?
Are citizens' jobs, housing, and welfare at risk because of 'new people' or do migrants' labour and spending boost the economy?
Should governments do more to restrict the entry of refugees, or do they have a duty to offer sanctuary?

Those who are 'for' immigration praise the cultural contributions of migrants, arguing that they enrich what would, in their view, otherwise be a bland, mono-cultural society. Those 'against' mourn the gradual loss of supposedly home-grown traditions and values; they long for a past perceived as less complex and threatening to identities. Advocates of immigration point to the economic success of many

E. Henrich (✉)
School of Humanities, University of Hertfordshire, Hatfield, Hertfordshire, UK

J. M. Simpson
Lancaster, Lancashire, UK

E. Henrich and J. M. Simpson (eds.),
History, Historians and the Immigration Debate,
https://doi.org/10.1007/978-3-319-97123-0_1

1

migrants, underscoring the social benefits of the skills and labour they bring. Critics express concern over limited funds and pressure on public services. And then there's the question of people seeking asylum. Some commentators favour a humanitarian response, arguing that resettled refugees become hard-working citizens and that societies should be judged by the way they treat their most vulnerable members. The alternative view is that hardline border policies are needed in the face of widespread abuse of laws aimed at protecting those facing persecution.

These questions frame a public discourse on immigration that is all too often about 'us' and 'them', sedentary citizens and rootless foreigners, or about the potential breaching of the 'sovereign borders' of nations whose own pasts of movement, emigration and conquest are conveniently forgotten. They also elide the real complexities behind these questions. Arguments around the pressures migration places on public services take little account of the roles immigrants have played in staffing public sector bodies. Asylum systems can both offer protection to survivors of persecution and be used by economic migrants to gain entry into a country. For that matter, there are no clear dividing lines between different types of migration.[1] Scholarly history's ability to embrace contradiction and inconvenient truths has the potential to make a significant contribution in this area.

However, debaters on both sides of the 'immigration question' don't just currently ignore migration's past in all its complexity. They, in fact, invent pasts to suit their current political or ideological purposes. On the one hand, immigrant founders or innovators are lauded as national heroes, when in reality, their trajectories tell us little about the realities of the lives of most migrants. On the other hand, we hear sometimes apocalyptical warnings against current migrant intakes by those who talk of historical periods with lower, more 'sustainable' numbers—when, as Donna Gabaccia notes in this volume, the global proportion of people living outside the countries where they were born has remained stable at just over 3% since the 1960s and may be slightly lower than it was a century ago. The stories told about the past fulfil a contemporary function—to bolster entrenched ideological positions and heighten their emotional resonance. Mobilising the past in these ways may make good political sense, but it does not promote good historical understanding nor does it contribute to informed public debate and policy-making.

This book is a response to the binary thinking and misuse of the past that characterise contemporary immigration debates. It argues that history, and historians, are uniquely placed to contribute to the discussion, and demonstrates the potential of doing so with chapters from scholars in the UK, Asia, Continental Europe, Australasia and North America. Through their work on global, transnational and national histories of migration, an alternative view emerges—one that complicates the entrenched lines of immigration debates and reasserts movement as a central dimension of the human condition. Millennia of human journeys are 'forgotten' in political debates—including those of immigrants, emigrants, sojourners, settlers, workers, colonisers, convicts, enslaved peoples and other forced migrants. Recovering the historical complexity and diversity of migration histories can provide a vital perspective on migration for our times. This book also makes a case for historians to more confidently assert themselves as expert commentators. It features chapters that reflect on how we write migration history today, and how we might do so in the future.

Our ultimate goal—to link scholarly understanding of migration history to current debates—is ambitious and optimistic, and unapologetically so. It has been inspired by a tradition of historical scholarship that takes the view that connecting academic research to contemporary debates forms an essential part of a scholar's remit. The US historian Theodore Roszak, writing in the 1960s, condemned academia's disengagement from wider social concerns as an 'act of criminal delinquency'.[2] In the same collection of *Essays criticizing the teaching of the humanities in American universities*, Staughton Lynd explained how his sense that history had to engage with the present world was the product of his experience of teaching black female students at the time of the US civil rights movement.[3] Historians have much to contribute to the debate on immigration at a time when immigration policy and identity politics are having such a profound effect on so many lives. In this context, it seems vital that we attempt to make our voices heard. In the words of the French sociologist Pierre Bourdieu:

> In Europe, at least, we are, as Edmund Husserl used to say, 'humanity's civil servants', paid by the government to make discoveries, either about the natural world or about the social world. It seems to me that part of our responsibility is to share what we have found.[4]

This quote is taken from *Sociology is a Martial Art*—a collection of Bourdieu's writings whose title was borrowed from a film about him called *La sociologie est un sport de combat*. The original French perhaps gives a better idea of the type of thinking that underpins our book. A *'sport de combat'* is a combat sport; it can indeed literally be a martial art, but the expression also hints at other battles to be fought, of a social and political nature, to which an academic discipline such as sociology can contribute. As Bourdieu put it in Pierre Carles' documentary, it can be a form of self-defence.[5] But this is to do with self-defence in a social and political context. It is in this sense that we use history here— not as a didactic tool deployed to enlighten the masses but as a political instrument that can inform, illuminate and encourage different types of thinking beyond the limited realm of academic research. It is a form of defence against the poverty of much contemporary discussion of issues around immigration.

If connecting scholarly research to public debates was simply a question of making information available, a selection of articles and book extracts taken from scholarly journals and the output of academic presses might have sufficed. However, the conventions of academic writing do not make such a task straightforward. Scholarly credibility is the main criterion for publication, sometimes at the cost of intelligibility: jargon is tolerated and a great deal of knowledge is assumed. Academia has its own internal reference points and debates which readers need to be familiar with in scholarly contexts. These are often of little interest to those looking for insights into wider social questions. There is a long-standing disconnect between the concerns of academia and the major questions of our time. It seems to us that it is urgent to address this issue and offer a response to the rhetorical questions asked by Roszak when, fifty years ago, he diagnosed a dysfunction at the heart of scholarly endeavour that is still in evidence today:

> The training of apprentice scholars and the pursuit of research – as these activities are presently handled – result in a great deal of mindless specialisation and irrelevant pedantry that ought not to be credited with intellectual respectability...Is it more 'knowledge' of this surplus kind, expertly gleaned by precise techniques, that we really require? Or, in the protracted emergency in which our civilisation finds itself, should our highest priority be placed on a scholar's ability to link his special knowledge or moral insight to our social needs?[6]

As well as contributing to debates about migration and the relationship between history and policy, we are therefore also engaging here in a broader conversation about the future of academic research and its audiences.

This is about content but also about form. There would be little point in seeking to reconnect scholarly work to social interrogations if the insights generated were not to be widely disseminated. As Angelika Bammer and Ruth-Ellen Boetcher Joeres argue in the introduction to their collection of essays *The future of scholarly writing*, the 'problem of communication' associated with academic work is a threat to its effectiveness and indicative of a 'writing "crisis"' in a context where 'established forms of scholarly presentation (the conventional monograph or peer-reviewed article) are no longer adequate to the needs of the contemporary academy, much less those of the world beyond it'.[7] In attempting to bring historical knowledge into the public debate on immigration, we have endeavoured to produce a book that speaks to social concerns and addresses at least some of the questions posed by this 'crisis'.

New forms of communication cannot be expected to emerge fully formed overnight, not least because the way people absorb information in the twenty-first century is constantly changing. The approach used here is necessarily experimental. As editors, we have sought to offer a way forward by encouraging researchers to think about the relationship of their work to contemporary policy debates and to write in a way that makes their thinking accessible to a non-specialist readership. This approach is distinct from traditional academic writing, in that the focus is no longer exclusively on the relationship between the findings of the research and established understanding. It is also at variance with other forms of writing that are not grounded in scholarly research and reflection. We are grateful to the academic historians who have agreed to contribute to this volume and have been open to working in a way that seeks to bridge the traditional divide between the scholarly and the public realms. We have also added editors' introductions to each section to guide readers through the book, highlight the policy relevance of the contributions and provide a thread of continuity which explains how the individual chapters all contribute to a greater whole.

We feel that this exercise has shown how much each of these often-separate spheres can contribute to the other. This book is for scholars interested in new ways of conceiving of their research agendas and communicating their work. It is for a general readership open to reflecting on how research into the past might help reshape our understanding of the present. It seeks to point the way to a more fruitful debate between scholars, policy-makers and the general public. The different chapters show that be it within national contexts in Europe, Asia or North America, or indeed at a global level, history has a major role to play: it can be a 'martial art', taking its place in political and social struggles surrounding immigration policy. By making these connections, we can also enrich scholarship by formulating new questions. In other words, this task is not solely about transferring knowledge from scholarship to the wider public sphere, it is also about encouraging historians to ask different questions of the past, in light of the challenges of the present.

BOOK STRUCTURE: GOING BACK TO WHERE WE CAME FROM

History, Historians and the Immigration Debate is structured geographically, with three central sections on Australia and New Zealand, Asia and Europe. Two additional sections bookend these case studies. The first addresses the profession of history, the role migration history plays within it and the choices historians make when framing their research. The last takes a step back to consider migration globally. The aim is to offer a global perspective on the relevance of migration history and its future. Naturally, it would be absurd to claim to provide an exhaustive perspective on such a topic. Future interventions from scholars working on Africa and Latin America would, for instance, be very welcome. What we offer here is a first step towards a global conversation on this topic.

A guiding idea throughout the writing and editing process has been to interrogate and subvert that most typical of injunctions directed at migrants: to 'go back to where you came from'. The notion that a person 'comes from' a single place, and therefore is 'out of place' when encountered elsewhere, is grounded in perceptions of race, nation and locality which are constructed and historically contingent. To reveal these contingencies, the historians featured here 'go back' chronologically and present evidence of human mobility which challenges, surprises or shifts perceptions of what is 'new' or 'natural' about migration. Their chapters further academic scholarship while informing debates about immigration and identity within their own national and regional contexts. The question of 'where we come from' has also prompted us to reflect on our own professional identities as historians of migration, and to trace how migration history has developed in relation to the broader field of historical studies. This is a theme that is addressed by a number of our contributors, making *History, Historians and the Immigration Debate* a useful source for both the past and possible futures of migration history.

Part I of this book, 'Moving Migration History Forward', addresses the challenges involved in trying to carve out a role for history in the politics of migration. In Chapter 2, 'From the Margins of History to the Political Mainstream: Putting Migration History Centre Stage', we begin by taking stock of the history of our own field, and of recent articulations of the immigration debate across the globe. Although different in context and detail, the politics of migration in countries including France, Germany, the USA, the UK, South Africa and Australia has in recent years been reinvigorated by popular nativist anti-immigration movements, and in some cases widespread protest against them. We argue that the expertise of historians has become sidelined in these popular discourses, partly as a product of a sub-discipline which has developed as an adjunct to, rather than as a central part of, the histories of nations and their politics. A move from the margins to the mainstream will involve reconnecting with a long tradition in our profession—reflecting on the past in order to inform the present. Leo Lucassen takes up these themes in Chapter 3, 'Beyond the Apocalypse: Reframing Migration History'. Migration scholars have a powerful opportunity to challenge narrow representations of 'migrants as trouble' in the media, politics and public discourse, but as Lucassen points out, uncritically reproducing or responding to that frame of reference can stymie any effective engagement. The 'cross-cultural migration rate (CCMR) approach' Lucassen advocates replaces the crisis of cross-border 'migration' with the phenomenon of 'human mobility' and shows how it has been a historical force for cultural and social change. As he argues, it is by changing the vantage point and therefore the terms of the debate that historians can 'use the full potential of their discipline and leave the imposed, but also self-chosen, ghetto'.

Part II features chapters on Australia and New Zealand, countries forged through settler colonialism which today proclaim themselves as modern, migrant nations with deep indigenous histories. In Chapter 4, 'Both Sides of the Tasman: History, Politics and Migration Between New Zealand and Australia', Lyndon Fraser shifts the familiar narrative of old-world to new-world migration by tracing the centuries of mobility between these two 'new worlds' across the Tasman Sea (reconfigured as the 'trans-Tasman highway'). This shared migration history is easily obscured by entrenched national narratives, and as Fraser argues, rarely finds public expression beyond the commemoration of joint military endeavours. The policy implications of recognising these historical connections are potentially transformative and offer crucial perspective to current political issues including social services reciprocation and deportation. If immigration debates too often assume the novelty of migration, in doing so they also elide the ability of migrants to be agents of their own future. In Chapter 5, 'Changing Migration Policy from the Margins: Filipino Activism on Behalf of Victims of Domestic Violence in Australia, 1980s–2000', Mina Roces traces a remarkable and largely unknown episode in Australia's migration history, where Filipina activists successfully campaigned for reforms to federal immigration law to protect the rights of marriage migrants who, post-arrival, became victims of domestic abuse by their Australian spouses. These events occurred during the golden age of Australian multiculturalism in the 1980s and 1990s, where a policy environment concerned with equality and access meant the work of ethnic minority organisations found mainstream government support. As Roces argues, this case study sets a 'powerful and optimistic precedent for the possibilities of migrant collaborations with the states of their host countries'. It also shows how migration histories can prove useful for the contemporary 'mainstream', as Australian authorities struggle to gather data to address the complexities of family, domestic and sexual violence that persist across all socio-economic and demographic groups.[8]

Part III turns to the Asian region, and to the role migration has played in the post-colonial nation-building narratives of India, Pakistan and Singapore. In Chapter 6, 'Not Singaporean Enough? Migration, History and National Identity in Singapore', John Solomon examines how migration in Singapore's history has been understood by both scholars and the public, with a focus on museum representations. Ethnic pluralism, multiculturalism or multiracialism (as it is variously described) has been part of the national framework in Singapore since independence in 1959, enshrined in the Chinese-Malay-Indian-Other model. But as Solomon argues, it is a selective history of immigration that is mobilised by the government in narrating the story of the nation, and historians have unwittingly supported such notions by largely neglecting migration to the country after the 1960s. Immigration debates in Singapore have in recent years seen a strong public backlash against government policies to increase immigration rates and create simpler paths to citizenship. There is an opportunity here, in Solomon's words, for 'new approaches to history' that can 'create space for the emergence of more inclusive understandings of national identity'. Chapter 7, '"They Don't Call Us Indian": Indian Muslim Voices and the 1947 India/Pakistan Partition', also traces identity narratives linked to independence from colonial rule, and how they have been represented in scholarship and public memory. The India/Pakistan partition of 1947 has been written and understood as a primarily migratory phenomenon, with millions finding themselves on the 'wrong' side of the newly created border and forced to flee. But as Anindya Raychaudhuri argues, this has created a shorthand for partition that entrenches simplistic notions of a Hindu India and a Muslim Pakistan, ignoring the experiences of those who decided *not* to migrate. Oral histories with Indian Muslims are thus an invaluable historical source, used by Raychaudhuri to complicate and nuance the picture and to question claims of a secular, postcolonial India. The recent 70th anniversary of Partition and the continuing memorialisation of the event are a salutary reminder of the need for scholarship that resists flattening complex histories into tidier storylines.

Part IV focuses on Europe, and begins with an essay by Gérard Noiriel, presented in Chapter 8 for the first time in English translation. Rather than a post-colonial phenomenon, migration—both within and across national borders—is an integral part of French history. Noiriel argues that if we wish to understand current rifts and divides within the working class, and the appeal of politicians who promote a xenophobic agenda, a longer historical perspective is essential. The detailed and clear analysis in 'The Role of Immigration in the Making/Unmaking of the French Working Class (Nineteenth and Twentieth Centuries)' is a powerful example of the value of historical inquiry in reframing politicised immigration discourses and informing understandings of contemporary issues, which in the case of France include social exclusion and urban violence. From class, we turn our attention to the other crucial category of historical analysis: gender. When it comes to public debates about rates of immigration and demographic change, migrant women often find themselves the reluctant subjects of projected anxieties about differences in culture and religion which stereotype them as submissive or oppressed. In Chapter 9, 'Was the Multiculturalism Backlash Good for Women with a Muslim Background? Perspectives from Five Minority Women's Organisations in the Netherlands', Margaretha A. van Es asks how women with a Muslim background experienced the negative turn of attitudes towards immigrant minorities, their cultures and religions in the past two decades. Van Es' observation that 'intense public debate about Muslim women's oppression has by no means always translated into substantial support for women in difficult situations' demonstrates the gap between rhetoric and reality that often exists when mainstream commentators voice concern about minority groups. Histories of the activism and involvement of migrant communities in Dutch society like van Es' can instead reveal the complex ramifications of political agendas on different groups, including Islamic feminists and women involved in secular organisations, and the agency of migrants which continues long after the news cycle moves on.

Part V offers global perspectives on migration history. In Chapter 10, 'Migrant Doctors and the "Frontiers of Medicine" in Westernized Healthcare Systems', Julian M. Simpson makes a case for a transnational approach to the migration of doctors. The labour of this migratory medical workforce has been essential to the functioning of a number of healthcare systems around the world, but previous scholarship on this phenomenon has tended to be ahistorical or framed within national narratives. Simpson argues that this topic can only be properly understood *across* borders and *throughout* history, and provides a model for understanding the professional impact of migrants over time. Such an approach can be instrumental in countering simplistic arguments which equate national identity, border control and the protection of jobs. In Simpson's words, 'by studying the history of migrants and work, we cast our gaze towards their interactions with the mainstream, rather than what defines them as outsiders'. The category of migrant that dominates today's migration controversies is the refugee or asylum seeker. In Chapter 11, Klaus Neumann demonstrates that the very concept of a right to grant or seek asylum has a complex and hidden international history. Taking Australia as a case study, Neumann traces the history of these ideas about asylum in public debate over the course of the twentieth century. When personal freedoms are at stake, an understanding of the genealogy of these legal instruments is crucial. Neumann's untangling of the use and misuse of the past in political debates about 'rights' starkly illustrates why policy understandings need to be informed by historical scholarship, rather than being based on the 'fickle emotion of compassion'. It also demonstrates the importance of history's 'dead ends', which 'allow us to imagine futures that are more than endlessly reproduced versions of the present'. This, ultimately, is where history and the work of historians can transform approaches to today's policy challenges. In the final chapter of the book, Chapter 12, Donna Gabaccia also looks to the future by way of the past to ask 'Will the Twenty-First Century World Embrace Immigration History?'. By tracing the origins of a proud and contested immigration historiography in the United States and contrasting it to the lack of such a tradition in Switzerland, a country with 'many foreigners, but few immigrants', Gabaccia reminds us that the projects of immigration history and nation-building are intertwined. The majority of the countries in the world have no field of 'immigration history', even though cross-border mobility may be a significant feature of their pasts and presents. Without the intention of turning foreign workers into citizens or subjects, there is no need for a national story of immigrant incorporation. The invisibility of migrants in the historiography and national mythology of countries like the United Arab Emirates, Qatar or Kuwait, who have some of the highest proportions of foreign-born residents, is a powerful example. Mobility does not promote the writing of immigration history, and its future beyond the handful of self-styled 'immigrant nations' is far from secure.

We are under no illusions that it will be straightforward to communicate an alternative message about migration by drawing on the past. Ultimately, however, a world such as ours, concerned as it is about migration, should really concern itself with migration history. The global immigration debate will remain ill-informed if it does not anchor itself in an understanding of our shared migratory past. This book is therefore a contribution towards a public and policy-relevant history of migration and an argument for placing migration history at the centre of the concerns of historians around the world. With the exception of a few countries, migration history remains a relatively marginal pursuit. The US historiographical model of the nation of immigrants is naturally not to be uncritically celebrated. The forced migration of African slaves has remained on the margins of this history which has also tended to privilege the Ellis Island story, giving a very partial view of who came to North America.[9] It is, however, a given that American history can only be understood in relation to migration history. Our aim here is to start a discussion about how migration history can become central to global history and help us rethink our current views of mobility.

NOTES

1. See, for instance, Christopher Kyriakides, 'Words don't come easy: Al Jazeera's migrant-refugee distinction and the European culture of (mis) trust,' *Current Sociology* 65, no. 7 (2017): 933–52.
2. Theodore Roszak, 'On academic delinquency,' in *The Dissenting Academy: Essays Criticising the Teaching of the Humanities in American Universities*, ed. Theodore Roszak (Harmondsworth: Penguin, 1969), 19.
3. Staughton Lynd, 'Historical past and existential present,' in ibid., 89–91.
4. Pierre Bourdieu, 'On Television,' in *Sociology is a Martial Art: Political Writings by Pierre Bourdieu*, Pierre Bourdieu, ed. Gisèle Shapiro (London and New York: The New Press, 2010).
5. Pierre Carles, *La sociologie est un sport de combat*, Documentary Film, C-P Productions, 2001.
6. Theodore Roszak, *The Dissenting Academy*, 38–39.
7. Angelika Bammer and Ruth-Ellen Boetcher Joeres, 'Introduction,' in *The Future of Scholarly Writing: Critical Interventions*, eds. Angelika Bammer and Ruth-Ellen Boetcher Joeres (New York: Palgrave Macmillan, 2015), 1–2.
8. Australian Institute of Health and Welfare, *Family, Domestic and Sexual Violence in Australia 2018* (Canberra: Australian Institute of Health and Welfare, 2018), ix. Available online, https://www.aihw.gov.au/reports/domestic-violence/family-domestic-sexual-violence-in-australia-2018/contents/table-of-contents.
9. Paul Spickard, 'Introduction: Immigration and race in United States history', in *Race and Immigration in the United States: New Histories*, ed. Paul Spickard (New York: Routledge, 2012), 1–12.

PART I

Moving Migration History Forward

As our aim is to relate migration history to contemporary political debates, we start by reflecting on why the former is currently not illuminating the latter, why this needs to change and how change might come about. It is not enough to just blame policy makers and the general public for not being sufficiently informed or expert to gain the level of understanding that scholarly researchers have. It is also important to interrogate scholarly assumptions, challenge traditional approaches to migration history and think about how to make connections with contemporary debates.

Henrich and Simpson's 'From the Margins of History to the Political Mainstream: Putting Migration History Centre Stage' makes the case for this paradigm shift. They argue that historical understanding has a major role to play in reframing immigration debates and that a number of historians have already demonstrated the relevance of historical research. Moreover, there is a long tradition of relating historical enquiry to contemporary concerns which has taken on new forms recently and has the potential to further evolve as new means of communication develop. This also implies that migration history needs to play a more central role in the discipline of history. Chapter 3, Leo Lucassen's 'Beyond the Apocalypse: Reframing Migration History' addresses itself specifically to this question. Noting the apocalyptic tone of much contemporary discourse about migration, he argues that this is fundamentally anchored in a misunderstanding of the nature of population movement. He shows how tracking historical movement across cultural boundaries rather than across national borders can reframe our understanding of the role of migration in the making of modern Europe.

CHAPTER 2

From the Margins of History to the Political Mainstream: Putting Migration History Centre Stage

Eureka Henrich and Julian M. Simpson

All humans are of migrant stock. Yet, at the same time, hostility towards migration is a powerful global political phenomenon. In the first part of this chapter, we survey the forms the immigration debate has taken in recent years in different parts of the world—including Europe, Australasia and Africa—and argue that engaging with these discourses, interrogating some of the assumptions that feed them and developing a different understanding of population movements through histori-cal enquiry is not just of interest but of vital importance worldwide. We then look back at the development of migration history and explore how it became a marginal pursuit within the wider discipline, despite migra-tion's central role in human societies and its contemporary relevance.

E. Henrich (✉)
School of Humanities, University of Hertfordshire,
Hatfield, Hertfordshire, UK

J. M. Simpson
Lancaster, Lancashire, UK

© The Author(s) 2019
E. Henrich and J. M. Simpson (eds.),
History, Historians and the Immigration Debate,
https://doi.org/10.1007/978-3-319-97123-0_2

15

The way forward, we suggest, is to draw on the tradition of connecting historical research to policy-making and public conversation, exploiting its 'utility' and offering not solutions, but fresh perspectives. Historians know that political debates are ahistorical; that they fail to sufficiently engage with immigration's past and reflect on its varying forms. But the profession has struggled to make a collective impact on the topic, and to assert its expertise and knowledge. To do so will involve putting migration history centre stage, both within the discipline of history itself and in the context of ongoing political debates.

Migration: A Global Issue

Immigration—and its supposed benefits and downsides—is now part of the global political discourse. It is generally portrayed as a symptom of modernity. It is also seen as something to be controlled and managed, rather than a natural dimension of the human condition. In a range of countries, political discourses and popular responses to migration have fed into each other and gradually led to major changes in both public attitudes and government policies. A case in point is the much-discussed backlash against multiculturalism in Western Europe in the face of an increasing belief in the fundamental antagonism between the cultures of migrants and those of host societies.[1] The growing preoccupation with the roles of migrants in European countries is a long-term trend. Surveys of twelve European countries showed a sharp rise in anti-for-eigner sentiment between 1988 and 2000, with the increase being particularly marked in the first six years of that period.[2] In practice, this meant an increase in xenophobia, ethnic tension, racism and at times ethnic violence with migrants seen as posing a threat to the homogeneity of European societies.[3]

These developments have resulted in fundamental shifts in the global political landscape, with migration and difference becoming a key theme in political debates, driving the rise of radical anti-immigration movements. Following the attack on the offices of the French satirical weekly *Charlie Hebdo* in 2015, the right-wing Dutch politician Geert Wilders claimed that Europe was 'at war' and argued that 'we have to close our borders, reinstate border controls, get rid of political correctness, introduce administrative detention, and stop immigration from Islamic countries'.[4] Opinion polls in the run-up to the 2017 elections suggested that his party could become the principal political force in the country.[5]

The fact that it did not can at least partly be attributed to the fact that his rhetoric has now permeated the mainstream—the centre-right Prime Minister Mark Rutte inviting migrants during the electoral campaign to 'be normal or be gone'.[6] In Germany, the Pegida (Patriotic Europeans against the Islamisation of the West) group has attracted thousands of sympathisers to street demonstrations.[7] In France, Marine Le Pen, whose *Front National* party was founded by her father Jean-Marie on an anti-immigration platform, was one of the main contenders in the 2017 presidential election. Although comfortably defeated in the second round of voting by Emmanuel Macron, she still obtained more than 10 million votes. It is a sign of the extent to which popular sentiment has evolved that such a result for a candidate whose appeal is so deeply entrenched in identity politics was seen as relatively disappointing. The impact of popular unrest and the rise of anti-immigrant movements is detectable in public policy. In 2010, France outlawed the wearing of burqas and niqabs in public places. And in the UK in 2016, years of controversy about the levels of migration from Eastern Europe and the rights of new migrants reached their zenith when the Conservative Prime Minister David Cameron held a promised referendum on the country's membership of the European Union. The result was a victory for the Leave campaign, Cameron's resignation and a surge in hate crimes recorded across England and Wales.[8]

This growing tension and resentment is mirrored elsewhere. Australian immigration policy has been described as having gone in recent years from being seen as an 'ideal benchmark' to achieving 'international infamy'.[9] It is now based around three core principles: preventing boats carrying refugees from arriving in Australia by turning or towing them back; housing refugees in detention centres in Nauru and Papua New Guinea; and undertaking to never resettle them in Australia.[10] In the US, official approaches to immigration altered dramatically after 9-11 with policy placing a greater emphasis on border security and the detention of immigrants.[11] A core aspect of Donald Trump's appeal during his campaign for the US presidency was his anti-immigrant and anti-Muslim rhetoric, both linked to his promise to 'make America great again'.[12] One of his first actions after becoming President was to sign an executive order titled 'Protecting the Nation From Terrorist Attacks by Foreign Nationals', effectively banning the arrival of citizens from seven Muslim-majority countries for 90 days, including refugees.

These shifts in discourses and in policy are not limited to the global North. In 1998, the leader of the South African Inkatha Freedom Party and then Home Affairs Minister Mangosuthu Buthelezi claimed that 'if we as South Africans are going to compete for scarce resources with millions of aliens who are pouring into South Africa, then we can bid goodbye to our Reconstruction and Development programme'.[13] Anti-immigrant sentiment in South Africa frequently takes the form of brutal attacks on migrants, as seen in the pogroms of early 2015.[14] In early 2017, police in Pretoria used rubber bullets, tear gas and water canons to disperse a violent anti-immigrant march.[15] The South African President Jacob Zuma felt compelled at the time to state what might in the past have been deemed obvious, pointing out that 'It is wrong to brandish all non-nationals as drug dealers or human traffickers'.[16] Michael Neocosmos has argued convincingly that there is a link between xenophobic responses and what he terms a 'politics of fear' in post-Apartheid South Africa. In his view, the politics of fear has at least three components: 'a state discourse of xenophobia, a discourse of South African exceptionalism and a conception of citizenship founded exclusively on indigeneity.'[17] Anti-immigrant rhetoric is a factor in politics elsewhere on the African continent. In Côte d'Ivoire for instance, the ultra-nationalist concept of *Ivoirité* (literally 'Ivorianess') gained credence from the 1990s, legitimating hostility towards migrants from other African countries and eventually fuelling a civil war.[18]

Similar processes are at play elsewhere as populations withdraw into narrowly defined identities which leave those marked as foreign and different on the outside. As the Algerian singer and musician Rachid Taha put it over twenty years ago in his song 'Voilà, Voilà': 'Wherever you go, the talk is the same/ Foreigner – for our problems, you take the blame.'[19] Although there is little agreement around the factors that shape negative attitudes towards migration, a significant number of studies have suggested that xenophobic attitudes are fuelled by recourse to exclusionary political rhetoric.[20] It is this persistent international phenomenon of popular and policy defensiveness that we want to address here. Not to deny or minimise the importance of migration and the issues that it raises, but to attempt to encourage the emergence of a critical debate which recognises that movement is part of the human condition. Taha also sang on that recording of lessons left unlearned and of culpable silences in lieu of memories—a clear allusion to where xenophobia has led in Europe's past that we also see as an invitation to historians to outline how the past might help us to think differently about the present. If anti-immigrant sentiment can be fuelled by political discourses expressing hostility towards immigrants, it is logical to assume that there is therefore a space that can be usefully occupied by proponents of a more measured understanding of the forces driving immigration and its place in the modern world.

If the speed at which migrants can move around the globe today may be unprecedented, and if today's migrants have more means than in the past to remain connected to the places they left behind, human history is nothing if not the history of a species on the move. Current scientific understanding is that early human beings evolved in various locations in the African continent.[21] Does the movement of our common ancestors to other parts of the world not compare in magnitude to the changes in today's world? Did the arrival of white settlers in sub-Saharan Africa, in the Americas or Australia not represent a revolution for the peoples already living there? Do the Roman, Mongol, and Ottoman Empires not offer illustrations of the fact that connected multicultural spaces predate the twenty-first century? The forced migration of slaves and the movement of indentured labourers shape contemporary demographics in the Americas, the Caribbean and elsewhere.

Indeed, this point is an even more straightforward one to make when one takes national borders out of the equation as the artificial creations that they are. The industrial revolution which has played such a part in making the modern world is predicated on the ability of employers to draw on a mobile workforce and its movement, across borders or from rural to urban areas. As Leo Lucassen notes in his contribution to this volume, this type of cross-cultural movement is not in its nature radically different from the transnational movement of people seeking employment.[22] In spite of this, political discourse constructs migration (of particular groups) as dysfunctional and historical enquiry has tended to treat it as a marginal preoccupation. We need to shift the terms of this debate, highlighting the importance of migration to the work of historians and the relevance of their findings to policy.

THE POLITICS OF MIGRATION HISTORY

To contribute to the immigration debate, we need to better understand the role of migration in shaping the modern world, and to reflect
critically on the significance of new understandings of the past. Two
traditions of historical work can assist in this task. A growing body of
research into the history of migration in countries where it had previously remained a marginal activity has added to the work done in countries (the US for instance) where migration has long formed a part of
national identity. We also aim to reconnect with a long history of using
historical scholarship to inform policy thinking which has been reinvigorated in recent years. The former shows that the history of immigration is of vital importance to understanding the world we live in; the
latter that history has much to offer to our understanding of human
migration, and the policies, both past and present, which attempt to
regulate it.

Our concerns about the tenor of current 'immigration debates', and
the general reluctance of historians to engage in them, are not with-
out precedent. Three decades ago, similar considerations prompted
Gérard Noiriel to write his landmark history of immigration in France,
The French Melting Pot: Immigration, Citizenship and National Identity.
As he recalls in the English-language translation:

> My purpose... was not to intervene directly in the public controversy but,
> rather, by setting the historical record straight, to confront these efforts to
> manipulate the past. I wanted to show that the indifference displayed by
> French historians on this issue had encouraged nationalist propaganda by
> fostering a genuine phenomenon of collective amnesia about the extraor-
> dinary role played by immigration in the renewal of the French population
> during the twentieth century.[23]

The 'collective amnesia' diagnosed by Noiriel recurs in the historical
record whenever an apparently 'new' group appears to resist integration
or assimilation—in this case, North African Muslim immigrants served
as the subjects of anxiety. Controverting the idea of migration as a problematic new phenomenon, and instead 'setting the historical record
straight', became the important project of many migration historians
working within nationalist historiographies from the 1980s onwards.
In European countries, which have historically been reluctant to accept

migratory movements as an integral part of their development, this was a radical proposal.[24] As Lucassen points out, 'Ellis Islands'—places that commemorate the entry of migrants into a country and create a context for remembering and reflecting on such processes—are hard to locate in the European landscape. The close links between the development in Western Europe of the concept of the nation-state, with a stable homogeneous citizenry, and the profession of history is one possible explanation that has been put forward to explain this lack of engagement.[25]

If historians had been blind to the centrality of migration in the development of contemporary nations, politicians were blissfully ignorant. As the British pioneer of migration history Colin Holmes noted: 'It might be convenient, an apt political rationalization of a policy decision, to proclaim that Britain is not "an immigration country". However, it is a remark that has no historical substance'.[26]

Whether asserting the positive economic and cultural contributions of migrant groups in the nation, or revealing preceding waves of various classes of newcomers, such as refugees, what united the wave of 'new migration historians' in the 1980s was a desire to demonstrate that migrants deserved a central place in nation-building narratives, rather than being relegated to the sidelines of historical change. This trend was inflected differently in settler societies such as the United States, Canada, New Zealand and Australia. There the positive narrative of the 'nation of immigrants', what Australian historian Graeme Davison calls 'the great voyage', was already a familiar, albeit benign, vehicle for celebrating national progress (official choreographed celebrations and 'birthdays' such as the annual Waitangi Day in New Zealand, the Australian Bicentenary in 1988 and the American Bicentenary in 1976 all drew on this archetypal story).[27] Rather than a drastic challenge to previous national narratives, social historians in these countries pointed to the silences and conflations within them—the violent conflict and dispossession of Indigenous peoples which made possible colonial expansions, the racial and ethnic diversity and changing composition of the migrant intake in supposedly 'white' settler societies, the forced migration of convicts, slaves and indentured labourers alongside free emigrants which made the imperial enterprise profitable, and the policies enacted by colonial governments to police their newly drawn borders. Race relations and attention to gender were key to these histories, and post-colonial theories challenged and reinvigorated the literature in the 1990s by questioning dominant Western-centric narratives.

Alongside this scholarship appeared ethno-specific studies. Historians of particular groups, such as the Scots, Chinese or Italians, were engaged in the important and validating project of writing minority migrant groups into the story of immigrant nations—a project that was shared by many family historians searching for their 'roots'. While some transcended national boundaries to consider the global flow of ethnic groups, most stuck to the nation—or destination—as the frame of analysis.[28] Their questions concerned who came, when, why and what they contributed to their adopted country—an approach that, however useful, tends to produce immigrant success stories in which newcomers successfully assimilate and become grateful citizens. Pushing against this celebratory narrative, or the 'Ellis Island paradigm' of immigration history, has in recent years become a priority for historians in post-colonial settler societies.[29]

Despite the efflorescence of many strands of migration history in recent decades, and the mission to bring migration from the periphery to the centre, the writings of migration historians have ironically remained on the margins of the mainstream historical discipline. In both avowedly 'immigrant' nations and those which resist that categorisation, there developed clusters of historians whose work spoke to small circles of like-minded specialists—be it in convict transportation, slavery, empire migration schemes or post-colonial migration—but rarely did this work influence broader theoretical or historiographical trends. The result is what has recently been dubbed 'the splendid isolation of migration history'—a splintering and sidelining of a literature which we believe has made it harder for specialists to come together and influence the increasingly anxious discourses on immigration outside the academy.[30]

In his 2012 book *The Battle of Britishness: Migrant Journeys, 1685 to the Present*, Tony Kushner traced the journeys of migrants to Britain, and the ways that those journeys have been remembered (or forgotten) in Britain today. Responding to a review of the book, he drew attention to the 'obsessive national and international concern about migration' and argued that in this context:

> ...historians have a role – professional and moral – to show that British history is about migration within its borders and also in relation to immigration and emigration. It is a history, like all national histories, that is about movement. For too long the study of migration in British history has been left to a handful of specialists... but ignored by the so-called mainstream.

The implication, reminiscent of Noiriel's argument concerning France in the 1980s, is that in the absence of a historical profession engaged publicly in the history of migration, the past has been vulnerable to those keen to 'exploit it with a restrictionist or discriminatory agenda'.[31]

Individuals like Noiriel and Kushner, by their choice of questions and thorough methods of social history research, have brought their work to bear on broader discussions outside their institutions. But as a group, the historical profession has not yet engaged confidently in debates about migration. Perhaps the most promising leap forward in the field in recent years has been the embrace of the global as a framework for historical analysis. 'Going global' has implications for how historians 'do history'—the further away from specialisation we go, the more we must rely on other experts and scholars, often outside our discipline. In *Migration History in World History*, Lucassen, Lucassen and Manning draw together sociological, historical and anthropological approaches to migration. By introducing historians to different methodologies and periods of study—often far beyond the comfort zone of written records—the authors are able to start a conversation about the nature of mobility in human history—one that has influenced the underlying arguments in this volume.[32]

Another important influence on our thinking about migration has been the work of historians engaged in the 'new imperial history'. Drawing attention to the political, cultural, ideological and demographic legacies of imperialism encourages us to recognise connections between imperial movements and contemporary migrations, such as post-war migration from Britain's former colonies to the UK. These connections have been repeatedly invoked by migrants themselves in the powerful slogan, 'we are here because you were there'. And crucially, as Antoinette Burton argues, the process of interrogating imperial legacies involves 'unmasking' national historiographies and their attendant national identities which are themselves products of empire.[33] Global or world history and the 'new imperial history' have the potential to reframe migration in ways that can influence public debate, but reaching that potential will require historians to write for, speak to and engage with audiences beyond their colleagues and students.

THE PAST IN THE PRESENT

The idea that historians should attempt to contribute to our understanding of the present is not a new one, although it has gone through a phase of being unfashionable. Recent decades have been characterised by the movement of historians away from 'big questions' of social transformation towards culture, ideas and individual historical experiences.[34] As the historians of immigration we have mentioned have shown, this shift is more to do with intellectual fashions than a reflection of the fact that history has little to contribute to our understanding of the world we live in. Large strands of historical inquiry are in fact the product of historians' desire to produce a type of historical understanding that would inform their own presents. In the UK, E.P. Thompson's pioneering work on social history was fuelled by his desire to gain a better understanding of social classes, and Sheila Rowbotham explicitly linked her interest in women's history with her political activism as a feminist.[35] More recently, a range of scholars have put forward strong arguments for the need to re-engage with the social and policy relevance of history. This is not to claim that history can provide clear-cut answers to political questions—it is more helpful as Ludmilla Jordanova has put it to see it as casting a different type of light on the present rather than as representing the discovery of a manual offering instructions on how to proceed.[36] History can provide *analogues* that support a reflection around similar issues that have arisen in the past; *direct evidence* that can be used to enhance our understanding of the present (e.g. environmental data); and a different *mode of thought*, one that is the product of a holistic engagement with a wide range of evidence and that embraces complexity.[37] In other words, as Pamela Cox has put it, historians can be the 'enlightened sceptics' of the knowledge economy.[38]

It is evident from these examples that historical thinking is a valuable tool not just for understanding the past, but for imagining alternate futures. But the question of how best to put history to work outside the academy is not straightforward to answer. One approach that has a long tradition in the discipline is connecting historical expertise to the work of policy-makers in government. There are a number of models for this kind of engagement. The History & Policy website, established by a group of leading UK historians in 2002, now offers a rich archive of opinion pieces and policy papers which effectively translate the research of historians into language more accessible to public servants and journalists and highlight its policy relevance. Their work is 'inspired by the belief that history can and should improve public policy making, helping to avoid reinventing the wheel and repeating past mistakes'.[39] As Alix Green points out, this model is one of 'knowledge transfer', which requires historians to articulate the relevance of their work to a range of policy contexts, packaging it as a resource that can be quickly consulted. An alternate model is 'knowledge exchange', where historians would work alongside policy-makers and experts in other disciplines to brainstorm solutions to policy problems.[40] The emphasis here is less on what historians know, than on how they acquire that knowledge:

> We may be 'content' experts – in foreign relations, health or welfare policy, for example – but we also bring distinctive habits of mind as historians, ways of questioning, seeking and reading evidence, checking assumptions and building arguments...[41]

These habits are invaluable to the process of assessing what has or hasn't worked in the past, and what might work in the future. Used well, they can serve to effectively 'past-proof' policy, ensuring that new initiatives take past experience and historical perspective into consideration.[42] But while historians have long worked with and for governments in many roles, from speech-writing to policy research, the types of insights offered by thinking 'with history' in policy have not been as obvious as those gained through disciplines such as economics and sociology. As Peter Stearns pointed out in the early 1980s, 'applied historians are not social scientists with a slightly unusual data set'. The policy 'product' they produce will have 'considerably less emphasis on the narrowest economic factors, considerably less claim to precise predictive power but considerably more utility as a result'.[43]

In asserting that historians can have a powerful voice in debates about migration in different national, regional and international contexts, we are consciously drawing attention to the policy 'utility' of migration history. Informing policy debate with historical perspectives is an important first step towards what might, in the future, become a genuine embedding of migration history into the development of policies ranging from immigration to health and social care, as chapters by Roces and Simpson in this volume suggest. History used in this way could serve to mount practical political challenges, from pointing out to Côte d'Ivoire's defenders of *Ivoirité* that they are in effect celebrating the borders defined by their former colonial rulers to answering claims that Muslim migrants pose a unique challenge of integration by pointing out that similar discourses of Irish Catholic exceptionalism used to abound. This is not to say that the answers to everything can be found in the past. The past can, however, serve to highlight the weaknesses of discourses that ignore it.

Thinking about the policy relevance of historical knowledge can encourage historians to articulate why their work matters. But there are also other ways and spaces in which we can bring history into public conversations about human movement. Immigration debates take place on television and in print, but it is in the online world where both forms of communication can be combined and shared, and where anyone with an internet connection and a device can add their opinions to the mix. The web is also the library of the twenty-first century, a resource to which people turn for clarification, information and education. A recent example of a scholarly intervention harnessing the power of an online platform is #ImmigrationSyllabus, an initiative of immigration historians affiliated with the Immigration History Research Center at the University of Minnesota and the Immigration and Ethnic History Society. The website, which was developed in response to the 2016 presidential election, provides readings, historical documents and multimedia in the form of a freely accessible 15-week course in US immigration history. The aim is to inform Americans not only about histories of immigration, but the history of the debate itself:

> This syllabus seeks to provide historical context to current debates over immigration reform, integration, and citizenship. Many Americans have a romanticized idea of the nation's immigrant past. In fact, America's immigration history is more contested, more nuanced, and more complicated than many assume. Then, like now, many politicians, public commentators, critics, and media organizations have greatly influenced Americans' understanding of immigration and the role that immigrants play in U.S. society.[44]

Providing and publicising access to historical scholarship tailored to contemporary concerns, such as border control, racism and nativism, can form an important antidote to misinformed and ill-tempered discourses. In the words of one of the historians involved, Adam Goodman, 'by normalising migration, rather than borders, US histories have the opportunity to depoliticize, to an extent, the highly controversial nature of public and academic debates about immigration'.[45]

From dedicated websites to blogs and news outlets like *The Conversation*, new media offers opportunities for scholarly engagement which can marry our own personal concerns 'as politically minded citizens living in the present' with our professional commitment to translating the complexity of historical understandings for a broad audience.[46] In other words, when our research throws new light on contemporary issues, and our own conscience tells us to 'do something', the web presents itself as an ideal stage for a timely intervention into the public debate. And, as is so often the case in today's continually churning news media landscape, timing is everything. #ImmigrationSyllabus launched on 26 January 2017, the day before President Trump signed an executive order to suspend the entry of refugees, as well as immigrants from seven Muslim-majority countries, one of three immigration-related executive orders passed in the week since his inauguration. Some news coverage of the 'travel ban' and associated protests at airports across the United States drew on the expertise of the historians involved in #ImmigrationSyllabus, in one instance enlisting them to annotate the text of the executive order itself.[47] This kind of detailed, historically informed and non-partisan analysis is often reserved for academic writing and publications, hidden behind paywalls or written in language that is excessively jargonistic. However, if given the right platform and publicity, historians' perspectives can come to influence the public conversations we have about immigration.

CONCLUSION

Historians of migration possess the expertise to provide a different perspective on current immigration debates, yet their ability to do so collectively has been hampered by the marginalisation of migration within the discipline of history, and, we suspect, the reluctance to offer complex historical explanations to media outlets where the politicisation of the topic seems to leave little room for nuance. Confronting these structural challenges and personal misgivings is, we have argued, not only necessary but also productive, as seeking to widen our intended audience from colleagues and students to policy-makers and the broader public involves rethinking what we do and why it is important.

In *The French Melting Pot*, Noiriel declared a belief in the historian's 'obligation to address the political issues of the time', while cautioning that 'he or she should refrain from developing a "habit of judgement" and keep an analytical distance from the passions provoked by current events'.[48] In the words of Marc Bloch, whom Noiriel was referring to:

> Unfortunately the habit of passing judgements leads to a loss of taste for explanations. When the passions of the past blend with the prejudices of the present, human reality is reduced to a picture in black and white.[49]

Writing history in full colour and complexity means putting the present to one side (as much as we can), immersing ourselves in the historical record and analysing sources with careful regard to their own temporal contexts—keeping our 'taste for explanations' sharp. It is a process that takes time, reflection, writing and rewriting, and cannot be fast-tracked to suit a political need or purpose. This is precisely why it is so valuable. The insights historians gain by seeking a better understanding of the past can offer crucial context to entrenched debates about migration in countries across the globe. And by sharing those insights, we lend visibility to historians as members of a profession which engages with the present, as well as the past. Practising this kind of 'critical public history' means publicly engaging with, discussing and challenging the simplistic and ahistorical assumptions which underlie global immigration debates.[50] The challenge now is to reflect on how we can draw on new and old media to make our voices heard in the public domain and in the corridors of power.

NOTES

1. Steven Vertovec and Susanne Wessendorf, eds., *The Multicultural Backlash: European Discourses, Policies and Practices* (Abingdon and New York: Routledge, 2010).
2. Moshe Semyonov, Rebeca Raijman, and Anastasia Gorodzeisky, 'The rise of anti-foreigner sentiment in European societies, 1988–2000,' *American Sociological Review* 71 (2006): 426–49.
3. Ibid.
4. Charlotte McDonald-Gibson, 'Europe's anti-immigrant parties make hay from Paris terrorist attacks,' *Time*, 8 January 2015.
5. Peter Cluskey, 'Poll puts Wilders far-right party on par with the Liberals,' *The Irish Times*, 13 November 2014.

6. Senay Boztas, David Chazan, and Peter Foster, 'Dutch prime minister warns migrants to "be normal or be gone", as he fends off populist Gert Wilders in bitter election fight,' *The Telegraph*, 23 January 2017, http://www.telegraph.co.uk/news/2017/01/23/dutch-prime-minister-warns-migrants-normal-gone-fends-populist/.
7. 'Why are thousands of Germans protesting and who are Pegida?,' *BBC News Online*, 13 January 2015, http://www.bbc.co.uk/newsbeat/article/30694252/why-are-thousands-of-germans-protesting-and-who-are-pegida.
8. Dominic Casciani, '"Record hate crimes" after EU referendum,' *BBC News Online*, 15 February 2017, http://www.bbc.co.uk/news/uk-38976087.
9. Jock Collins, 'Rethinking Australian immigration and immigrant settlement policy,' *Journal of Intercultural Studies* 34, no. 2 (2013): 160–77.
10. Paul Farrel, 'Could Australia's "Stop the Boats" policy solve Europe's migrant crisis?,' *The Guardian*, 22 April 2015, http://www.theguardian.com/world/2015/apr/22/could-australia-stop-the-boats-policy-solve-europe-migrant-crisis.
11. Michelle Mittelstadt, Burke Speaker, Doris Meissner, and Muzaffar Chishti, 'Through the prism of national security: Major immigration policy and program changes in the decade since 9/11' (Washington: Migration Policy Institute Fact Sheet, August 2011), http://migrationpolicy.org/research/post-9-11-immigration-policy-program-changes.
12. Donald Trump, 'Immigration reform that will make America great again,' Presidential Positions Document, 2016, https://assets.donaldjtrump.com/Immigration-Reform-Trump.pdf.
13. Quoted in Michael Neocosmos, 'The politics of fear and the fear of politics: Reflections on xenophobic violence in South Africa,' *Journal of Asian and African Studies* 43, no. 6 (2008): 588.
14. Daniel Magaziner and Sean Jacobs, 'South Africa turns on its immigrants,' *New York Times*, 24 April 2015, http://www.nytimes.com/2015/04/25/opinion/south-africa-turns-on-its-immigrants.html?_r=0.
15. Norimitsu Onishi, 'South Africa anti-immigrant protests turn violent,' *New York Times*, 24 February 2017, https://www.nytimes.com/2017/02/24/world/africa/immigrant-protests-south-africa.html?mcubz=1.
16. Ibid.
17. Neocosmos, 'The politics of fear,' 587.
18. Beth Elise Whitaker, 'Playing the immigration card: The politics of exclusion in Côte d'Ivoire and Ghana,' *Commonwealth and Comparative Politics* 53, no. 3 (2015): 275.
19. Authors' translation.

20. Whitaker, 'Immigration card,' 275.
21. Jean-Jacques Hublin, Abdelouahed Ben-Ncer, Shara E. Bailey, Sarah E. Freidline, Simon Neubauer, Matthew M. Skinner, Inga Bergmann, Adeline Le Cabec, Stefano Benazzi, Katerina Harvati, and Philipp Gunz, 'New fossils from Jebel Irhoud, Morrocco and the pan-African origin of *Homo sapiens*,' *Nature* 546 (2017): 289–93. This theory has been contested but remains dominant. See, for instance, Julien Benoit, 'There's not enough evidence to back the claim that humans originated in Europe', *The Conversation*, 25 May 2017, https://theconversation.com/theres-not-enough-evidence-to-back-the-claim-that-humans-originated-in-europe-78280.
22. Leo Lucassen, 'Beyond the apocalypse: Reframing migration history,' this volume.
23. Gérard Noiriel, *The French Melting Pot: Immigration, Citizenship and National Identity* (Minneapolis: University of Minnesota Press, 1996 [1988]), xii.
24. Leo Lucassen, *The Immigrant Threat: The Integration of Old and New Migrants in Western Europe Since 1850* (Urbana and Chicago: University of Illinois Press, 2005), 19.
25. Ibid.
26. Colin Holmes, *John Bull's Island: Immigration and British Society 1871–1971* (Basingstoke: Palgrave Macmillan, 1988), 276.
27. Graeme Davison, *The Use and Abuse of Australian History* (St. Leonards, NSW: Allen & Unwin, 2000), 56–79.
28. For an example of the global history approach, see Donna Gabaccia and Fraser Ottanelli, eds., *Italian Workers of the World: Labor Migration and the Formation of Multiethnic States* (Urbana and Chicago: University of Illinois Press, 2005).
29. See, for instance, Paul Spickard, ed., *Race and Immigration in the United States: New Histories* (New York: Routledge, 2012).
30. Jan Lucassen, Leo Lucassen, and Patrick Manning, 'Migration history: Multidisciplinary approaches,' in *Migration History in World History: Multidisciplinary Approaches*, eds. Lucassen, Lucassen, and Manning (Leiden and Boston: Brill, 2010), 6.
31. See author's response, http://www.history.ac.uk/reviews/review/1566.
32. Lucassen, Lucassen, and Manning, *Migration in World History*, 17–19.
33. Antoinette Burton, 'Introduction: On the inadequacy and the indispensability of the nation,' in *After the Imperial Turn: Thinking Through and With the Nation*, ed. Antoinette Burton (Durham, NC and London: Duke University Press, 2003), 8.

34. Eric Hobsbawm, *How to Change the World: Tales of Marx and Marxism* (London: Little Brown, 2011), 392.

35. E.P. Thompson, *The Making of the English Working Class* (London: Penguin Books, 1991 [1963]); Sheila Rowbotham, *Hidden from History: 300 Years of Women's Oppression and The Fight Against It* (London: Pluto Press, 1977).

36. Ludmilla Jordanova, *History in Practice* (London: Hodder Arnold, 2006), 3.

37. Lucy Delap, Simon Szreter, and Paul Warde, 'History and Policy: A Decade of Bridge-Building in the United Kingdom,' *Scandia* 80, no. 1 (2014): 97–118.

38. Pamela Cox, 'The Future Use of History,' *History Workshop Journal* 75, no. 1 (2013): 125–45.

39. 'Who We Are,' History & Policy website, http://www.historyandpolicy.org/who-we-are.

40. Alix Green, 'History as expertise and the influence of political culture on advice for policy since Fulton,' *Contemporary British History*, 29, no. 1 (2014): 40–41.

41. Alix Green, 'History, policy and public purpose: Historians and historical thinking in government,' History & Policy website, June 2016, http://www.historyandpolicy.org/historians-books/books/history-policy-and-public-purpose-historians-and-historical-thinking-in-gov.

42. J.M. Simpson, K. Checkland, S.J. Snow, K. Rothwell, J. Voorhees, and A. Esmail, 'Adding the past to the policy mix: An historical approach to the issue of access to general practice in England,' *Contemporary British History* 32, no. 2 (2018): 276–99.

43. Peter N. Stearns, 'History and policy analysis: Toward maturity,' *The Public Historian* 4, no. 3 (1982): 6.

44. '#ImmigrationSyllabus, Essential Topics, Readings, and Multimedia that Provide Historical Context to Current Debates Over Immigration Reform, Integration, and Citizenship,' 26 January 2017, http://editions.lib.umn.edu/immigrationsyllabus/.

45. Adam Goodman, 'Nation of migrants, historians of migration,' *Journal of American Ethnic History* 34, no. 4 (2015): 9.

46. Marilyn Lake, 'On history and politics,' in *The Historian's Conscience: Australian Historians on the Ethics of History* ed. Stuart Macintyre (Carlton, VIC: Melbourne University Press, 2004), 96.

47. Angilee Shah, 'We've been here before: Historians annotate and analyse immigration ban's place in history,' *PRI*, 1 February 2017, https://www.pri.org/stories/2017-02-01/we-ve-been-here-historians-annotate-and-analyze-immigration-bans-place-history. See also Maura Lerner,

'Immigration crackdowns led to regrets, say University of Minnesota experts launching new website,' *Star Tribune*, 8 February 2017, http://www.startribune.com/immigration-crackdowns-led-to-regrets-say-university-of-minnesota-experts-launching-new-website/413108563/.

48. Noiriel, *The French Melting Pot*, xiii.
49. Marc Bloch, *The Historian's Craft*, trans. Peter Putnam (Manchester: Manchester University Press, 1954), 140.
50. John Tosh, *Why History Matters* (Basingstoke: Palgrave Macmillan, 2008), 23.

CHAPTER 3

Beyond the Apocalypse: Reframing Migration History

Leo Lucassen

MIGRANTS AS TROUBLE

As the editors of this volume have explained in their introduction, current public debates on migration and integration in Western Europe are fraught with misunderstandings, selective perceptions, and deliberate misrepresentations. Whether it regards the Brexit discussion[1] or the so-called 'refugee crisis', the tone is often outright apocalyptical. Not only among politicians and journalists, but in some cases also among serious commentators and scholars, like David Goodhart, Paul Collier and David Miller.[2] But mainstream migration scholars, often unintentionally, contribute to this alarmist atmosphere as well, by too uncritically reproducing the frame that migrants constitute a problem that should be solved. Or that we should look at the 'root causes' of migration and prevent people from leaving the global South in the first place. This perspective treats migration not only as a predicament, but also

L. Lucassen (✉)
International Institute of Social History, Amsterdam, The Netherlands

L. Lucassen
Leiden University, Leiden, The Netherlands

© The Author(s) 2019
E. Henrich and J. M. Simpson (eds.),
History, Historians and the Immigration Debate,
https://doi.org/10.1007/978-3-319-97123-0_3

as an anomaly for modern sedentary states, who therefore should stop unwanted migrants wherever possible. More recently climate change and the high fertility in the Arab world and Sub-Saharan Africa are added to this pool of negative associations and root causes.[3]

From a broader historical perspective, there are two major problems with this framing. First of all, it reflects a myopic view of what migration as a human phenomenon constitutes, by only concentrating on those forms of migration that are—believed to be—negative: both for receiving societies (cultural and financial costs),[4] the migrants themselves (who would be uprooted and disoriented), and for sending regions, often portrayed as suffering from 'brain drain'. Hence, the search for 'root causes' in order to stop migration. The second problem is that migration is often perceived as a natural phenomenon like earthquakes and hurricanes, devoid of human agency, leading poor regions of the world to 'empty out' (Collier) and set in motion mass migrations, unless harsh measures and tight migration controls are put in place. It is no coincidence that 'water speak' (i.e. talk of streams, flows or tsunamis) is so popular in the current discussions on migration.

When it comes to the current, politicised discussion on migration in Europe and North America, historians are often lured into narrow debates on the alleged failed integration of specific low-skilled groups of migrants and their descendants, like the former guest workers in Western Europe or Mexican labour migrants in the United States. Within these confines, which leave out the majority of migrants who are not seen as a problem, the most common reflex of migration scholars is to bring nuance into the discussion by pointing out differences between groups and generations. They rightfully stress that integration processes take time, can only be judged properly over several generations, and draw parallels with previous clashes between immigrants and natives that in the end led to incorporation and the blurring or disappearance of ethnic boundaries.[5]

Comparing then and now is not undisputed. Especially when it comes to current political debates on immigration, historians who draw on earlier experiences to nuance or debunk ideas about uniqueness and unprecedentedness are often accused of being naïve, activist or both. And sometimes rightly so. German immigrants to Great Britain and the Netherlands in the nineteenth and early twentieth centuries, for example, arrived in another context and were differently selected than Turkish and Moroccan labour migrants a century later. Scholars therefore have to be cautious in drawing parallels, and should also have an eye for dissimilarities and 'newness', especially where it regards the opportunity structure of the society. For the post-war period, this regards among other things the rise of the welfare state, secularisation, and the accelerating process of globalisation.[6] In short, we have to be explicit about our assumptions, the specific historical context, and about the variables we measure in the past and the present.

Another problem that we confront when making comparisons in time is that the past often assumes a different guise and adopts the sepia colour of the documents that are left to study. This easily leads to nostalgia and may unduly soften experiences of people in the past. Or in the words of Perlmann and Waldinger, we tend to be too optimistic about the past and too pessimistic about the present.[7] Of course, not all past occurrences are wrapped in nostalgia. Think more broadly about the Holocaust and other traumatic episodes, such as the Vietnam War, the mass killings of so-called communists in Indonesia in 1965/1966, the Chinese Cultural Revolution, or state terrorism in Latin America during the 1970s and 1980s. And also earlier events, like American slavery, can still incite deeply felt emotions and outrage. When it comes to most recollections of Europe's migratory past, however—as far as people are aware of it—nostalgia tends to dominate. It is as if the layers of time polish and smoothen its sharp and ugly edges.

This distortion is related to a bias that posits earlier migrants as the opposite of the current ones. The argument then runs as follows: back then, they were Europeans, (Judeo) Christians, frugal, entrepreneurial, skilled, and willing to adapt, whereas nowadays, they threaten our culture, refuse to integrate, and are primarily drawn by our welfare state. Such juxtapositions not only belie historical facts, but also are a recurring phenomenon in the history of immigration. In his 1897 book *Alien Immigrants to England*, the economic historian William Cunningham, for example, warned against the dangerous and parasitic Jewish migrants from Eastern Europe, whom he deemed 'incomparable' with the thrifty Walloons and French who found refuge in England in the sixteenth and seventeenth centuries.[8] Nowadays, many argue that the post-war immigration of (non-white) people from the colonies and labour migrants from Islamic countries has changed the game fundamentally. Western Europeans, and their so-called 'Judeo-Christian' civilisation, are believed to have never been exposed to such high numbers of people with a fundamentally different culture and physical appearance. If we look at the numbers and regions of origin, this seems a truism. Whereas in the first half of the twentieth century the three million immigrants from other continents barely constituted 1% of the European population, after the Second World War, this number rose to almost 25 million, or on average 5%. As we know, these immigrants were not evenly spread over Europe, but concentrated in the (North) West. Added to intra-European migrants, this pushed percentages of foreign-born people up to more than 10% in countries like France, Great Britain, Austria, Belgium, Germany, Sweden, and the Netherlands.[9]

The main aim of this chapter is not to repeat the well-known 'then and now' discussion, but to put the spectacular increase of immigrants from Asia and Africa in the second half of the twentieth century in a much broader conceptual perspective, thus counterbalancing the rather narrow view of migration that dominates the media and politics and that limits 'immigrants' to those newcomers who for whatever reason are seen as a problem. As will be shown, the most recent groups of immigrants are part of a much larger and structural phenomenon that has characterized human history from its very first beginnings.[10] In order to really appreciate and understand the function of migrations for human societies, a long-term perspective is therefore key. Mobility, both local, regional and over longer distances, was (and still is) the rule, and largely determined not by anonymous climatic or economic push and pull forces, but by conscious decisions within households, throughout the world. Only with this vantage point can historians use the full potential of their discipline and leave their imposed, but also self-chosen, ghetto.

THE DEFINITION GHOST

To understand the role of migration in human societies, scholars are—to borrow Karl Marx and Friedrich Engels' imagery from the *Communist Manifesto*—haunted by the spectre of state definitions.[11] This gaze not only ignores internal and temporary migrants, but focuses only on foreign immigrants who are perceived as a problem by contemporaries. The result is a self-fulfilling prophecy that defines migrants as a burden, threat or nuisance, or a combination of the three. In itself, limiting ourselves to groups that fit this definition, as I did in my book *The Immigrant Threat*, can be legitimate and produce interesting conclusions, but often such choices are not explicitly motivated and easily strengthen the prevailing negative framing of migration. Moreover, this trap is difficult to avoid, because we are highly dependent on sources and national and racial categories produced by states, like 'non-Western migrants'.

With these reminders and possible pitfalls in mind, this chapter will offer a much broader perspective of people on the move, which goes beyond current political and societal obsessions and media frames. As Leslie Moch did in her excellent overview of European migrations (at least until the twentieth century),[12] I will transcend conventional definitions of migrants as those coming from other states with the intention to stay, and include internal and temporary migrants as far as they crossed cultural boundaries. In the cross-cultural migration rate (CCMR) approach, we distinguish four core types of migration: (1) people moving from the countryside to cities, either within states or coming from abroad (to cities); (2) people who move within the countryside to culturally and ecologically different settings (colonisation); (3) people who move temporarily as seasonal workers from peasant areas to much more commercial farming regions; and (4) people who migrate temporarily and stay away for several years (temporary multi-annual migrants), like soldiers, sailors, skilled workers, and missionaries. In order to arrive at the total number of cross-cultural migrants in Europe, we finally have to add all those who entered the continent (immigrants) and those who left with the aim to stay away for good (emigrants).[13]

With the CCMR approach, a rather different picture emerges of Europe's migration history since 1800 than we get from the mainstream scholarship, which limits itself largely to those who cross international borders, or to migrants from the so-called 'non-West'. Where Stephen Castles and Mark Miller in their well-known handbook on international migration write that the age of migration basically started after the Second World War, and particularly in the 1980s when international migration grew in volume and significance, they take a very contemporaneous perspective. Although they acknowledge that migration has been a structural part of human societies, it is clear that in their eyes, it is only in the last decades that this phenomenon has become *really* important. But even if we accept their predilection for international migrations, this account is fraught with an ahistorical bias.[14] Historians, but also social scientists, like Nancy Foner, Caroline Brettell, Roger Waldinger, and Joel Perlmann, have shown that especially during the period 1880–1920 North America witnessed similar levels of international migration as a century later.[15] And also the problematization of migrants who are perceived as culturally different was equally strong in the past. The discrimination and racism endured by the Irish and by Eastern European Jews in the United Kingdom and the United States in the nineteenth and early twentieth centuries, as well as Italians and Chinese worldwide, offer ample evidence.[16] Like the present day low-skilled migrants from abroad, be they Mexicans in the United States, Moroccans in the Netherlands or Pakistanis in England, earlier examples ignited similar fears and opposition. Only, the sepia colourisation has done its job, so that now few people can still imagine that Catholicism, Judaism, or 'Asian races' once were considered insurmountable cultural barriers to integration. The current 'Jewish-Christian roots of our civilization' amalgamation, frequently used as the ultimate opposite of Islam, would have been inconceivable before the 1960s. The fault lines of the 'Clash of Civilizations' ran very differently, not too long ago.

This chapter will not recall those earlier histories of frictions between immigrants and natives, but take a more radical departure from the dominant nation state paradigm and use the CCMR approach as a point of departure. The main idea is that this enables us to take a much broader look at how migrants with different cultural backgrounds change the places they go to, but often also the places they leave. Because most moves are not simply from A-to-B, but much more messy, involving (repetitive) return migrations—also after several generations—and circular and serial moves. So how do the long-term migration patterns for Europe look if we take the CCMR approach instead of the conventional, nation-state-driven, international-cum-problematisation angle? Well, quite different from the standard representation, as Table 3.1 shows.

What immediately catches the eye is the all time high in the first (instead of the second) half of the twentieth century. The reason is quite simple: war. The two world wars did not only uproot millions of civilians, as refugees and displaced persons, but also involved tens of millions of young men (and women) who were drafted as soldiers and sent to fight and occupy other countries, often far away from home. As the following paragraph will show, there are good reasons to consider such soldiers as cross-cultural migrants whose moves wrought fundamental and unexpected changes.

Table 3.1 Cross-cultural migration rates in Europe (without Russia) as a percentage of the average population per half century (1801–2000)

	1801–1850	1851–1900	1901–1950	1951–2000
To cities*	7.7	12.3	7.2	5.7
Colonisation	0	0	2.6	0
Seasonal	1	2.6	0.8	0.2
Temporary multi-annual	6.7	3.3	25.6	5
Immigration	0	0	0.8	4.8
Emigration	1.6	7.4	7.1	2.9
Total CCMR	17	25.6	44.1	18.6

Source Lucassen and Lucassen, *Globalizing Migration History.* Table 170 on p. 86
*For the twentieth century, we excluded internal moves to cities, assuming that the cultural differences between the countryside and cities due to the process of national homogenisation had become insignificant

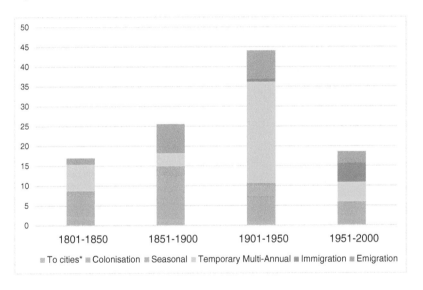

SOLDIERS AND OTHER ORGANISATIONAL MIGRANTS

Only recently, we are beginning to grasp the cross-cultural influences of mass migrations of soldiers, temporary as they may have been and often resulting in 'death by migration'. Not only for the soldiers themselves, but also for those they temporarily interacted with, violently or not, and for the societies those who survived returned to. To start with, armies, also during peacetime, were places where young men were brought together and confronted with peers from very different class and religious and ethnic backgrounds. This was especially true for multicultural empires like Russia and China, but also in early modern states like France.[17] In times of war, moreover, soldiers and the broader occupation forces they were part of often introduced new institutions and policies, from discrimination and genocide to obligatory health insurance, in the case of Nazi Germany.[18] Furthermore, they were instrumental in massive deportations, and other types of social engineering, forcing millions to move (and work) elsewhere and deliberately killing millions of others. Let us take a brief look at the effects on European societies in the twentieth century, both at destination (where soldiers went to), and at origin (where soldiers came from).

Soldiers were instrumental in forcing millions of people to relocate, both during and after the two world wars, thus dramatically changing the demographic and cultural make-up of Europe,[19] especially due to the ethnic cleansing in Eastern Europe. In this process, people were not only moved against their will but also deliberately killed. The genocide of the Jews, only possible by the military conquest of large parts of Europe, reduced the share of Jewish Europeans, and their culture, from roughly 10 million in 1939 to 4 million in 1979. The change in Eastern Europe was much greater. Before the war, 75% of Jewish Europeans lived in Eastern Europe, whereas nowadays, only a few hundred thousands are left. Poland is by far the most extreme case. At the outbreak of the war, in September 1939, almost 10% of the population was of Jewish faith, some three million citizens, of whom only 6000 were left after the Nazis surrendered six years later.[20] As a result, an entire culture was extinguished, which—combined with the resettlement of 'national minorities' directly after 1945 and the emigration to Israel of the survivors—resulted in much more homogenous nation states in Eastern Europe than ever before. This created and enhanced an ethno-national social and political climate in countries like Poland, Hungary, Romania, and Czechoslovakia which may partly explain the xenophobic attitudes towards African and Asian guest workers during the Communist era and more recently the Islamophobia directed against Muslim refugees from the Middle East.[21]

Two other demographic effects of war that deserve mentioning are first of all the mass emigration of Turkish-speaking Ottoman subjects from the Balkans. Due to the defeat of the Ottoman army in the Balkan

War of 1912–1913, the Ottomans lost 80% of their European territory, which at one point almost reached Vienna. Some 400,000 Muslims citizens fled to what was to become modern Turkey, with Anatolia as its new heartland. Under the leadership of the Young Turks, many of them—including Mustafa Kemal Atatürk—refugees from the Balkans, a programme of ethnic cleansing forced 20,000 Greek Orthodox Christians to leave for Greek islands in the Aegean Sea. After World War I, the former Ottoman empire had lost even more territory and a much larger 'population exchange' started, resulting in 1.2 million Greek Orthodox Christians from the Ottoman empire settling in Greece and 60,000 Muslims relocating from Greek territory to Turkey.[22] Even more traumatic, but part of the same extreme nation-building process, were the deliberate mass killings of around one million Armenians and Syrian Christians in 1915.

The second example of a fundamental reshuffling of populations through social engineering with soldiers and police troops as executioners, was the millions of Russians forced to resettle in parts of the Soviet Union, as ordered by Stalin. Again, war not only uprooted millions of soldiers, many of whom had never left their home region, but also turned a considerable part of the population into forced migrants, who either died or were moved to Central Asia and Kazakhstan, thousands of kilometres away in culturally and ecologically entirely unknown terrains.[23]

Soldiers as migrants not only influenced the empires they fought for and the states they occupied, but also the societies of origin. An interesting example concerns African-American GIs who liberated Europe and subsequently became part of a huge and floating mass of men—and a small minority of women—who fulfilled their (2-year) tour of duty on military bases in Japan, Italy, the United Kingdom, the Netherlands, and foremost West Germany. In the latter country, their function was to safeguard the process of denazification, and more importantly, they acted as a physical and symbolic force in the fast developing Cold War. Although racial segregation also determined daily life at American military bases abroad, black soldiers soon realized that the surrounding German society, not long ago the racial state par excellence, offered much more freedom than the segregated US South where many of them originated from, or the ghettos in the North for that matter. Dating white women and being served without discrimination in bars and restaurants was a totally new experience and made them aware that the institutionalised racism back home was not normal. The impact of their tour of duty was immense and their experiences were transmitted through letters to their friends and relatives at the other side of the Atlantic. Moreover, upon return, many of them became politically active, joined the National Association for the Advancement of Colored People (NAACP), and thus infused their overseas experience as cultural and social capital in the emerging Civil Rights Movement.[24] If we want to understand the post-war social and political history of the United States, the foreign encounters of hundreds of thousands of black American soldiers are crucial, and therefore the often-neglected temporary migrations of these 'organisational migrants', defined as people whose migratory patterns are primarily defined by the organisation they work for, deserve serious study.[25]

Other organisational migrants who crossed cultural borders were at least as important in forging social, cultural and political changes. Think of sailors, missionaries, aid workers, diplomats, high-skilled technicians, and expats working for large multinational corporations, like Shell or Philips. Often invested with power and status, their influence on the culture of the people they temporarily interact with is often overlooked and underrated. Yet, they are also an integral part of migration flows and thereby of migration history. Ignoring them not only uncritically adopts the myopic gaze of the state, which is primarily interested in migrants they consider as a (potential) problem, but also makes the impact of migration at large invisible and reproduces the idea that migration is the exception and—as Gérard Noiriel already noticed at the end of the 1980s—societies are determined by *longue durée* native structures.[26] Migration history offers a necessary antidote, but in order to deploy its full potential, it should not limit itself to the traditional low-skilled A-to-B migrants. Nancy Green's recent study on the American business and diplomatic community in Paris, numbering around 60,000 in the interwar period, is an excellent example of questioning assumptions of fixed national (and local) traits, unimpaired by outside influences.[27]

SEASONAL MIGRANTS

The second category of temporary migrants in the CCMR model concerns those who move seasonally, determined by climatic cycles in agriculture, forestry and—in the past more than in the present—construction. Although nowadays Polish and Romanian seasonal migrants are a topic of debate in several member states of the European Union, they have largely been invisible in migration history, apart from specific cases like the Bracero Program (1942–1964) to bring in Mexican manual workers on a temporal basis to the United States, or a similar scheme the Prussian state developed in the 1880s for Polish agricultural workers in the East of the German empire.[28] These examples are only the tip of the iceberg, especially when we look at the millions of seasonal workers who moved around in the past centuries.[29] Most seasonal workers were free to move, especially when they remained within their country (like in Spain, France and Italy), and alternated between their own small family farm, where wife and children remained, and the region where they temporarily earned money—a pattern that is still visible for the Eastern Europeans who come to Western Europe nowadays to harvest asparagus and strawberries.

The main reason to consider seasonal migrants as people who cross cultural boundaries is that they become familiar with more developed market economies than they are used to back home. From historical studies, we know that earning wages and being exposed to commercial-isation and new consumption patterns, along with a range of other new cultural experiences, not only changed the migrants but also changed the home communities. Investment of money into home villages by those members who have the opportunity to earn extra wages stimulates con-spicuous consumption, to use Torsten Veblen's term, and may very well increase social inequality, and the loosening of family bonds, leading to a loss of communal solidarity. Once again, this example shows that social changes through cross-cultural migrations (CCM) may have positive and negative effects, depending on one's perspective.

Another cross-cultural effect of seasonal migrations is illustrated by the experience of inhabitants of the Indian village of Ranapuram in Andhra Pradesh state who every year temporarily moved to the prov-ince of Karnataka for harvesting work. Not only did they earn wages and save money, but they also brought back knowledge and experience that changed agricultural patterns back home:

> The knowledge gained by seasonal migrants from working elsewhere also increased the adoption of new varieties of grain that fit the local environ-mental conditions and provided additional income. In the process of man-aging crops according to the rainfall conditions, there is a shift from local variety of jowar to the Raichur jowar, which was brought by the seasonal migrants as part of their wage labour. The local variety of jowar is usually sown by the villagers as a substitute crop if there are no rains till the end of August to sow groundnut. The local variety of jowar is grown only for fodder at present.[30]

CITY DWELLERS

For a long time, cities, both within and outside Europe, could only exist and grow through continuous immigration from the countryside. But when mortality levels declined in the course of the nineteenth century, cities remained a primary target for migrants. Many of them stayed only temporarily and either returned or moved onwards to other cities, but a considerable number of them stayed for good. Moving to cities brought villagers into a very different cultural and social environment. Apart from working opportunities and the possibility to earn one's own money, the much broader public space and institutions offered in general more possibilities for individuals to increase their autonomy from the family. In the countryside, they were more dependent on kin and subject to stricter social controls. For women, this often meant more possibilities to act on their own and reach a greater extent of agency, albeit within the prevailing gender norms.

Urban historians have recently argued along similar lines with respect to the greater public role of women in English and Dutch cities in the early modern period, leading to higher criminality rates,[31] whereas economic historians stress the relationship between gender equality in urban areas and economic growth.[32] Research on Western Europe, Korea, and Japan shows that there are causal links between gender relations, family systems, and economic development, illustrating that constraints on powerholders (men, parents) at the micro level advanced the motivations of women—and thus their agency—which positively impacted economic growth. These studies did not factor in migration, but it is clear that this was a crucial condition for cities in this period to exist, let alone grow.

Although these examples concern the early modern period, the liberating effect of rural to urban migrations through the reduced role of patriarchy, possibilities for education and earning one's own money have been attested for many European regions for the nineteenth and twentieth centuries. Most recently, the massive migration of men and women to Chinese cities has attracted the interest of social scientists who observe similar cultural changes.[33] This relationship, however, is not straightforward and depends on the extent to which patriarchal family systems erode under the influence of city air and on the specific urban 'membership regime' that sets the (gendered) formal and informal rules pertaining to the access of migrants to urban institutions and public spaces.[34]

The degree of 'open access' varies through time and space and—together with the extent of the homogenisation of national cultures—determines the salience of the rural–urban boundary. From the twentieth century onwards, in most parts of Europe, the process of nation-state building and the ensuing homogenisation through centralised education systems severely weakened cultural differences between the countryside and villages. In Table 3.1, internal migrations to cities after 1900 are therefore not considered as 'cross-cultural' anymore. For other parts of the world, however, especially in large states like India, Russia, and China with much greater internal ethnic, linguistic and religious diversity, there are good reasons to include internal moves. A good example is China. Not only are cultural differences between various parts of the country much bigger, but rural migrants have only limited access to urban institutions, such as schools and housing due to the discriminatory 'hukou system'.[35]

COLONISATION

In large empires like China, Russia, the Ottoman and the Habsburg empires, but also in overseas 'plantations' in the Americas and Oceania, people who moved as farmers to culturally and ecologically different (rural) areas were a recurrent phenomenon, both in the early modern and the modern periods. Such colonising migrations were often organised and supported by the state. Some of the migrants were coerced, such as French and British convicts and Russian dissenters,[36] whereas others saw no other option than leaving for unknown destinations as indentured migrants or redemptioners, often treated as virtual slaves at destination until they had repaid their debt (money borrowed for the journey). By far the largest group of forced colonists were some ten million Africans who were taken against their will to the Americas to work on plantations as hereditary chattel slaves. These examples show that, within this category, the full range of free to unfree migrations is represented, with 'free' migrants as the exception until the mid-nineteenth century. They have in common that they migrated not to cities but to land and that it was often institutions like states and commercial firms who organised their displacement and exploitation.

When we take a look at Western Europe in the modern period, at first glance, colonisation seems a more or less extinct phenomenon. By that time this region was so urbanised and densely populated that very little uncultivated or 'empty' land was left. Moreover, the democratising nation-states did not have the intention and need to organise such migrations, except for stimulating their citizens to emigrate outside Europe. An exception is Hitler's Germany, not by coincidence a self-declared empire and dictatorship. In its 'Drang nach Osten' to create 'Lebensraum', starting in 1939, the Nazis resettled about 500,000 German citizens and co-ethnics from the Baltic, Bessarabia, Alpine Italy, Galicia, Wolhynia and Transylvania in formerly Polish and Russian territory, many of them as farmers or villagers. The prerequisite was that about 1.2 million Poles were expelled, half of whom were soon exterminated, because they were Jewish.[37]

The Second World War and the horrific decision by the Nazi leadership to destroy all Jews in Europe brought about huge migrations, not only of soldiers—as we saw—but also a peculiar type of forced colonists: almost eight million coerced workers sent to labour camps and factories in Germany, where they mixed with companions from all over Europe. The cross-cultural effects of this experience for those who were lucky enough to return after the war, and for those to whom they returned, have not yet been systematically mapped and the topic begs for research. This leaves us with about three and a half million Jews and some 220,000 Roma and Sinti who were killed in concentration camps. Although many of them did not travel very far, they can be considered migrants, albeit not of the cross-cultural type, because the genocide prevented them from developing any contacts with others whatsoever.[38] The impact on Europe as a whole was nevertheless huge. Not only in cultural and demographic respects, as we discussed before, but also politically, as it created a deeply felt awareness, one could even say an ethical revolution, that started in the 1960s in Western Europe, that racism, discrimination, and stigmatisation represented the ultimate evil and should be discouraged and banned.[39] In recent decades, however, the force of this revolution is waning, due to the rise of radical and extreme right political parties that essentialise cultural features of migrants from Muslim countries and blame political correctness that ensued from the ethical revolution.[40]

CONCLUSION

How does the CCM approach help us to put the current polarised debate about immigration and integration into perspective, and more generally when it comes to the relation between people on the move and social change in the long run? To start with, it may offer a more balanced view on and understanding of the transforming effects of migration, whether one interprets these as positive or negative. Whereas the political discussion of migrants focuses one-sidedly on negative outcomes, such as the alleged (failing) integration of immigrants and their threat to free speech and liberal values, this chapter stresses that migration is a much more systemic phenomenon and in order to understand the impact of people who cross cultural boundaries, we should not reproduce prevailing selective—and biased—views of what constitutes geographical mobility.

The CCM methodology highlights much broader societal changes, both in Europe and in the regions where migrants came from and partly returned to. Its added value is that it contributes to general debates, from economic growth to state formation and the Civil Rights Movement in the US. Therefore, the CCM approach has the potential to free migration studies and migration history from a (sometimes self chosen) academic ghetto that focuses on very specific migrants, their ethnicity, and the reactions of receiving societies to these 'problematic' newcomers. CCM stresses the normality of human mobility and its structural function for forging social change.[41]

Although we are only at the very beginning of appreciating the relationship between CCM and social change, the main building stones of a theoretical model have been identified. Apart from the four key types of migration as defined in the CCM approach, they include the various sorts of 'capital' (social, cultural, economic, and political) that migrants embody and the prevailing 'membership regime' (from open access to rigid segregation), which determines to what extent receiving societies enable migrants to interact freely with those already present.[42] Finally we have to be precise when it comes to what kind of social change we are interested in, which ranges from political and institutional transformations to technological innovations and alterations in family systems, both at destination and back home. Irrespective of what specific question we focus on, the CCM approach frees us from the prevailing conceptual political straitjacket and opens up a new and exciting field of study.

NOTES

1. Jonathan Wadsworth, *Immigration and the UK Labour Market* (London: LSE, 2015).
2. David Goodhart, *The British Dream: Success and Failures of Post-War Immigration* (London: Atlantic, 2013); Paul Collier, *Exodus:*

Immigration and Multiculturalism in the 21st Century (London: Allen Lane, 2013); and David Miller, *Strangers in Our Midst: The Political Philosophy of Immigration* (Cambridge, MA: Harvard University Press, 2016).

3. For balanced and nuanced studies on these issues, see: Étienne Piguet, Antoine Pécoud, and Paul de Guchteneire, eds., *Migration and Climate Change* (New York: Unesco and Cambridge University Press, 2011); Paul Puschmann and Koen Matthijs, 'The demographic transition in the Arab world: The dual role of marriage in family dynamics and population growth,' in *Beyond the Demographic Divide: Population Change in Europe, the Middle-East and North Africa*, eds. Koen Matthijs, Karel Neels, Christiane Timmerman, and Jacques Haers (Farnham: Ashgate, 2015), 119–65; and Alex Sager, 'Book review: Strangers in our midst: The political philosophy of immigration by David Miller,' *LSE Blog Review of Books* (London: LSE, 2016), http://blogs.lse.ac.uk/lsereviewofbooks/2016/09/06/book-review-strangers-in-our-midst-the-political-philosophy-of-immigration-by-david-miller/.

4. Leo Lucassen and Jan Lucassen, 'The strange death of Dutch tolerance: The timing and nature of the pessimist turn in the Dutch migration debate,' *The Journal of Modern History* 87, no. 1 (2015): 72–101.

5. Nancy Foner, *From Ellis Island to JFK. New York's Two Great Waves of Immigration* (New Haven: Yale University Press, 2000); Richard Alba and Victor Nee, *Remaking the American Mainstream: Assimilation and Contemporary Immigration* (Cambridge, MA: Harvard University Press, 2003); Leo Lucassen, *The Immigrant Threat: The Integration of Old and New Migrants in Western Europe Since 1850* (Urbana and Chicago: The University of Illinois Press, 2005); and Klaus J. Bade, Pieter C. Emmer, Leo Lucassen, and Jochen Oltmer, eds. *The Encyclopedia of Migration and Minorities in Europe: From the 17th Century to the Present* (New York: Cambridge University Press, 2011).

6. James Hollifield, *Immigrants, Markets, and States: The Political Economy of Postwar Europe* (Cambridge, MA: Harvard University Press, 1992); Lucassen and Lucassen, 'The strange death'; and Leo Lucassen, 'Migration, membership regimes and social policies: A view from global history,' in *Handbook of Migration and Social Policy*, eds. Gary Freeman and Nikola Mirilovic (Cheltenham and Northampton: Edward Elgar Publishing, 2016), 64–84.

7. Joel Perlmann and Roger Waldinger, 'Second generation decline? Children of immigrants, past and present—A reconsideration,' *International Migration Review* 31, no. 4 (1997): 893–922.

8. William Cunningham, *Alien Immigrants to England* (London and New York: Swan Sonnenschein & Co. and The Macmillan Co., 1897).

9. Nancy Foner and Leo Lucassen, 'Legacies of the past', in *The Changing Face of World Cities: Young Adult Children of Immigrants in Europe and the United States*, eds. Maurice Crul and John Mollenkopf (New York: Russell Sage 2012) 26–43.

10. Patrick Manning, *Migration in World History*, 2nd ed. (Abingdon and New York: Routledge, 2013).

11. Karl Marx and Friedrich Engels, *Manifest der Kommunistischen Partei* (London: J. E. Burghard, 1848).

12. Leslie P. Moch, *Moving Europeans. Migration in Western Europe Since 1650* (Bloomington: Indiana University Press, 2013).

13. Jan Lucassen and Leo Lucassen, 'The mobility transition revisited, 1500–1900: What the case of Europe can offer to global history,' *The Journal of Global History* 4, no. 4 (2009): 347–77; Lucassen and Lucassen, eds., *Globalising Migration History. The Eurasian Experience (16th–21st Centuries)* (Leiden and Boston: Brill, 2014); and Lucassen and Lucassen, 'Theorizing cross-cultural migrations: The case of Eurasia since 1500,' *Social Science History*, 41, no. 3 (2017): 445–75. This cross-cultural approach leaves out migrants whose mobility is limited to the same cultural realm.

14. Already noticed by Ewa Morawska, 'The sociology and historiography of immigration,' in *Immigration Reconsidered: History Sociology, and Politics*, ed. Virginia Yans-McLaughlin (Oxford: Oxford University Press 1990), 187–240.

15. Foner, *From Ellis Island to JFK*; Joel Perlmann, *Italians Then, Mexicans Now. Immigrant Origins and Second-Generation Progress, 1890 to 2000* (New York: Russell Sage Foundation, 2005); Lucassen, *The Immigrant Threat*; and Roger Waldinger, 'Did manufacturing matter? The experience of yesterday's second generation: A reassessment,' *International Migration Review* 41, no. 1 (2007): 3–39.

16. Donna Gabaccia, 'The "yellow peril" and the "Chinese of Europe": Global perspectives on race and labor, 1815–1930,' in *Migration, Migration History, History: Old Paradigms and New Perspectives*, eds. Jan Lucassen and Leo Lucassen (Bern: Peter Lang), 177–96; See also Adam McKeown, *Melancholy Order: Asian Migration and the Globalization of Borders* (New York: Columbia University Press, 2008).

17. Joshua A. Sanborn, 'Unsettling the empire: Violent migrations and social disaster in Russia during World War I,' *The Journal of Modern History* 77, no. 2 (2005): 290–324; Christopher J. Tozzi, *Nationalizing France's Army. Foreign, Black, and Jewish Troops in the French Military, 1715–1831* (Charlottesville and London: University of Virginia Press, 2016).

18. Götz Aly, *Hitler's Beneficiaries: Plunder, Racial War, and the Nazi Welfare State* (New York: Henry Holt, 2006).

19. Christopher Rass, *Militärische Migration vom Altertum bis zur Gegenwart* (Paderborn: Ferdinand Schöningh, 2016).

20. Alex Bein, *The Jewish Question. Biography of a World Problem* (Rutherford, NJ: Fairleigh Dickinson University Press, 1990), 25–27.

21. Stephen M. Saideman and R. William Ayres, *For Kin or Country: Xenophobia, Nationalism, and War* (New York: Columbia University Press, 2005); and Jan C. Behrends and Patrice G. Poutrus, 'Xenophobia in the former GDR—Explorations and explanation from a historical perspective,' in *Nationalisms Across the Globe. An Overview of Nationalisms in State-Endowed and Stateless Nations*, eds. Wojciech Burszta, Tomasz Dominik Kamusella, and Sebastian Wojciechowski (Poznań: Wyższa Nikoła Nauk Humanistycznych i Dziennikarstwa, 2005), 155–70.

22. Erik-Jan Zürcher, *Fighting for a Living: A Comparative History of Military Labour in Europe and Asia, 1500–2000* (Amsterdam: Amsterdam University Press, 2011).

23. Pavel Polian, *Against Their Will: The History and Geography of Forced Migrations in the USSR* (Budapest: CEU Press, 2004).

24. Maria Höhn and Martin Klimke, *A Breath of Freedom: The Civil Rights Struggle, African American GIs, and Germany* (New York: Palgrave Macmillan, 2010). For more in general on soldiers as migrants, see Rass, *Militärische Migration* and Sanborn, 'Unsettling the empire'.

25. Leo Lucassen and Aniek X. Smit, 'The repugnant other: Soldiers, missionaries and aid workers as organizational migrants,' *The Journal of World History* 26, no. 1 (2015): 1–39.

26. Gérard Noiriel, *Le Creuset Français: Histoire de l'Immigration, XIXe-XXe Siècles* (Paris: Éd. du Seuil, 1988); and Noiriel, *La Tyrannie du National: le Droit d'Asile en Europe (1793–1993)* (Paris: Calmann-Lévy, 1991).

27. Nancy L. Green, 'Americans abroad and the uses of citizenship: Paris, 1914–1940,' *Journal of American Ethnic History*, 31 no. 3 (2012): 5–34.

28. Lucassen, *The Immigrant Threat*, 59–61.

29. Jan Lucassen, *Migrant Labour in Europe. The Drift to the North Sea* (London: Croom Helm, 1987).

30. Purendra Prasad, *Famines & Droughts. Survival Strategies* (Jaipur and New Delhi: Rawat Publications, 1988), 132–33.

31. Ariadne Schmidt and Manon van der Heijden, 'Women alone in early modern Dutch towns: Opportunities and strategies to survive,' *Urban History*, 42, no. 1 (2016) 21–38.

32. Alexandra M. de Pleijt, Jan Luiten van Zanden, and Sarah Carmichael, 'Gender relations and economic development: Hypotheses about the reversal of fortune in EurAsia,' CGEH Working Paper No. 79 (Utrecht: Utrecht University, 2016); See also Tine de Moor and Jan Luiten van Zanden, 'Girlpower: The European marriage pattern (EMP) and labour

markets in the North Sea region in the late medieval and early modern period,' *Economic History Review*, 63, no. 1 (2010) 1–33.

33. Hong Zhang, 'Labor migration, gender, and the rise of neo-local marriages in the economic boomtown of Dongguan, South China,' *Journal of Contemporary China* 18, no. 61 (2009): 639–56.

34. Leo Lucassen, 'Population and migration,' in *The Oxford Handbook of Cities in World History*, ed. Peter Clark (Oxford: Oxford University Press, 2013), 664–82.

35. Martin King Whyte, *One Country, Two Societies: Rural Urban Inequality in Contemporary China* (Cambridge, MA: Harvard University Press, 2010).

36. Nicholas B. Breyfogle, *Heretics and Colonizers: Forging Russia's Empire in the South Caucasus* (Ithaca: Cornell University Press, 2005).

37. Klaus J. Bade, *Migration in European History* (Malden and Oxford: Blackwell, 2003), 210–11.

38. Leo Lucassen, Jan Lucassen, Rick de Jong, and Mark van de Water, 'Cross-cultural migration in Europe 1901–2000: A preliminary estimate,' IISH Research Papers (Amsterdam: International Institute of Social History, 2014), 50.

39. Lucassen and Lucassen, 'The strange death'.

40. Cas Mudde, 'Three decades of populist radical right parties in Western Europe: So what?' *European Journal of Political Research* 52, no. 1 (2013): 1–19.

41. Manning, *Migration in World History*.

42. Lucassen and Lucassen, 'Theorizing cross-cultural migrations'.

PART II

New Zealand and Australia

If we are to 'reframe' migration history, we need to address two of its traditional weaknesses: the tendency to focus on problematic, poor, male and non-white migrants and to ignore migrant agency. This section shows how this can be done through the prism of migration in Australia and New Zealand. Lyndon Fraser's contribution 'Both Sides of the Tasman: History, Politics and Migration between New Zealand and Australia' points the way to a 'trans-Tasman' history encompassing the connections and movements across the sea that lies between the two countries. This would in Fraser's view encourage us to think beyond the nation as a way of defining the world and our past. In 'Changing Migration Policy from the Margins: Filipino Activism on Behalf of Victims of Domestic Violence in Australia, 1980s–2000s', Mina Roces puts migrant women and their agency centre stage, moving away from a focus on victimhood. By highlighting the way in which activists were able to shape Australian policy she puts migrants at the heart of policy-making processes, subverting the traditional distinctions between history from above and from below and highlighting the transnational dimension of policy-making. Her work also acts as a reminder that in a different political climate, dialogue and collaboration between migrant groups and government bureaucracy were possible, offering a contrast to twenty-first-century approaches.

CHAPTER 4

Both Sides of the Tasman: History, Politics and Migration Between New Zealand and Australia

Lyndon Fraser

In her recent book *Playing for Both Sides*, New Zealand-born novelist Stephanie Johnson offers 'a kind of memoir' about her relationship to Australia, a place that has 'loomed large' in her own life, 'just as it has in the lives of many New Zealanders'.[1] Although the sunburnt country held 'little fascination' before her departure, she is drawn to Sydney by 'a Kiwi erstwhile boyfriend who had come back to New Zealand briefly with short-lived declarations of undying love'.[2] Johnson recalls being struck by the sexist remarks and brazen racism of many Australians she encountered, as well as the legion of Kiwi sheep and 'dole bludger' jokes.[3] But she falls heavily for Sydney's 'new quality of light', the old sandstone buildings, the beauty of Hyde Park and the harbour with 'water the colour of kerosene'. There were flying foxes in the Morton Bay fig trees at the Botanic Gardens and an array of native birds that she thought had adjusted far better to

L. Fraser (✉)
University of Canterbury, Christchurch, New Zealand

L. Fraser
Canterbury Museum, Christchurch, New Zealand

© The Author(s) 2019
E. Henrich and J. M. Simpson (eds.),
History, Historians and the Immigration Debate,
https://doi.org/10.1007/978-3-319-97123-0_4

city life than their Auckland counterparts: 'lizard-headed ibis, raucous cockatoos, rosellas and kookaburras'.[4] Johnson deals with isolation and fear by writing again. She feels liberated, finds work as an assistant in a news-clipping room and ends her disastrous love affair. She also acquires an Australian accent during a brief stint in Melbourne and returns to Sydney where the dust jacket on the Australian edition of her first book of short stories describes her 'as one of their own'. It is back here, in a shared house at Centennial Park, that she finds love with her 'Aussie' flatmate and future husband, Tim, 'a curly-haired, blue-eyed' editor at the Australian Broadcasting Corporation. After the birth of their first child, Stan, the couple decide to settle in Auckland where they believe they can make a better life for their son. 'For several years after our return', she says, 'I had the eerie feeling that my Sydney life continued, that I had somehow split in half and lived two lives at once; I had only to somehow find the money for a plane fare and I could slip back inside that other skin'.[5]

Johnson's experiences and feelings as both migrant and returnee would strike a chord with a great many New Zealanders. Like thousands of others, she has a wider trans-Tasman family. Her son, Stan—the first grand-child on either side—was born at the Royal Women's Hospital in Paddington, Sydney, grew up in Auckland and now lives in Melbourne. A daughter, Maeve, has recently returned from Australia 'and may well go back again'. Both have relatives and friends in 'the West Island'.[6] Many would also share Johnson's sentiment that if she was unable to visit Australia in the future, she would feel as though she had lost a part of her heart. Large numbers of Kiwis live their lives going back and forth across the Tasman Sea for work, family, holidays, sport, love, lifestyle and adventure. Brisbane, Perth, Bondi, the Gold Coast and—in my case a little slice of St Kilda in Melbourne—can make us feel as much at 'home' (and sometimes more so) than Christchurch, Hokitika or Hamilton.

Trans-Tasman migration connections are deeply woven into our everyday existence, emotions and imaginations in ways that historians are only really beginning to explore. They have also become a significant political issue. At the heart of the matter is a perception among many New Zealanders that Australia betrayed 'the ANZAC spirit' in 2001 by entering into 'mean-spirited' arrangements over social security entitlement, medical care, tertiary education and citizenship for Kiwi migrants.[7] Australians living in New Zealand, meanwhile, have continued to receive these benefits without disruption. More recently, there has been anger over the incarceration of New Zealanders at Villawood and Christmas Island detention centres, the mandatory deportation of convicted criminals (some of whom grew up in Australia), and the solitary confinement of Afghanistan veteran Lance Corporal Ngati Kanohi Te Eke Haapu in a maximum security prison after the revocation of his visa for his links to an outlaw motorcycle gang.[8] Immigration, by contrast, has generated little heat in what Australians refer to as 'the shaky isles' (on account of New Zealand's frequent earthquakes) for more than a decade, despite record intakes. New Zealand has no equivalent to the Cronulla 'race' riots, the anti-Islamic Reclaim Australia protests, a reinvigorated One Nation (a conservative political party that has been extremely critical of current immigration policies), the detention of asylum seekers, or confrontations around Islam and multiculturalism, all of which cast long shadows across the political landscape of its nearest neighbour. Yet, this does not mean that local historians should resign themselves to playing the role of street-corner spectators. Their work in transnational, public and oral history can inform contemporary debates over the status of New Zealanders in Australia (and vice versa) by placing them in wider perspective and highlighting the human dimension to the story of trans-Tasman mobility.

I

It is supremely ironic, given New Zealand's reputation for having one of the most mobile populations in the world, that its national icon, the endangered Kiwi, is a flightless, nocturnal and near-blind bird that spends most of its adult life in a defined territory. At the time of writing, as many as one million New Zealanders are resident overseas with around three-fifths living in Australia. Roughly one-in-six New Zealand-born people currently live outside their country of birth and relative to its population size—over 4.6 million—it has one of the largest diasporas per capita in the world.[9] In a very real sense, then, growing up in New Zealand means preparing oneself to leave at some future point.

Trans-Tasman migration has deep historical roots dating back to the eighteenth century, something that is too often obscured in recent commentary. Historian and educationalist Rollo Arnold captured its essence when he coined the phrase 'the Perennial Interchange' to describe the long-standing movement of people, flora, fauna and ideas between Australia and New Zealand.[10] After the formation of a penal colony at Port Jackson in 1788, the eastern islands were seen through an imperial lens as an extension of the New South Wales colonial frontier. New Zealand provided much needed timber, flax, naval stores and, later, whales for oil. An increasing volume of trans-Tasman traffic and inter-actions with foreign visitors ensured that Māori (those indigenous to the islands) were drawn into trade and significantly to European tech-nologies, ideas and commodities. But these early exchanges were geo-graphically concentrated in the far north and around the southern coast. European deserters, for example, lived with Hauraki Māori, learned their language, and worked in the timber trade.[11] Sealing gangs, meanwhile, were active in Fiordland in 1791 and in Rakuira and the Chathams by the early 1800s.[12] One of the most extraordinary outcomes was the establishment of one of the first trans-Tasman communities by Ngai Tāhu leaders who gave Whenuahou (Codfish Island) to a mixed group of European sealer 'overstayers' and their indigenous partners. As the Ngāi Tāhu archaeologist and writer Atholl Anderson explains, the settle-ment provided the 'foundation for an emerging mixed-race population' in the region that 'transformed the nature of southern Māori descent and experience in the nineteenth century'.[13] Cross-cultural encounters were even more dramatic in the north of Te Ika a Māui with the estab-lishment of Protestant missions among Māori in 1814 and the reshaping of local power relations as the area became incorporated into the politi-cal, religious and commercial networks of empire.[14]

The formation of large expatriate Māori populations in Australia is in many ways the culmination of two centuries of Māori travel and engagement with the outside world that began in this period.[15] The young chiefs Tuki Tahua and Huru Kokoti were 'the first OE [Overseas Experience] pioneers' to set foot on Australian soil. They were kidnapped in 1793, transported to Port Jackson and then transferred to Norfolk Island where they were expected to instruct convicts in flax-dressing.[16] They established close reciprocal bonds with the Lieutenant-Governor, Philip Gidley King, 'living in [his] house, dining at his own table and mixing freely with the local élite'. Moved by their lamentations for kinsfolk and home, King escorted the two rangatira [chiefs] back to Doubtless Bay on the *Britannia* in 1795.[17] They brought pigs, potatoes and the knowledge that 'there were kindly strangers out there who might protect and befriend Māori travellers in need'.[18]

If the element of duress makes this story unique, the theme of rela-tionships is one that endures across the *longue durée*. One of the most famous cases involves the powerful Bay of Islands chief, Te Pahi, whose son, Matara, joined a British whaling ship in 1804 and returned from Sydney with gifts which King (now the Governor of New South

Wales) had sent for his father in recognition of his generous hospitality to whalers and local power.[19] When Te Pahi travelled to Port Jackson ('Poihakena') one year later with four of his sons, he stayed for several months with King at Government House. This episode was akin to 'a diplomatic or state visit' given the chief's senior status. He returned to New Zealand 'with his mana high', and, in the Governor's estimation, as 'the Greatest Monarch that ever left it'.[20] There is a beautiful medal presented to Te Pahi by his host in January 1806 that still survives. But the gift was a bad omen. Within four years, the great chief was dead, a victim of inter-tribal conflict over the control of the lucrative European trade. His youngest daughter died of dysentery just weeks earlier in Sydney, leaving a child in the Female Orphan School. It is also significant that Te Pahi had met and impressed Reverend Samuel Marsden, who rose to become principal chaplain, a landholder and local notable in New South Wales. His model farm at Parramatta became 'an important Māori offshore base' with a constant flow of guests and visitors.[21] Marsden's plans for the establishment of a Church Missionary Society presence in New Zealand were only realised through personal relationships and ties of reciprocity with high-ranking chiefs such as Ruatara and Hongi Hika. Missions, then, were dependent on Māori patronage and protection, and indigenes partly set the terms for cross-cultural engagement in Australia as well as at home in Te Ika a Māui, a region shaped by complex political rivalries, genealogies, alliances and conflicts.[22]

Hongi Hika carved a self-portrait from one of Samuel Marsden's Parramatta fenceposts before his return to New Zealand in 1814.[23] It is an extraordinary piece and one that speaks not only to the idea of relationships, but also to the crucial trans-Tasman dimension to colonisation. Marsden noted that Ruatara, Hika and their companions became sullen on their departure from Sydney Cove aboard the *Active*, having been warned by a 'gentleman' that many more Europeans would follow the missionaries and they 'would possess themselves of the whole island, and either destroy the natives, or reduce them to slavery'.[24] This prophesy was not entirely fanciful. Historians have shown how Ruatara's last sojourn in Sydney had inexorably 'spun the thread' which would soon bind New Zealand within the webs of empire. Māori did make gains from the fluctuating mercantile trade and some chiefs opened agencies at Port Jackson for the purpose. But the trans-Tasman commerce also led to the introduction of muskets, the formation of whaling stations, and the arrival of young settlers from the Australian colonies. Trade also had a darker side, nowhere more so than in 1830 when Ngati Toa chief Te Rauparaha hired Captain John Stewart and the brig *Elizabeth* in Sydney to take him and his warriors to Akaroa where they extracted a grisly revenge on Ngāi Tahu for the blood price of a cargo of flax.[25] The outrage that ensued highlighted the question of New Zealand's legal relations with New South Wales. The appointment of James Busby as the British Resident in New Zealand (1833), financed by the state's treasury, set in motion a complex chain of events that take us from the choice of the first national flag (1834)—allowing locally registered ships to enter Australian ports—to the Declaration of Independence of the United Tribes (1835) and, ultimately, the signing of the Treaty of Waitangi (1840).[26] Perhaps Judith Binney offers the most compelling summary of deepening relationships within the trans-Tasman world: 'The many travellers to Poihakena had been entertained, and wined, and dined, and fed sweet cakes. They had entered contracts, both knowingly and unknowingly. They had brought back new images of power and of justice. They were not innocent travellers, but they could not know the extent to which their world was being altered'.[27]

The contribution of Australian colonies to the systematic colonisation of New Zealand persisted long after its formal acquisition by the British Crown in 1840. Public and academic histories have understandably given sustained attention to the great migrations of the nineteenth century that brought so many newcomers to the colonies from Britain, Ireland, parts of Europe, India and southern China. State assistance was a key distinguishing feature of the increasing flows of people that so surprised Māori, just as it had been in Australia.[28] Nonetheless, the crucial trans-Tasman dimension to mobility and colonialism has been obscured in the national histories of both countries.[29] Between the 1840s and the late 1870s, the Australian colonies provided a substantial proportion of migrants to New Zealand and a majority in particular years. I think here of early South Island pastoralists, Waikato militia recruited to fight in the Land Wars, the activities of church professionals, mobile business women seeking fresh opportunities, and, especially, Charles Thatcher's 'noisy, drinking, smoking, cursing crowd' chasing the latest El Dorado on the mining frontier.[30] Large numbers of people moved in the opposite direction during tough times in the 1880s, lured by higher wages and better living conditions in places like Victoria. This flow was reversed in the last decade of the nineteenth century and into the twentieth when Australian arrivals greatly exceeded those travelling from Britain and Ireland.

Among these newcomers were New Zealand's future Prime Minister Michael Joseph Savage and his fellow Australian-born migrants Paddy Webb, Bob Semple, Mark Fagan and Bill Parry, who formed part of the first Labour government's cabinet in 1935.[31]

The Tasman Sea, then, is perhaps best seen as 'bridge' across which people travelled backwards and forwards at a time when land presented the greater barrier to mobility. We have already seen examples of its operation in the cases of the chiefs such as Te Pahi or Hongi Hika, the 'offshore base' at Parramatta, and in the activities of sealers, deserters and colonial officials. It endured long beyond the first part of the nineteenth century to the golden age of Māori trans-Tasman entrepreneurialism, the migrant super-highway of the 1860s and the labour movements of the turn-of-the-century era. In my own goldfields research, I was struck by the ease with which someone like Irish-born Sarah Gillin, who spent time in Melbourne and Hokitika before marrying a man she had not spoken to until the morning of her wedding, could cross from the West Coast of New Zealand to shop in the splendour of the Victorian capital in the 1860s.[32] As Philip Ross May once famously noted, the physical isolation of the region from which she set sail helped turn it into 'an economic dependency of Victoria' in the period and made its capital, Hokitika, into 'a trans-Tasman suburb of Melbourne'.[33] More recently, scholars have identified long-standing economic and cultural connections centred on the flourishing entrepot that linked localities in Victoria, Otago, northern Tasmania and the South Island's rugged West Coast. Ideas, identities, news, industrial practices, organisational and government structures circulated throughout this Tasman world.[34] The ties that bind were also deeply personal. Transnational families spanned the sea in all directions and the story of people on the move cannot be told fully without taking these relationships into account.

II

There were powerful continuities in terms of mobility, connections and interactions across the Tasman world after the transition from sail, steam and sea-spray to the great age of flight. New Zealand experienced a small net loss to people to Australian states soon after the Second World War but it soon became the main recipient of trans-Tasman movement. Between the years 1952 and 1967 as many as 36,000 Australians migrated to New Zealand, lured by a golden economy with plentiful jobs and higher standards of living.[35] A collapse in wool prices and growing unemployment brought harder times and led to a dramatic change. From the late 1960s onwards, far more Kiwis made their way to 'the West Island' than vice versa. The pattern has persisted for several decades and still constitutes the main slice of a larger New Zealand abroad.

We need to turn to the work of demographers to explain this trend. In the first instance, the New Zealand economy weakened. The major recession of the late 1960s featured not only significant job losses, but also rapid inflation and, tellingly, the devaluation of the New Zealand dollar by twenty percent.[36] Second, the rapid expansion of commercial air travel during the decade made trans-Tasman flights a more affordable option for larger numbers of people. A third contributing factor was an emerging trend for New Zealand 'baby boomers' to go on their 'OE' as young adults.[37] Australia, for some, was the first step on a longer journey. It required little preparation and very few savings. Kiwis could move there on short notice and were able to settle without applying for permanent residence or citizenship. The New Zealand-born poet, ethnographer and novelist Michael Jackson, for example, fled to Melbourne after a pub full of drinkers he had invited to Auckland University after closing time wrecked the Anthropology Department.[38] An air ticket was affordable, even for students like Jackson, and so Kiwi migrants came from a broad cross-section of New Zealand society. Both cost and closeness meant that visits home, return migration and circular movements were very real possibilities.

A closer look at the ebbs and flows shows that there were five peaks in trans-Tasman migration between the late 1960s and today. Around 21,000 New Zealanders made their way west each year from 1967 to 1971. The Trans-Tasman Travel Arrangement of 1973 formalised long-standing agreements and practices whereby citizens from each country had unrestricted rights to live and work on either side of 'the ditch'. A second major wave took place between 1978–1979 and 1980–1981, when a whopping 32,000 people moved across the ditch annually. The exodus led to one of the most famous sledges in modern Australasian history when the then New Zealand Prime Minister, Robert Muldoon—deflecting concern about the exodus—quipped that Kiwis leaving for Australia 'raise the IQ of both countries'.[39] Numbers fell by about one-third in the early 1980s at a time of recession and higher unemployment in Australia. As economic conditions there improved and New Zealand's continued to worsen, the exodus regained its momentum.

The third major wave of migration peaked at over 44,000 in 1988–1989. Australia experienced another recession in the following decade and permanent and long-term migration from New Zealand dropped again.[40] Widespread political concerns about the rising cost of Kiwi 'dole-bludgers', the refusal of the New Zealand government to pay a larger share of their maintenance and fears about 'back door entry' for those who might otherwise not have been admitted to the country were factors behind Australia's decision to withdraw the automatic access of New Zealanders to a welfare safety-net on arrival. Australian officials thought that the numbers of Kiwis in the 'lucky country' would decline markedly as a result of these changes.[41] Towards the end of the 2000s, however, movement from New Zealand to Australia surged once again and sparked renewed anxiety about a 'brain drain'. It was followed by a new record high of 53,900 in the twelve month period from August 2011, a loss for which the Canterbury earthquakes of 2010–2011 must be taken into account.[42] Whether or not the relatively low level of departures and high level of arrivals in 2015 heralds something quite new remains to be seen. What we can say with greater confidence is that since the 1960s the numbers of New Zealand citizens departing to Australia has always exceeded those arriving from the west.[43]

Population economist Jacques Poot has characterised trans-Tasman migration patterns over recent decades as cyclical, circular and increasingly permanent. He argues convincingly that the streams have been remarkably consistent since the 1960s, with peak net outflows to Australia towards the end of every decade other than the late 1990s (in 1969, 1979, 1989 and 2008). Moreover, the timing of departures has been mirrored to some degree in the rhythm of arrivals from Australia, of whom as many as two-thirds are returnees.[44] We can go even further than this. The sheer growth in the numbers of Kiwis in Australia has meant that New Zealanders and their Australian families dominate the flow of migration from Australia to New Zealand.[45] Australian demographer Graeme Hugo has traced the extraordinarily high rates of circularity in trans-Tasman migration, with many people moving frequently between east and west, much as they did in the nineteenth and early twentieth centuries.[46] At the same time, scholars have revealed a significant change from long-term to permanent movement among flying Kiwis as well as a sizeable return flow.[47] Leaving 2015 aside, the steady stream of returnees has never entirely 'offset the larger, more erratic surges' of those going abroad.[48]

There is no doubt that the direction and volume of trans-Tasman traffic has been linked to the relative health of the two economies in the post-war period. Yet economics, demography, politics and policy—though vitally important—can only take us so far. Recent scholarship in New Zealand, like migration histories internationally, has revealed the centrality of personal relationships in encouraging and facilitating mobility. Oral histories, for example, show that these ties played a key role in decision-making for Kiwis 'on the wing'. Australian-based contacts provided information for newcomers and helped to organise accommodation or jobs. This could be quite a simple matter. One of historian Rosemary Baird's informants was sent a copy of *The Age* every couple of weeks by her Melbourne-based brother so that she could explore the 'situations vacant' section. A young reporter left Taumarunui after landing a job in Townsville in the 1960s, a move that was eased by the support of his cousin's family who lived there. Invercargill-born mechanic, David Cavanagh, on the other hand, enjoyed a wild life of parties, alcohol and cars. After narrowly avoiding drink driving convictions and buoyed by the stories of his mates in Perth, he went to Melbourne where he had access to a 'community car' left for new migrants by his Western Australia-based friends.[49] Relationships based on kinship, locality or acquaintance remain crucial in shaping places of first settlement and in bringing about further departures, just as they did for these late twentieth-century migrants. Such ties could also work in a negative sense: Australian destinations offered—and continue to provide—an easy refuge from annoying parents, abusive partners, divorce, or the pain of death. When referee Steve Walsh was sacked by the New Zealand Rugby Union in 2009 after a well-publicised battle with alcohol, for example, he went to Sydney and worked as a labourer. There, he eventually resurrected his international career, becoming Australia's leading official at elite level by 2010.[50]

New Zealanders now constitute the second largest migrant category in the West Island and fifteen out of every one hundred people born in the shaky isles live across the ditch. The impact of these numbers on both the sending and receiving society is highly significant. I have found in my classes at the University of Canterbury in Christchurch—and in presentations at other places—that few people indicate that they have no relatives or friends in Australia. This response has increased quite dramatically since I first began teaching in 2000, despite growing numbers of overseas-born students. It has been pure gold from a pedagogical point of view. An otherwise arcane concept like transnationalism becomes an aspect of everyday experience and a topic for sustained discussion and reflection. Families are stretched across the Tasman. Visits take place in both directions and homesickness or a sense of 'missing out' persists even with Facebook, Skype and all the other wonders of modern digital technologies. It is also clear that trans-Tasman migration affects men and women 'in gender specific ways' and places a heavy burden on the latter who usually 'undertake the meshing of work and family systems'.[51] Historical work shows that how this was so when Kiwi women migrants had children. The early stages of motherhood were very hard and they usually enjoyed emotional support from transnational networks but missed having sisters, grandparents and, especially, mothers physically present. Later in the life course, as migrants face the challenges of ageing parents at home, there has been a gendered expectation that women will take on transnational caring roles. The ease and relative cheapness of flights across the Tasman has done little to diminish the challenges of long-distance aid. On the contrary, the geographical closeness of Australia may have increased women's obligations in caring for the elderly, as there is often a tacit assumption that they will visit more regularly. In times of family crisis, through death, accident, break-ups or illness, the Tasman Sea must have seemed much wider to many Kiwis.[52]

If an historical perspective offers much in these areas, it is surely crucial when exploring the question of return migration. I have already noted the circularity of contemporary trans-Tasman migration and the substantial flow of returnees. Historians are notoriously susceptible to 'turns' of one kind or another—linguistic, cultural and so on—but current interest in emotions holds promise for the study of this kind of mobility. The need for extended family, the shame of divorce, the enticement of love and perceived opportunities for children were just some of the feelings that Rosemary Baird's oral history interviewees described when they talked about going home. In our joint research, we found that return was often a more disorientating and difficult experience for Kiwis than policy-makers, politicians and other commentators would lead us to believe. They had changed in the sunburnt country and so had New Zealand during their absence in ways that could be surprising and disappointing. Past relationships were less meaningful or comfortable than before. For some returnees, everyday life was much harder financially than it had been in Australia, especially in terms of pay. Migrant children missed their friends and warmer weather, as did many of their parents. It is not surprising that Kiwis re-migrated frequently.

'Home' could be an ambiguous notion. One circular migrant, living in Canberra, captured this beautifully when he described that place as somewhere 'in the middle of the Tasman … I'm an Australian, I'm a New Zealander. I can pretty much live anywhere'.[53]

III

In *The Age of Migration*, Stephen Castles and Mark Miller describe international mobility as a 'transnational revolution' that is reshaping societies around the world.[54] As the chapters in this volume suggest, historians have much to contribute to global and local political debates around issues such as refugee policy, racism, citizenship, multiculturalism, indigenous rights, and the 'management' of super-diversity. Their work also provides a better understanding of regional migration systems like the trans-Tasman highway by placing developments in a wider context and drawing attention to patterns of continuity and change. There are certainly opportunities here for collaborative public histories that highlight personal stories, emphasise the experiences of transnational Australasian families and raise tough questions about equity and injustice.[55] Most importantly, perhaps, our scholarship has policy relevance because it introduces a crucial historical dimension that has been sadly lacking in Australia's approach to contemporary Kiwi migration. The experiences of people like Te Pahi and Stephanie Johnson, separated by two centuries, speak to the long-standing connections that bind people and places on both sides of the Tasman. A failure to take these links into account has led to short-term policy solutions like deportation that create genuine hardship and lead to more problems than they were designed to solve. One of the key challenges in overcoming this historical amnesia about the role of the Tasman Sea in our shared migration history, however, is the fact that the nation remains powerfully entrenched as a way of representing, framing and understanding the social world. This 'methodological nationalism' obscures important aspects of the past.[56] As Peter Hempenstall has astutely noted, 'writers on both sides of the Tasman have produced national histories that talk past one another, ignore shared pasts and neglect historical parallels'.[57] To understand the diverse experiences of contemporary trans-Tasman migrants, however, we need transnational histories that promote deeper understandings of regional mobility, encourage more nuanced debate, and contribute to greater compassion in immigration policy.

Notes

1. Stephanie Johnson, *Playing for Both Sides: Love Across the Tasman* (Wellington: Bridget Williams Books, 2016), 9.
2. Johnson, *Playing for Both Sides*, 19.
3. The derogatory term 'dole bludger' is used informally in New Zealand and Australia to refer to people who choose to take the unemployment benefit (or 'dole') rather than work.
4. Johnson, *Playing for Both Sides*, 32.
5. Johnson, *Playing for Both Sides*, 16.
6. New Zealand has two main islands: the North and the South. Some Kiwis use the phrase 'the West Island' or 'our West Island' playfully to refer to Australia and its relationship to New Zealand.
7. The Returned Servicemen's Association (RSA) of New Zealand states that the ANZAC spirit 'was forged when Australians and New Zealanders (Australian and New Zealand Army Corps) stood side by side as comrades through two world wars. The term stands for values of courage, camaraderie, compassion and commitment'. See https://rsa.org.nz/Community/Living-the-Anzac-Spirit.
8. See, for example, *Sydney Morning Herald*, 29 September 2015; *New Zealand Herald*, 11 November 2015.
9. For an incisive introduction, see Julie Fry and Hayden Glass, *Going Places: Migration, Economics and the Future of New Zealand* (Wellington: Bridget Williams Books, 2016).
10. Rollo Arnold, 'The dynamics and quality of trans-Tasman migration, 1885–1910,' *Australian Economic History Review* 26 (1986): 1–20.
11. Atholl Anderson, Judith Binney, and Aroha Harris, *Tangata Whenua: An Illustrated History* (Wellington: Bridget Williams Books, 2015), 158.
12. On sealing, see Ian W. G. Smith, *The New Zealand Sealing Industry: History, Archaeology, and Heritage Management* (Wellington: Department of Conservation, 2002).
13. Atholl Anderson, 'Whenuahou: A Southern community', in *Tangata Whenua*, eds. Anderson, Binney, and Harris, 161–62.
14. Tony Ballantyne, *Entanglements of Empire: Missionaries, Māori and the Question of the Body* (Auckland: Auckland University Press, 2014).
15. Vincent O'Malley, *Haerenga: Early Māori Journeys Across the Globe* (Wellington: Bridget Williams Books, 2015). For a highly suggestive reading of 'mobility' in maritime empires, see Tony Ballantyne, 'Mobility, empire, colonisation,' *History Australia* 11 (2014): 7–37.
16. Judith Binney, 'Tuki's universe,' *New Zealand Journal of History*, 38 (2004): 215–32.
17. See Philip Gidley King, Letterbook, c187, 225, Mitchell Library, State Library of New South Wales, Australia.

18. O'Malley, *Haerenga*, 7, 8. See also Vincent O'Malley, *The Meeting Place: Māori and Pākehā Encounters, 1642–1840* (Auckland: Auckland University Press, 2012).

19. On Te Pahi, see Angela Ballara, 'Te Pahi', first published in the *Dictionary of New Zealand Biography*, 1, 1990. Te Ara—the Encyclopedia of New Zealand, updated 30 October 2012, http://www.TeAra.govt.nz/en/biographies/1t53/te-pahi.

20. Philip Gidley King, Journal, 8 January 1806, MSS 720/2, Alexander Turnbull Library, Wellington, quoted in Binney, 128.

21. O'Malley, *Haerenga*, 26.

22. See Ballantyne, *Entanglements*, Chapter 1.

23. See http://www.radionz.co.nz/news/regional/292387/long-lost-treasures-return-to-waitangi.

24. Binney, 'Tuki's universe', 219–20.

25. Anderson, Binney, and Harris, *Tangata Whenua*, 184.

26. The classic text here is Claudia Orange, *The Treaty of Waitangi* (Wellington: Allen and Unwin, 1988).

27. Binney, 'Tuki's universe', 230.

28. For an entry point, see Jock Phillips and Terry Hearn, *Settlers: New Zealand Immigrants from England, Ireland and Scotland, 1800–1900* (Auckland: Auckland University Press, 2008).

29. Notable recent exceptions include Catherine Bishop, 'Women on the move: Gender, money-making and mobility in mid-nineteenth-century Australasia,' *History Australia* 11 (2014): 38–59; Rosemary Baird and Philippa Mein Smith, 'Australia as New Zealand's western frontier, 1965–95,' in *New Zealand's Empire*, eds. Katie Pickles and Catharine Coleborne (Manchester: Manchester University Press, 2016), 213–28; and the essays in Lloyd Carpenter and Lyndon Fraser, eds., *Rushing for Gold: Life and Commerce on the Goldfields of Australia and New Zealand* (Dunedin: Otago University Press, 2016).

30. Charles R. Thatcher, 'Our own correspondent,' reprinted in Robert Hoskins, *Goldfield Balladeer: The Life and Times of the Celebrated Charles R. Thatcher* (Auckland and London, 1977), 167–69.

31. See Peter Franks and Jim McAloon, *The New Zealand Labour Party, 1916–2016* (Wellington: Victoria University Press, 2016).

32. Lyndon Fraser, *Castles of Gold: A History of New Zealand's West Coast Irish* (Dunedin: Otago University Press, 2007), 88–89.

33. Philip Ross May, *The West Coast Gold Rushes* (Christchurch: Pegasus Press, 1962), 480.

34. Chris McConville, Keir Reeves, and Andrew Reeves, '"Tasman world": Investigating gold-rush-era historical links and subsequent regional development between Otago and Victoria,' in *Rushing for Gold: Life and Commerce*

on the Goldfields of Australia and New Zealand, eds. Lloyd Carpenter and Lyndon Fraser (Dunedin: Otago University Press, 2016), 23–40.

35. W.D. Borrie, 'The peopling of Australia, 1788–1988: The common heritage,' in *Tasman Relations: New Zealand and Australia, 1788–1988*, ed. Keith Sinclair (Auckland: Auckland University Press, 1987), 207–8.

36. John Gould, *The Rake's Progress? The New Zealand Economy Since 1945* (Auckland: Hodder and Stoughton, 1982), 118; Jim McAloon, *Judgements of All Kinds: Economic Policy-Making in New Zealand, 1945–84* (Wellington: Victoria University Press, 2013), 127–29.

37. See Jacques Poot, 'Trans-Tasman migration, transnationalism and economic development in Australasia,' *Asian and Pacific Migration Journal* 19 (2010): 319–42.

38. Michael Jackson, *The Accidental Anthropologist: A Memoir* (Dunedin: Longacre Press, 2006), 64–70.

39. Harry Orsman and Jan Moore, eds., *Heinemann Dictionary of New Zealand Quotations* (Auckland: Heinemann, 1988), 488.

40. Gordon A. Carmichael, 'History of Trans-Tasman population movement,' in *Trans-Tasman Migration: Trends, Causes and Consequences*, ed. Gordon A. Carmichael (Canberra: Australian Government Publishing Service, 1993), 47.

41. See Alan Gamlen, 'Creating and destroying diaspora strategies,' Working Paper No. 31, International Migration Institute, University of Oxford, April 2011.

42. *New Zealand Herald*, 21 September 2012.

43. Statistics New Zealand, 'Kiwi exodus to Australia bungees back,' 21 July 2016, accessed 9 September 2016, http://www.stats.govt.nz/browse_for_stats/population/Migration/international-travel-and-migration-articles/kiwi-exodus-australia.aspx.

44. Poot, 'Trans-Tasman migration'. See also Richard Bedford and Jacques Poot, 'Changing tides in the South Pacific: Immigration to Aotearoa New Zealand,' in *Immigration Worldwide: Policies, Practices and Trends*, eds. Uma A. Segal, Nazneen S. Mayadas, and Doreen Elliot (New York: Oxford University Press, 2009).

45. Carmichael, *Trans-Tasman Migration*, 122.

46. Graeme Hugo, 'New Zealanders in Australia in 2001,' *New Zealand Population Review* 30 (2004): 75.

47. On the latter, see Jacqueline Lidgard, 'Return migration of New Zealanders: A rising tide?' (MA thesis, University of Waikato, 1992). For Māori, see Paul Hamer, 'One in six? The rapid growth of the Māori population in Australia,' *New Zealand Population Review* 33, no. 34 (2008): 153–76; and Paul Hamer, *Māori in Australia: Ngā Māori i Te Ao Moemoeā* (Wellington: Te Puni Kokiri, 2007).

48. Alan Gamlen, 'Making hay while the sun shines: Envisioning New Zealand's state-diaspora relations,' *Policy Quarterly* 3 (2007): 12. See also Wendy Larner, 'Expatriate experts and globalising governmentalities: The New Zealand diaspora strategy,' *Transactions of the Institute of British Geographers* 32 (2007): 331–45.
49. See Rosemary Baird, 'Across the Tasman: Narratives of New Zealand migrants to and from Australia, 1965–95' (PhD thesis, University of Canterbury, 2012).
50. See http://www.rugby.com.au/news/2016/02/05/steve-walsh-to-retire-from-rugby.
51. Janet Salaff and Arent Greve, 'Can women's social networks survive?,' *Women's Studies International Forum* 27 (2004): 160.
52. Rosemary Baird and Lyndon Fraser, '"Kiwis 'on the wing": The continuing migration experiences of New Zealanders in Australia from the 1960–1990s,' in *On The Wing: Mobility Before and After Emigration to Australia*, Visible Immigrants Series, No. 7, eds. Margrette Kleinig and Eric Richards (Adelaide: Anchor Books 2012), 163–65.
53. Baird and Fraser, 'Kiwis "On the wing,"' 171–73, 175.
54. Stephen Castles and Mark Miller, *The Age of Migration: International Population Movements in the Modern World* (Basingstoke: Palgrave Macmillan, 2009), 7.
55. See Paul Ward and Elizabeth Pente, 'Let's change history! Community histories and the co-production of historical knowledge,' in *History Making a Difference*, eds. Katie Pickles, Lyndon Fraser, Marguerite Hill, Sarah Murray, and Greg Ryan (Cambridge Scholars Publishing, 2017).
56. Giselle Byrnes, 'Nation and migration: Postcolonial perspectives,' *New Zealand Journal of History* 43 (2009): 123–32.
57. Peter Hempenstall, 'Overcoming separate histories: Historians as "ideas traders" in a trans-Tasman world,' *History Australia* 4 (2007): 1.

CHAPTER 5

Changing Migration Policy from the Margins: Filipino Activism on Behalf of Victims of Domestic Violence in Australia, 1980s–2000

Mina Roces

Between 1980 and 2011, 44 Filipino women in a cross-cultural marriage were killed by their husbands in Australia.[1] The murdered women were all sponsored as wives or fiancées of Australian nationals and a number of them were the second or third wives sponsored by the same individual. A study commissioned by the Centre for Philippine Concerns-Australia (CPCA) that was funded by the Human Rights and Equal Opportunity Commission (HREOC) delivered the shocking statistic that Filipino women in Australia were nearly six times more likely to be victims of spousal homicide than Australian women in general.[2] The timing of these stories and their locations across several states in New South Wales, Victoria, and South Australia, underscored the point that it was a national issue and a serious concern for the Filipino and the Australian community.

M. Roces (✉)
University of New South Wales, Sydney, NSW, Australia

© The Author(s) 2019
E. Henrich and J. M. Simpson (eds.),
History, Historians and the Immigration Debate,
https://doi.org/10.1007/978-3-319-97123-0_5

71

Filipina Australians were the first to call attention to domestic violence as an issue facing the Filipino Australian community and they were the driving force in the campaign to alter the laws and provide services to those who became victims of abuse. However, they did not do this alone. They found allies in the Australian government who provided funding for research and organised forums to meet with fellow Filipinas to discuss possible solutions to the problem. This chapter argues that the advocacy on behalf of Filipina victims of domestic violence in Australia was a *joint* project between Filipina Australian activists and the Australia government. It is a case study of how a minority group was able to introduce new laws in the host country. Writing this history directly challenges the tendency to provincialise the woman migrant as peripheral to the centre (read Australia) and reveals the contribution this unique group has brought to the host country. These advocates were also pioneers in the area of transnational organising for a feminist issue since the practical side of the advocacy required navigating the Australian legal bureaucracy and liaising with the Australian Embassy in Manila and the Philippine government. I also argue that the success of the advocacy could be explained not just by the relentless energy and robust actions of the Filipina Australians, particularly the Filipino Women's Working Party (FWWP) and the CPCA, but also because of the unique Australian historical context of the 1980s and 1990s.

I will focus on the strategies deployed by Filipina activists to address the issue of Filipino victims of domestic violence in Australia from the late 1980s until the end of the 1990s. These Filipina good Samaritans— composed of community and welfare workers, psychologists, social workers, and educators who were permanent residents or Australian citizens—lobbied vigorously, demanding not just protection and services for the victims but a change in Australian perceptions of Filipino women. Almost all of these women were married to white Australian nationals and were Australian permanent residents or Australian citizens. Their location in a cross-cultural marriage gave them access to both the Filipino community and the Australian one. All were highly educated. Some were able to take courses in Australia primarily in the fields of social work and welfare. Some of these women worked in the migrant resource centres that mushroomed in this period and it was through their positions as migrant settlement officers that they encountered the victims. Hence, while these Filipina advocates were not victims themselves, their educational background in social work or psychology (one of them was a former Catholic nun), or their previous involvement as activists protesting the martial law regime of President Marcos in the Philippines meant that they had a track record as advocates for social justice.

Filipino migrant activism has been a popular topic tackled by social scientists, especially those writing about the post-1970s migration. The literature has tended to focus on NGO activism on behalf of Filipino overseas contract workers primarily because of their particularly vulnerable situation as non-permanent residents without citizenship rights, and in the case of domestic workers or entertainers, their living situation as highly susceptible to employer abuse and exploitation.[3] The scholarship has to its credit moved away from depicting these migrants as victims, showcasing instead the robust nature of their resistance particularly as NGO activists and union leaders.[4]

In this body of work, Filipino activists were positioned in direct conflict with host countries in their task of empowering the marginalised Filipino ethnic group.[5] Activist NGOs assumed combative positions in order to compel governments of host countries to protect the rights of their guest workers. But defiance against the host country was not the only strategy deployed by Filipino activists to achieve their goals. The histories of migrant engagement with host states did not always conform to a neat dichotomy of activists = good and governments = bad. This chapter shifts the way the fault lines of migrant activism have been imagined in the existing scholarship by analysing how Filipino migrants *worked in partnership* with the government of the host country in the *joint* project of empowering the Filipino ethnic group. In doing so, it challenges long-held views that legal and policy changes do not come 'from below'. It contributes to the historiography of Australian migration by showing that activism initiated by migrants themselves can alter migration law. Finally, by lifting the taboo on discussing the delicate issue of domestic violence, this case study also unsettles the usual heroic narrative of migration where stories of struggle end with triumph. It departs from the usual trope that either documented the contributions migrants made to the host country or celebrated the refashioning of migrant identities. Although the activism I discuss here has achieved legislative success, the topic of Filipina victims of domestic violence was and continues to be a sensitive issue for the Filipino community (and perhaps the Australian community as well) because of the 'shame' attached to this extremely private form of abuse.

Domestic violence is defined as 'the abuse, coercion and control of one of more persons over others and includes physical, emotional, verbal and sexual abuse, financial deprivation, social isolation and control of environment'.[6] In the specific context of Filipina Australian marriages, Filipina Australian activists and scholars writing on its most extreme form—homicides of Filipina partners—pointed out that a fundamental factor in the abuse was 'the relationship between Australian men and what they understand to be Filipino women'.[7] In other words, the abuse occurred partly because the men 'constructed their wives in particular ways and then resorted to violence when the women did not live up to their expectations'.[8]

While there is a critical mass of scholarship on Filipino migrants for marriage in Australia, these studies have been more preoccupied with the gendered and racial experience of migration including discourses on Filipina brides rather than on advocacy on behalf of the Filipino ethnic group.[9] Social scientists writing specifically on Filipina marriage migration to Australia tended to focus on analyses of the reasons for international marriage migration between the two countries,[10] Filipina 'brides' as victims of domestic violence and homicide,[11] and the ways in which Filipinas there have been subjected to Orientalist stereotyping as 'mail-order brides' or highly sexualised mercenaries.[12] This social science scholarship delivers a powerful narrative of Filipina women's victimisation in the hands of white male patriarchy. But there has been little attempt to date to document the activism that Filipinas initiated to address the problems of migrants who became victims of violence. This chapter is a first step towards addressing this gap in the scholarship. Historians analyse unique historical eras in detail, and this method can illuminate what opportunities and challenges these times offered for migrants and migrant activists alike. The period I analyse here was unprecedented in the history of Australian immigration.

MIGRANT SETTLEMENT POLICIES IN AUSTRALIA—FROM ASSIMILATION TO MULTICULTURALISM

Filipina migrant activism followed a period of massive change in Australian government approaches to migrant settlement. In the 1950s and 1960s, the policy of assimilation meant that non-Anglo immigrants were expected to discontinue the language and culture of their parents and absorb the Anglo-Australian culture. By the mid-1960s, this shifted to a policy of 'integration' wherein the non-Anglo immigrants were considered part of mainstream society but could keep their language and culture.[13] The policy of multiculturalism launched in the 1970s completely altered the way ethnic minorities were viewed. It became the responsibility of government to support (and this included funding) the language and culture of diverse groups and to provide special services and programmes for all migrants.[14] In this perspective, the individuals had the right to their language and culture within the framework of the Australian legal system.[15] In May 1978, the Frank Galbally report made a number of recommendations that reflected this new attitude of openness and interest in working with ethnic communities.[16] The report self-consciously articulated its brief that: 'it is now necessary for the Commonwealth Government to change the direction of its involvement in the provision of programs and services for migrants and to take further steps to encourage multiculturalism'.[17] It recommended 'a special program of multicultural resource centres... involving the local communities to the greatest extent in their management and operation'[18] and an increase of ethnic welfare workers 'through an extension of the grant-in-aid scheme' from 1 to 3 years as well as a special programme to provide 'once only' grants of up to $5000 to assist with special projects.[19] The same report also recommended extending ethnic (i.e. non-English) radio to all states and the establishment of ethnic television (this later gave birth to the television station SBS).[20] Furthermore, the report also recommended that the Department of Immigration and Ethnic Affairs appoint more grant-in-aid coordinators to assist with migrant settlement.[21] The establishment of Migrant Resource Centers (from 1978) and the Ethnic Affairs Commission of New South Wales (from 1976) generated the need for seed grants specifically targeted at minority groups, and the employment of social and community workers from ethnic communities. For the first time, Filipinas could apply for and be hired as community workers in Migrant Resource Centres and in the Ethnic Affairs Commission: entry points into the government bureaucracy that was once closed to them. Filipinas embraced these new opportunities for social inclusion. Filipino organisations applied for the funds, particularly state funds that were available for ethnic organisations.

The 1980s–2000 was also the period where ethnic organisations flowered in Australia, many of them run by the second-generation or

Australian-born children of immigrants. Umbrella organisations called Ethnic Communities Councils across the nation reflected greater organisation of migrant groups and the government's interest in working with them. However, the male-dominated leadership of these groups inspired the immigrant women to secure funding to have their own lobby group to address gender-specific immigrant issues in their landmark conference: Immigrant Women Speak Out.[22] In the 1980s, Filipinas were still at the fringes of the ethnic community lobby groups.[23] But by the 1990s, Filipinas had linked up with the Immigrant Women's Speak Out group.[24]

DEMOGRAPHIC CONTEXT

The 1980s also coincided with the dramatic increase of Filipino migration to Australia, particularly that of spousal migration or women sponsored as fiancées. Filipino migration was unique because of the sex ratios favouring women. Australian Bureau of Statistics data revealed that in 2006, 42,680 Philippine-born residents were male while 77,854 were female. The gender gap of almost 2:1 reflected the marriage migration pattern in which Filipinas arrived as wives, or fiancées of Australian permanent residents, a trend that reached its apogee in the years between 1974 and 1998. In 1991, for example, approximately 70% of Filipino women migrants in Australia were sponsored as fiancées of men who were Australian residents.[25] The profile of Filipinos in Australia showed that Filipino females outnumbered the males by a ratio of 2.2:1 and was more pronounced in the 20–29 and 30–54 age groups where the ratio difference increased to 3.5:1 and 2.9:1.4, respectively.[26] The 1991 census of New South Wales was the first to include the numbers of people born overseas even if they totalled less than 50. An examination of these statistics revealed that Filipinas were scattered in small rural towns all over the state. For example, in Grafton, there were zero males but 24 females; in Lismore, there were 14 men and 26 women; in Albury, there were 28 males and 68 females; and in Shellharbour, there were 38 males and 128 females.[27] Since one could assume the majority of them were married to Australian men, their location in remote areas made them even more vulnerable as new migrants.[28]

Domestic Violence in Cross-Cultural Marriages as an Issue Affecting the Filipino Australian Community

The history of advocacy on behalf of Filipina victims' of domestic violence is inextricably linked to the beginnings of the Australian government's establishment of Migrant Resource Centres. Using sources coming from interviews and the personal papers of the activists themselves, historians are able to trace individual women's lives, placing them as actors within the broader political and institutional contexts. These collective biographies are critical for social historians who want to analyse how activism can begin from the margins since their life stories would not otherwise be available in the government archives. These women, almost all of whom had some activist experience in the Philippines, were assertive, confident and resourceful. They knew how to use the language of human rights to get the attention of the legislators and they learned how to navigate the Australian bureaucracy.

In 1985, Lilia McKinnon bested 31 other applicants to win the job of Community Welfare Officer for migrant and refugee women at the then Illawarra Migrant Resource Centre, funded by the Department of Immigration. Born in the Philippines, McKinnon moved to Wollongong because she married a local Australian, and although she completed a Bachelor's degree in Library Science from Far Eastern University in Manila and had worked for the Christ the King Seminary Library and the Columban Fathers Library there, her overseas qualifications were not recognised in Australia. In 1983, she took several short courses at the TAFE (as 'technical and further education' institutions in Australia are called) including one on financial and community management and administration, while volunteering as an officer of the Australian Filipino organisation in Wollongong.[29] Della Ipong arrived in Sydney in the 1970s. A trained psychologist, in 1987, she was a welfare worker for the Filipino community in the Sydney area filling a grant-in-aid position funded by the Department of Immigration.[30] Joan Dicka, a social worker and former nun who obtained her qualifications in the Philippines with more than 20 years of experience working with the Catholic Church in southern Philippines, wrote a proposal to the Department of Immigration in 1983 to create a position of social worker to attend to the Filipinas married to Australian men. The Department offered her a half-time position in Adelaide, South Australia (where she lived with her Australian husband).[31] Joan had previously worked with the Jesuit missions in Bukidnon, Mindanao, in Southern Philippines in 1962 where she looked after the indigenous peoples in remote areas. Her tireless efforts earned her the label 'the Joan of Arc of Mindanao'. When she joined the order of the Oblates of Notre Dame as a Catholic nun she worked with Bishop Gerard Mongeau OMI working with the homeless (both Muslims and Christians) in Cotobato City. When she left the religious order in 1972, she moved to Baguio's Pelletier High School, run by the Good Shepherd nuns, as a caseworker for troubled children, unwed mothers or students with drug problems. She then moved to a job with the Department of Social Welfare rising to the ranks of Provincial Social Welfare Officer and President of the Philippine Association of Social Workers. She migrated to Australia in January 1981 to join her husband Stefan Dicka whom she married in 1980. Thus, even before her migration to Australia, Joan already had an impressive career in social welfare and a distinguished track record for helping society's marginalised sectors.[32] In 1990, Conception 'Chat' Ramilo was hired by the Ethnic Affairs Commission as a community liaison officer for the Asia Pacific Community. Ramilo had a degree in psychology from the University of the Philippines but left the country for Australia in 1986 because she was an activist against the Marcos dictatorship.[33] Hence, by the end of the 1980s, there was already a small group of Filipina women trained social workers, psychologists or community welfare workers who worked in the Migrant Resource Centres or the NSW Ethnic Affairs Commission, whose job portfolio was to help Filipina/o migrants and provide information and services with regard to settlement issues, housing, language and education—matters that were connected to life in the new country.

What came as a huge surprise to these Filipino women was the number of cases of domestic violence brought to their attention. These took several forms from physical harm to verbal abuse, emotional blackmail, withdrawal of financial support, and prohibiting them from speaking their own language.[34] While working as a case manager in the Migrant Women's Shelter Service in Adelaide between 1983 and 1989, Joan Dicka was inundated with cases involving Filipina victims of domestic violence.[35] In 1987, for example, 55 Filipino women sought help from women's shelters and the Migrant Women's Emergency Support Service in Adelaide. Considering that there were only 900 married Filipinos in South Australia, this was a significant percentage.[36]

Once the Filipina community workers and social workers became aware of the magnitude of the problem, those in the state of New South Wales took the issue up with their Ethnic Affairs Commission (EAC NSW). Within the EAC NSW, they found allies in Filipina community liaison officer Chat Ramilo and then senior policy officer Rosa Droescher whose roles were to develop interaction with the migrant communities themselves.[37] The EAC NSW sponsored a Filipino Women's Consultative Meeting held on November 28, 1989, that led to the formation of the Filipino Women's Working Party (hereafter FWWP) to carry out the recommendations that came out of that meeting. The formation of the FWWP launched the first serious advocacy for changes in legislation that were directly related to the issue of Filipina migrants for marriage who were victims of domestic violence. The 20 recommendations that emerged from the 1989 consultative meeting that was organised by the EAC NSW and co-convened by the New South Wales Immigrant Women's Coordinating Committee and the Women's Advisory Council set the agenda and priorities for the future. The first priority was to lobby for changing the laws regarding (1) Serial Sponsorship (defined as the practice of men sponsoring a succession of women to Australia as fiancées or spouses) and (2) an amendment to the domestic violence provisions to grant permanent residency to victims of domestic violence who came as spouses or fiancées who had not yet fulfilled the 2-year permanent residency requirement.[38] The fear of deportation prevented women from asking for help or leaving abusive partners thereby risking women's lives. McKinnon noted the poignant stories of Filipino women who were deported back to the Philippines because they had left violent husbands before their two-year residency requirement.[39] They had to deal with the stigma associated with a failed marriage (divorce is not recognised in the Philippines), and the shame of an unsuccessful migration endeavour. Serial sponsorship was raised because the community workers and social workers noticed a pattern in which several victims of domestic violence all arrived as fiancées of one man. The other priorities were the need to address the negative representation of Filipinas in the Australian media, provision of support services for victims, and the need to disseminate information about services to the community.[40] In Adelaide, Joan Dicka formed the Filipino Brides Working Party in 1989. She talked to the media to disseminate her findings about the domestic violence cases she handled.[41]

In 1989, Charles Schembri strangled Generosa 'Gene' Bongcodin in Newport, Victoria. Filipinos in Melbourne were outraged not only by the circumstances of her death (Gene was a popular member of the community there) but also by the relatively light sentence that the perpetrator received, primarily due to representations of the victim in both the media and trial as a 'dangerous woman—a gold-digging opportunist who used Schembri as a passport for a better life in Australia'.[42] Schembri was sentenced to eight years' imprisonment with a minimum of five and a half years, and he was released on 11 July 1993.[43] The death of Gene, the light sentence bestowed on her murderer, and the misrepresentation of her character mobilised another group of Filipina activists in Melbourne who campaigned under the general theme of 'Justice for Gene'.[44] Melba Marginson led 30 Filipino Australians in a demonstration to denounce the decision of the Australian legal system for the verdict of manslaughter influenced by the image of the victim as 'a loose woman' who 'used him as a passport to Australia, and who was not morally fit to be a mother to their child'.[45] An organisation called the Collective of Filipinas for Empowerment and Development (CFED) was formed in the wave of the 'Justice for Gene' campaign 'to look for strategies to get Filipino women to engage in discussions of possible victimization'.[46] The next step was to have a national organisation and in November 1991 the CPCA was formally established as 'a national network of Filipino individuals in Australia committed to advancing the Filipino people's interests'.[47] Its aims included addressing the issues of Filipino women in cross-cultural marriages and the negative public images of Filipinos in Australia.[48] Melba Marginson persuaded the organisation to focus on violence against Filipino women in Australia.[49] Educated at the University of the Philippines at the height of student activism against President Ferdinand Marcos (she enrolled in 1970), after graduation Marginson taught at the Philippine High School while actively involved in the Philippine national democratic movement. In 1982, she became a member of the Alliance of Concerned Teachers, a militant teachers' union and was elected Secretary General in 1985. She married Simon Marginson and arrived in Australia in 1990.[50] Thus, Marginson already had an impressive track record as a militant activist at the time of the Marcos dictatorship and experience leading a major union with a membership of 50,000 of which 85% were women.[51]

In 1994, the Australian government's Office of the Status of Women awarded a grant to CPCA to conduct a National Conference on stopping violence against Filipino women. Held in Melbourne on October 6–7, it resulted in the formation of the Filipino Women's Network of Australia (FWNA).[52] CPCA also focused on accumulating data on the number of spousal homicides of Filipina victims in its drive to promote greater public awareness of this pattern of extreme domestic violence experienced by the Filipino ethnic group in Australia.[53] In 1993, Marginson presented the grim statistics of 23 victims in the years 1987–1993 to Irene Moss, the Race Discrimination Commissioner.[54] Her response was to ask the Institute of Criminology, University of Sydney, to complete a research project on the topic funded by the HREOC.[55] The findings that Filipino women were nearly six times more likely to be victims of spousal homicide than Australian women alarmed both the Filipino and Australian communities and caught the attention of the Australian media.[56] In 1995, the *Sydney Morning Herald Magazine* published a leading story on the Serial Sponsorship of Filipinas.[57]

Strategies and Successes

The Filipina activists' crowning achievement was the passage of two crucial pieces of legislation. In chronological order, they were the Immigration Law (Migration Regulations 1994 first introduced on 14 April 1991) 'which provides that women migrants will no longer be deported if they have left violent fiancées, defactos [those who live together as man or wife outside legal marriage] or husbands' even if they had not yet completed the two-year residency requirement, and the Serial Sponsorship law that limited the number of partners that an individual could bring to Australia to 2 (Migration Regulations 1994-REG 1.20J).[58] These two pieces of legislation had an impact on all women migrating to Australia as a spouse or fianceé of an Australian national. In addition, FWWP lobbied for increased services for Filipino women.[59] More funding was made available for Filipino Grant in Aid workers and there was a focus on more culturally appropriate domestic violence services and programmes.[60] In Adelaide, Joan Dicka was able to work with the local police, giving them information on how they can be sensitive to Filipino cultural attitudes towards domestic violence.[61]

The Department of Immigration and Ethnic Affairs produced the short films *Marrying and Migrating to Australia: The Filipino Australian Experience* (1995) and *Marrying and Migrating...You Have to Work at it* (1996).[62] The two videos were compulsory viewing for all those who attended the pre-departure seminars conducted by both the Australian Embassy in Manila and the Commission of Filipinos Overseas (CFO), the Philippine government body tasked with preparing Filipino citizens for permanent migration overseas.[63] Even though by the time Filipinas watched the videos they would have more or less decided to migrate, about 5% of women who had seen the video changed their minds about marrying and migrating to Australia.[64]

Filipino women activists also aspired to empower victims by critiquing Filipino cultural expectations of women as obedient wives and dutiful daughters sending regular remittances. Dawn House was a women's domestic violence service located in South Australia. It inspired the establishment of a survivors' theatre group that called itself *Buklod* (Buklod Kababaihang Filipina). Joan Dicka was a Non-English Speaking Background (NESB) worker in Dawn House and she worked with the Filipina survivors in workshops over a five-month period. They helped to increase women's confidence and self-esteem and participants took steps to empower themselves including enrolling in full-time tertiary study, obtaining drivers' licences, joining other community groups and gaining part-time or full-time employment.[65] *In 1997*, Buklod produced and performed a play 'For Better or Worse... Till Death Do Us Part...?' raising awareness of domestic violence as an issue experienced by Filipinas married to Australian nationals in South Australia.[66] The play was performed at the Adelaide Women's Community Health Centre, and a number of venues including a national conference in Melbourne entitled Stopping Violence Against Filipino Women in Australia.[67]

The FWWP also produced a radio programme in Filipino/Tagalog language. The 12-episode radio series funded by the Department of Immigration and Ethnic Affairs (Migrant Access Projects Scheme) and the Department of Primary Industries and Energy (Rural Access Program) aimed to reach Filipinas in rural areas 'to increase the level of awareness of Filipino women in cross-cultural marriages about the community and welfare services available to them through a radio information campaign; and to evaluate the effectiveness of radio as a medium for the delivery of settlement information'.[68] The programme in Tagalog language was aired on the SBS radio network in the major cities of Sydney, Melbourne, Adelaide, Brisbane, Perth, and Darwin, in the afternoon, three times a week, for four consecutive weeks on 11 stations.[69]

In addition, cassette tapes of the series were also sent out to community stations in country towns that had no local community radio stations.[70]

The radio programme (entitled *Ngayon Aussie Ka Na Manay* or *Now that you are an Aussie*) aspired to empower women listeners by encouraging them to assert themselves, a project that required them to transcend Filipino cultural constructions of the feminine that expected women to accept their suffering without complaint. It advised women not to tolerate domestic violence (both physical and psychological) alerting them to the new law that granted victims permanent residency even though they had not yet fulfilled the two-year residency requirement. The radio programme's directives were radical in the sense that they advised Filipino women to break away from their gender socialisation as obedient wives and fashion themselves into strong, assertive women.

Filipina activists who were employed as settlement officers, migrant workers, social workers or community welfare workers also conducted information seminars, and held workshops addressed specifically to Filipino women marriage migrants. These lectures, seminars, and workshops had a huge impact on attendees, some of whom only realised after attending that they were victims of psychological abuse.[71]

Conclusion

By the end of the 1990s, the Filipina activists moved to other issues that were trans-ethnic rather than Filipino-centred, and this shift signified the end of the period of this robust activism. For example, in 1991, Debbie Wall became interested in issues affecting Indigenous Australians joining the Redfern Residents for Reconciliation, the Action for World Development (AWD) and the Women's Reconciliation Network.[72] In 1998, Melba Marginson became founding chairperson of the Victorian Immigrant and Refugee Women's Coalition. Her portfolio changed from advocacy for Filipino women to representing the needs of immigrant and refugee women from all over the world.

This handful of women advocates were relentless and persistent in putting up grant and proposal submissions, devoting a lot of their time and energies to this campaign. They were a unique coterie of assertive, feisty, strong, and tough women. Filipina Australian Welfare workers who rescued domestic violence victims had to brave the wrath of the victims' husbands. Estrella McKinnon could not go from her office to the car park without a chaperone and recalls hiding under the table in her office when an irate husband stormed into the migrant resource centre looking for her because he did not know the whereabouts of his wife who was secretly taken to a women's refuge centre.[73] Della Ipong was accosted by the furious husband of one Filipina woman she helped to place in a refuge centre, who barged into in her office confronting her with: 'Where is my wife? What did you do to her?'[74] Incidents such as this have happened more than once prompting Ipong to admit: 'Our work can be dangerous because we are dealing with angry men'.[75]

Relationships between the Australian bureaucracy and the Filipina advocates—particularly those affiliated with the migrant resource centres—were symbiotic: the Ethnic Affairs Commission did not have the legitimacy to speak on behalf of the Filipina community so they needed those in the ethnic community, and the Filipinos needed the help of the bureaucracy to initiate legal change and to fund their projects.[76] According to Debbie Wall, 'without the Ethnic Affairs Commission and the facilitation of the other agencies (such as the Migrant Resource Centres etc.), the FWWP would not have been founded and our work would have been in limbo'.[77]

Filipino women who were victims of abuse did find empowerment—they received information on how and where to seek help, survivors processed their trauma through finding their voice and performing in plays where they told their stories. In Joan Dicka's personal papers, I discovered one statement and two letters written by three different survivors to the Department of Immigration and Citizenship and the Women's Shelter in Adelaide naming their husbands as abusers, and imploring these agencies to do all that was possible to prevent the men from sponsoring more Filipina women as brides.[78] One of the women declared that she was the seventh wife.[79] The sheer act of 'writing upwards' (whether or not they were coached by a Filipina activist) showed that they were no longer silenced victims but strong assertive survivors acting to prevent further abuse.[80] Others formed their own organisations for emotional and social support, running workshops and activities funded by grants they won from the Australian government.

This case study is an intervention in the field of Australian migration history because it demonstrates that a handful of Filipino women first-generation migrants can alter legislation in the host country. In illustrating the fruitful ways that migrants have been able to work jointly with the Australian government bureaucracy, it sets a powerful and optimistic precedent for the possibilities of migrant collaborations with the states of their host countries. It shows that at least in the 1980s and 1990s, the Australian bureaucracy was open to addressing issues of migrant rights and the sensitive subject of domestic violence. Finally, it documents the way policy can be changed from below—from an ethnic minority viewed as marginal or peripheral—proving that they can be at the very centre of legislative history in Australia.

Notes

1. Solidary Philippines Australia Network, 'Violent deaths and disappearances of Filipino women and children in Australia since 1980. Summary of data compiled by the centre as at 6th August 2011,' CPCA Website, http://cpcabrisbane.org/CPCA/Deaths.htm.
2. Chris Cunneen and Julie Stubbs, *Gender, 'Race' and International Relations. Violence Against Women in Australia* (Sydney: Institute of Criminology Monograph Series No. 9, University of Sydney, 1997), ix, 31.
3. Ligaya Lindio-McGovern, *Globalization, Labor Export and Resistance, A Study of Filipino Migrant Domestic Workers in Global Cities* (London: Routledge, 2012); Stefan Rother, 'Transnational political spaces: Political activism of Philippines labor migrants in Hong Kong,' in *State, Politics and Nationalism Beyond Borders: Changing Dynamics in Filipino Overseas Migration*, ed. Jorge V. Tigno (Quezon City: Philippine Social Science Council, 2009), 1–23; Nicole Constable, 'Migrant workers and the many states of protest in Hong Kong,' *Critical Asian Studies*, 41, no. 1 (2009): 143–64; and Hsiao-Chuan Hsia, 'The making of a transnational grassroots migrant movement,' *Critical Asian Studies* 41, no. 1 (2009): 113–41.
4. For a history of Filipino unions in the USA's Pacific Northwest see Dorothy Fujita-Rony, *American Workers, Colonial Power Philippine Seattle and the Transpacific West, 1919–1941* (Berkeley: University of California Press, 2003); Chris Friday, *Organizing Asian American Labor. The Pacific Coast Canned-Salmon Industry, 1870–1942* (Philadelphia: Temple University Press, 1994); Thomas Churchill, *Triumph Over Marcos: A Story Based on the Lives of Gene Viernes & Silme Domingo, Filipino American Cannery Union Organizers, their Assassination and the Trial that Followed* (Seattle: Open Hand Publishing, 1995). For unions in other parts of the US see Dorothy Fujita-Rony, 'Coalitions, race and labor: Rereading Philip Vera Cruz,' *Journal of Asian American Studies* 3, no. 2 (2000): 139–62; Howard de Witt, *Violence in the Fields: California Filipino Farm Labor Unionization During the Great Depression*

(Unknown Binding: Century One Publishing, 1980); John E. Reinecke, *The Filipino Piecemeal Sugar Strike of 1924–1925* (Honolulu: Social Science Research Institute, University of Hawaii, 1996); Melinda Tria Kerkvliet, *Unbending Cane: Pablo Manlapit, A Filipino Labor Leader in Hawaii* (Honolulu: Office of Multicultural Student Services, University of Hawaii at Manoa, 2002). For post-1970s migrant activism see Ligaya Lindio-McGovern, *Globalization, Labor Export and Resistance, A Study of Filipino Migrant Domestic Workers in Global Cities* (London: Routledge, 2012); Constable, 'Migrant workers,' 143–64; and Hsia, 'The making of a transnational grassroots migrant movement,' 113–41.

5. See especially Lindio-McGovern, *Globalization, Labor Export and Resistance.*

6. Women's Coalition Against Family Violence, 1994, 1–2 quoted in Cleonicki Saroca, 'Violence against migrant Filipino women in Australia: Making men's behavior visible,' *Review of Women's Studies* XV, no. 2 (2005): 117.

7. Ibid., 118; and Cunneen and Stubbs, *Violence,* 119.

8. Saroca, 'Violence,' 120.

9. See, for example, Cleonicki Saroca, 'Filipino women, migration, and violence in Australia: Lived reality and media image,' *Kasarinlan: Philippine Journal of Third World Studies* 1, no. 1 (2006): 75–110; Cleonicki Saroca, 'Woman in danger or dangerous woman? Contesting images of Filipina victims of domestic homicide in Australia,' *Asian Journal of Women's Studies* 12, no. 3 (2006): 35–74; Saroca, 'Violence'; Cleonicki Saroca, 'Filipino women, sexual politics, and the gendered discourse of the mail order bride,' *JIGS (Journal of Interdisciplinary Gender Studies)* 2, no. 2 (1997): 89–103; Desmond Cahill, *Intermarriages in International Contexts. A Study of Filipina Women Married to Australian, Japanese and Swiss Men* (Quezon City: Scalabrini Migration Centre, 1990); Elizabeth Holt, 'Writing Filipina-Australian brides: The discourse on Filipina brides,' *Philippine Sociological Review* 44, no. 1–4 (1996): 58–78; and Kathryn Robinson, 'Of mail-order brides and "Boys Own" tales: Representations of Asian-Australian marriages,' *Feminist Review* 52 (1996): 53–68.

10. Cahill, *Intermarriages;* F.M. Cooke, *Australian-Filipino Marriages in the 1980s: The Myth and the Reality* (Griffith University School of Modern Asian Studies, Center for the Study of Australia-Asian Relations, Research Paper 37, 1986); J. Pendlebury, 'Filipino brides in remote areas,' Occasional Paper no. 5, Department of Social Security, Darwin, 1990; and C. Boer, *Are You Looking for a Filipina Wife? A Study of Filipina-Australian Marriages* (Sydney: General Synod Office, 1988).

11. Cunneen and Stubbs, *Violence.*

12. Holt, 'Writing Filipina-Australian,' 58–78; Robinson, 'Of mail-order brides'; Saroca, 'Hearing the voices'; Saroca, 'Filipino women'; Saroca, 'Woman in danger'; Saroca, 'Violence'; and Saroca, 'Filipino women'.

13. Interview with Rosa Droescher former Senior Policy Officer, Ethnic Affairs Commission of NSW, Sydney, 8 January 2015.

14. Ibid.; and Elsa Koleth, 'Multiculturalism: A review of Australian policy statements and recent debates in Australia and overseas,' Research Paper no. 6, 2010–2011, Parliament of Australia, 3, http://www.aph.gov.au/About_Parliament/Parliamentary_Departments/Parliamentary_Library/pubs/rp/rp1011/11rp06#_Toc275248116.

15. Rosa Droescher interview.

16. Frank Galbally, *Migrant Services and Programs, Report of the Review of Post-arrival Programs and Services for Migrants* (Canberra: Australian Government Publishing Service, 1978).

17. Ibid., 4.

18. Ibid., 9.

19. Ibid., 9–10.

20. Ibid., 12.

21. Ibid., 70.

22. Droescher interview.

23. Ibid.

24. Interview with Della Ipong, Sydney, 27 April 2014.

25. Cunneen and Stubbs, *Violence*, 13.

26. Quoted in Maria Eleanor Guanio-Bartels and Rogelia Pe-Pua, *The Development of a Radio Information Package for Filipino Women* (Sydney: Filipino Women's Working Party, 1994), 3.

27. See *The People of New South Wales, 1991 Census* (Sydney: Ethnic Affairs Commission, 1994); and ibid., 3.

28. The sources consulted included (1) Ethnic Affairs Commission Annual Reports (1986–2009), (2) the personal papers of Debbie Wall, Melba Marginson, Joan Dicka and Lilian McKinnon, (3) interviews, (4) the complete episodes of the FWWP—sponsored radio programme 'Now that you are an Aussie', and (5) the video on marrying and migrating to Australia.

29. Interview with Estrella McKinnon, Wollongong, 1 March 2013.

30. Ipong interview.

31. Interviews with Joan Dicka, Adelaide, 10–11 June 2014.

32. 'Joan Dicka—Shortlisted for a 2009 Australian Human Rights Award,' *Kasama* 24, no. 1 (January–March 2010): 1–5.

33. Interview with Concepcion 'Chat' Ramilo, Quezon City, 5 August 2014.

34. Dicka interviews, Ipong interview, McKinnon interview.

35. Dicka interviews.

36. Kym Tilbrook, '55 Filipino women have sought help: Bannon', *The Advertiser*, 28 November 1987, no page numbers, from the personal papers of Joan Dicka, Adelaide.
37. Ramilo interview.
38. Ethnic Affairs Commission of NSW, *Filipino Women: Challenges & Responses (1988–1991)* (Sydney: Ethnic Affairs Commission of NSW, 1992), 7.
39. McKinnon interview.
40. Ethnic Affairs Commission of NSW, *Filipino Women: Challenges & Responses (1988–1991)* (Sydney: Ethnic Affairs Commission of NSW, 1992). Report prepared by Chat Ramilo and Rosa Droescher, Officers of the Ethnic Affairs Commission of NSW.
41. Dicka interview, 10 June 2014.
42. Saroca, 'Woman in danger', 35–74.
43. Ibid.
44. Ibid., 48.
45. Quoted in ibid.
46. Ibid., 53; and interview with Melba Marginson, Melbourne, 25 September 2007.
47. CPCA Website, http://cpcabrisbane.org/CPCA/. Accessed 10 August 2015.
48. Ibid.
49. Marginson interview.
50. Ibid.; and Melba Marginson, 'Not for the money,' in *Breaking Through—Women, Work and Careers*, ed. Jocelynne A. Scutt (Melbourne: Artemis, 1992), 115–23.
51. Marginson, 'Not for the money', 120; Marginson interview.
52. Melba Marginson, 'Increasing access for Filipina survivors of domestic violence,' in *Not the Same: Conference Proceedings and a Strategy on Domestic Violence and Sexual Assault for Non-English Speaking Background Women* (Brunswick Victoria: Office of the Status of Women, 1996), 20–21.
53. Cunneen and Stubbs, *Violence Against Filipino Women in Australia*, 1; Interview with Deborah Wall and Rosa Droescher, Sydney, 2 August 2012.
54. Melba Marginson, 'Immigrant and refugee women as victims of crime,' paper presented to the Conference on Support of Victims of Crime, Meeting the Challenges of Diversity: Different Cultures, Different Needs', 21 April 1999, Melbourne, 2, from the personal papers of Melba Marginson, Melbourne; Marginson interview.
55. Cunneen and Stubbs, *Violence*, 1; Marginson interview; and Zita Antonios, Race Discrimination Commissioner to Melba Marginson,

16 March 1995, 1, from the personal papers of Melba Marginson, Melbourne.

56. Cunneen and Stubbs, *Violence*, 1, 31.

57. Nikki Barrowclough, 'The shameful story of Australia's serial husbands,' *Good Weekend The Sydney Morning Herald Magazine*, 6 May 1995, 46–67.

58. Elizabeth Evatt, 'Serial sponsorship and abuse of Filipino women in Australia,' in *Serial Sponsorship: Perspectives for Policy Options* (Sydney: Ethnic Affairs Commission of NSW, 1992), 17; Clause 801.221 (6) of Sch 2 to the Migration Regulations 1994: 'Under the Migration Regulations 1994 of the Migration Act 1958, applicants on certain Partner visas, who have experienced domestic violence after arriving in Australia and whose relationship with the sponsoring partner has broken down because of domestic violence, remain eligible for Permanent Residence if they can demonstrate that the relationship with their sponsoring partner was genuine and broke down because of domestic violence. A victim must prove that the relationship was genuine and ongoing and that domestic violence occurred in Australia.'

59. Ibid.

60. Evatt, 'Serial sponsorship,' 17.

61. Dicka interview, 11 June 2014.

62. Department of Immigration and Multicultural Affairs, *Marrying and Migrating... You have to Work at It*, VHS Video, produced by Kestrel Film and Video for the Department of Immigration and Multicultural Affairs, 1996.

63. Interview with Marie del Rosario-Apattad and Rodrigo Garcia, CFO, Manila, 25 July 2014.

64. Dicka interview, 10 June 2014; and 'Smoothing the path for migrants,' *Post Migration*, 17 June 1995, from the personal papers of Joan Dicka, Adelaide.

65. 'Dawn House S.A. Inc' in *Good Practices in SAAP Services*, eds. Joanne Baulderstone and Catherine Scott (Adelaide: Flinders Institute of Public Policy and Management, Flinders University of South Australia, 1999), 107–18.

66. Jenny Clark, *The Art of Health: Using the Arts to Achieve Health* (South Australia: SA Health Commission, 1997), 15; Baulderstone and Scott, eds., 'Dawn House S.A. Inc,' 107–18; and 'Filipino Women and the Murray Mallee Support Group,' in Tahereh Ziaian, *Celebrating Our Success, Responses to Violence Against Non-English Speaking Background Women, The Report of the NESB Women and Violence Project* (South Australia: Women's Health Statewide, 1997), 28–31.

67. Clark, *The Art of Health*, 15.

68. Guanio-Bartels and Pe-Pua, *The Development of a Radio Information Package*, ix.
69. Ibid., 15. The programme was aired from 8 March to 18 July 1994.
70. For example, in Mudgee, Lithgow and Grafton in ibid., 16–17.
71. Ipong interview; and Dicka interviews.
72. Interview with Wall and Droescher, Sydney, 2 August 2012.
73. McKinnon interview.
74. Ipong interview.
75. Ibid.
76. Droescher interview.
77. Email communication from Deborah Wall, Tuesday, 6 January 2015. Della Ipong also described their activism as collaborative (Ipong interview).
78. Letter to the Information Collection Unit, Department of Immigration and Citizenship, 30 July 2012; and handwritten letter to the Women's Emergency Center, no date, both from the personal papers of Joan Dicka in Adelaide.
79. Statement, no date, from the personal papers of Joan Dicka in Adelaide.
80. I am indebted to Martyn Lyons for the label 'writing upwards'. See Martyn Lyons, 'Writing upwards: How the weak wrote to the powerful,' *Journal of Social History* 49, no. 2 (2015): 317–30.

PART III

Asia

Underpinning much of the contemporary unease around immigration is the tension between economic agendas that see population movement and globalisation as a necessity, and political responses that privilege the defence of what is perceived as a coherent national identity. In his chapter, 'Not Singaporean Enough? Migration, History and National Identity in Singapore', John Solomon explores this dynamic in a nation that is a symbol of the global economy. He argues that more recent patterns of movement tend to be treated as forming part of a 'long present' rather than integrated into settled understandings of the national story. For Solomon, historians have an important part to play in challenging received ideas about contemporary citizenship by producing more fluid and dynamic accounts of the city-state's past that integrate recent movements and do justice to the complexity of the distant past.

Anindya Raychaudhuri's contribution to this volume, '"They Don't Call Us Indian": Indian Muslim Voices and the 1947 India/Pakistan Partition', lays the ground for another shift of focus in migration history, looking at non-movement as a decision in itself. We are quick to assume that mobility should be the locus of enquiry—that it is in a way abnormal, of interest by definition. Focusing on decisions of Indian Muslims not to leave their country in spite of Partition and the divide between a majority Muslim Pakistan and a majority Hindu India, Raychaudhuri shows how listening to those who stayed and their reasons for doing so can also act as a counter to the political agendas that underpin hegemonic national narratives.

CHAPTER 6

Not Singaporean Enough? Migration, History and National Identity in Singapore

John Solomon

Situated along an important maritime corridor, Singapore's modern history has been defined by its openness as a port-city, and its connections to global networks of people, trade and ideas. Today, it positions itself as a global city, attracting new waves of visitors and settled and transient migrants. Singapore is, however, relatively unique amongst global cities, in that it is has for the last half century existed as a sovereign nation-state. The island therefore operates within two distinct discourses that have also influenced its migration and development policies, its recent politics, as well as the writing of its history. On the one hand, Singapore is a nation with territorial borders, a body politic of citizens, and it has attempted to consolidate a defined cultural identity. Yet, its economic and strategic interests also dictate that it retains its historical character as an open and fluid cosmopolitan city.

One area in which these two paradigms have been in tension is in the state's recent immigration policies. On the one hand, immigration is described as necessary in order to overcome the negative repercussions of Singapore's low birth rates and to ensure economic competitiveness.

J. Solomon (✉)
National University of Singapore, Singapore

© The Author(s) 2019
E. Henrich and J. M. Simpson (eds.),
History, Historians and the Immigration Debate,
https://doi.org/10.1007/978-3-319-97123-0_6

However, immigration policies remain unpopular amongst large sections of the population who have, alongside economic grievances, expressed anxieties about the potential loss of culture and identity that accompany certain aspects of globalisation.

Despite widespread negative sentiment towards contemporary immigration policies, the vast majority of Singapore's ethnically plural citizenry traces its roots to the large-scale migrations that occurred in the nineteenth and twentieth centuries; migrations that have fundamentally shaped the island's social and cultural characteristics. This raises a number of questions about how migration and its parts in Singapore's history is understood by the public, studied in scholarship and portrayed by public institutions, and how understandings of historical migration shape attitudes to contemporary migrants and newly naturalised citizens.

To understand the relationship between histories of migration and national identity in Singapore, therefore, we must take into account ideas of race, collective social experiences and historical periodisation. This chapter examines how these factors have not only had an impact on shaping public discourse about migration, identity and citizenship, but have also obscured the layered complexities of migration in Singapore's history. This, in turn, has led to the emergence of problematic notions of authenticity and inauthenticity in the public sphere, corresponding to inaccurate categories of 'old' and 'new' citizens. I argue that new approaches to history can help bring to the fore a complex past and offer a challenge to this kind of binary thinking. They, thus, have the potential to create space for the emergence of more inclusive understandings of national identity.

RACE, MIGRATION AND HISTORY

Singapore's recent past is imbricated in colonial migration, but unlike other 'migrant nations' like Australia and the United States, it was intended from the outset of its colonial history to be an ethnically plural society.[1] Although Singapore's discontinuous history of human settlement stretches back for at least 700 years, the island's contemporary population demography and cultural characteristics have been shaped by waves of migration that followed British settlement in 1819.[2]

From that period onwards, amongst the most numerically significant migrant communities to emerge in the settlement were the Chinese, Malays and Indians.[3] These communities together compose the largest segment of Singapore's citizenry today, their relative proportions within the entire population having more or less solidified by the late nineteenth century. Apart from these major groups, as well as European communities, there were other regional communities like the Eurasians, who remain an important and visible ethnic community today, receiving state recognition and heritage representation.[4] Other smaller communities like the Japanese were present in Singapore from its earliest colonial days, but remained largely regarded as transient communities that underwent significant fluctuations in population size and character. Several other communities like the Armenians, Jews and Arabs merged into other communities or became less numerically significant due to external migration.

The Chinese-Malay-Indian-Other (CMIO) framework was adopted by the People's Action Party after it came to power in Singapore in 1959, and it was subsequently utilised to shape the ethnic contours of the newly independent nation. Today, the categories are deployed in popular images of Singaporean multiculturalism, and in public celebrations like the annual National Day Parade. The government also uses this categorisation to manage language policies, access to public housing, statistical and census data and public holidays. Several scholars such as Chua Beng Huat and Sharon Siddique have argued that CMIO classifications serve to enforce frozen and essential categories that gloss over the heterogeneity of Singapore's 'racial' communities.[5] This is particularly true with regard to the first three categories of Chinese, Malay and Indian. However, even though the 'Other' category is meant to serve as a catch-all for minorities outside of the primary categories, it, too, has in the past operated in a somewhat exclusionary manner. The Eurasian community in particular has been traditionally highlighted as the fourth piece in Singapore's multiculturalism.

The use of this framework has implications for new citizens who fall outside CMIO categories. In a recent news article, a Singapore citizen of Filipino descent, Emily Tolentino, described that lack of acceptance she felt amongst her fellow citizens because of the fact that she did not fit into prescribed CMIO categories:

I told her I'm Singaporean but I'm Filipino. She laughed and said, 'Then you're not a real Singaporean, what.' After that, whenever I introduced myself as a Singaporean, she would interject that I'm Filipino. Eventually I just started introducing myself as Filipino. It was easier... I think to some people, it doesn't matter that I have a red passport or that this place is home to me. I'm not Chinese or Malay or Indian or White. I'm visibly Filipino and for them, I can never be Singaporean enough.[6]

The quote highlights the argument that geographers Natalie Oswin and Brenda Yeoh make about how CMIO models 'not only privilege essentialist categories tied to "ancestral cultures"', they also 'popularize the notion that these building blocks of Singapore's citizenry are fixed and sedentary'.[7]

Migration in Scholarship

Within the last two decades, there has been sustained scholarly attention on the issue of contemporary migration into Singapore from scholars working in a diverse range of fields. In the field of public policy, for example, a growing body of statistical surveys and qualitative interviews has provided insights into attitudes, institutions and processes of migrant integration or migrant attitudes towards their own mobilities. Framed and shaped by public policy considerations, the migrant-receiving nation-state looms large within these studies. Sociologists and geographers have also provided valuable input from a range of other perspectives, and conceptual and theoretical lenses, utilising the growing interdisciplinarity of fields like diaspora studies or mobility studies.

Such works have been pivotal in shedding light on contemporary Singaporean anxieties and debates surrounding national identity and migrant integration and assimilation. Within this body of work, however, issues relating to identity and citizenship are largely framed as contemporary problems that have arisen as a result of recent globalisation. As a result, scholars dealing with contemporary migration often fall short of historically contextualising current trends, or drawing connections with migrations in Singapore's past.

At the same time, historians have tended to neglect migration in Singapore after the 1960s. Within historical scholarship, most works that address the issue of migration focus on the pre-war period, with some work discussing a final wave of migration that occurred between the end of the war and the introduction of Singapore citizenship when it became a self-governing colony in 1959. Faced with unemployment, inadequate housing and a young population, the People's Action Party introduced citizenship legislation aimed at zero to low population growth.[8] As early as the late 1960s, in response to the growth of labour demand, the Singapore government began relaxing migration policies to facilitate the incorporation of labour in the form of temporary permit holders as well as highly skilled professional and managerial workers.[9] By the 1990s, liberalised policies facilitated a shifting emphasis towards high-skilled professional migration with increased pathways to permanent residency and citizenship, beginning the shift towards the current demographic distribution.

The implicit division of migration between these scholarly disciplines has led to the emergence of a way of thinking that divides Singapore's history of migration into two distinct periods. The older period of migration that has been the focus of historians is associated with the colonial era, which ends at the start of the nation-building decades that began with independence in 1965. At the same time, the newer phase, associated with the post-Cold War era of globalisation after Singapore's economic status as a developed nation had been established, is often treated as being part of a long present rather than as a subject of history. This is despite the fact that this period of migration began more than 25 years ago and the earliest wave of migrants who arrived during this phase, many of whom have since adopted Singapore citizenship, have been in Singapore for more than half of the country's existence as a sovereign nation state.

The omission of these later waves of migration from historical scholarship has been noted by scholars who contend that this period of migration should be featured in historical understandings of Singapore's society and community. Vineeta Sinha, for example, has argued that the last two decades marked by a new wave of migration constitute a 'critical phase' in the history of the Indian community in Singapore.[10]

However, migration between 1965 and the present period has not been the focus of any major work of social or cultural history. Although attracting international talent was the focus of government migration policies from only 1990 onwards, a significant number of permanent residencies and citizenships were already being granted at a steady rate before the 1990s, particularly from the 1970s onwards. For example, by 1989, the year the Singapore government had articulated a plan to begin attracting skilled professionals from around the world, almost 3% of the population, or 79,590 individuals, had received citizenship in the preceding nine years alone.[11]

These silences and omissions are significant because they have led to the problematic division of Singapore's history into discrete, unrelated periods, a framework that then has then been used in popular discourse to construct a notion of 'authentic citizenship'. This has been achieved in part, argues sociologist Terrence Chong, through the use of nostalgia as an affective tool to create a shared history. Specifically, Chong argues that nostalgia in Singapore is steeped in the social memory of, amongst other things, major events in Singapore's past (i.e. Singapore's separation from Malaysia in 1965, the relocation of communities from *kampongs* (villages) to Housing Development Board flats in the 1970s, and memories of spaces and public buildings that no longer exist) and more recent political and cultural events in the 1980s and early 1990s. Whilst the creation of these social memories is not solely a response to immigration, Chong argues that it functions to exclude newer citizens who have little or no access to these memories or events.[12]

Public history institutions, moreover, often exclude narratives of post-1965 migration in their representations of the nation's history. At the same time, earlier migrations are frequently represented through racial tropes that are organised according to the CMIO racial classification system that marks Singapore's unique approach to multiculturalism. One consequence of the use of this is the exclusion and under-representation of the migration histories of communities that are not commonly represented in discourse about Singapore's 'racial' make-up. Communities that arrived after independence, too, are excluded; communities that have contributed to what sociologist Steven Vertovec has described as the shift between long-established diversities and newer more complex configurations of class, ethnicity and mobility and legal status, or what he terms 'old' and 'new' diversities.[13]

CONTEMPORARY MIGRATION IN SINGAPORE

In recent years, the issue of foreign migration into Singapore has generated considerable public debate. Non-resident migrants who come from a broad spectrum of social classes, educational backgrounds and countries and have entered the country on a range of different work permits and temporary visas presently comprise roughly a third of the inhabitants of the island (Table 6.1).[14]

Table 6.1 Current proportion of Singapore citizens, permanent residents, non-residents

Total population in Singapore (as of June 2015)	5.54 million
Citizens	3.38 million
PRs	0.53 million
Non-residents	1.63 million

Source: *Population in Brief 2015* (Singapore: National Population and Talent Division, Prime Minister's Office, Singapore Department of Statistics, Ministry of Home Affairs, Immigration and Checkpoints Authority, 2015), 5

This is representative of a significant increase in both the total population size as well as the proportion of non-Singaporeans within the country in the last two decades. Amongst Singaporean citizens, many are naturalised citizens, or in local parlance 'new citizens', most of whom acquired citizenship at various times since the early 1990s. The falling proportion of local born Singaporeans from 78% in 1980 to 57% three decades later is indicative of the scale and speed of change.[15]

This change, moreover, is expected to continue. A Singaporean government White Paper released in 2013 revealed that officials expected the total population to reach 6.9 million by 2030, with a significant amount of this increase projected to come from immigration.[16]

The liberalisation of immigration policies in the last two decades and the demographic impact of new population growth strategies has resulted in rising tensions between not only Singaporean nationals and non-nationals, but also between Singaporean citizens by birth, and naturalised Singaporean citizens and permanent residents. New arrivals are sometimes regarded as 'scroungers' or economically motivated actors who are merely using Singapore as a 'stepping stone' before migrating once more to economically advanced countries in the West.[17] A survey of 1001 Singapore-born citizens conducted by the Institute of Policy Studies revealed that six out of ten respondents agreed or strongly agreed with the statement that new citizens were likely to use Singapore as a stepping-stone to settling in other countries.[18]

The release of the White Paper figures in 2013 triggered the largest public protests that Singapore had seen in decades as a few thousand people turned out to voice opposition to the government's planned immigration increase. Immigration was also a significant topic during the last two general elections in 2011 and 2015. Apart from questions about population size in relation to infrastructure, employment opportunities, state resources and quality of life, much debate has centred on the nature of Singapore's national identity in the context of contemporary migration.[19]

Government attempts to persuade Singaporeans of the merits of continuing to position the nation as a global city and of remaining open to immigration have involved reminding voters that Singapore has long been a city of migrants, and that its citizens are largely descended from migrants. Yet, the acknowledgement of a migrant lineage for most citizens, and the concomitant appeal for an acceptance of diversity, stands in tension with popular historical discourses that represent Singaporean identity as something racially and temporally situated in the past, into which new migrants must assimilate.

Since modern independent Singapore is just over 50 years old, ethnically heterogeneous, with no ancient past held in common by its citizens, the construction of national identity is a relatively recent, conscious activity. It is only since the 1960s, as part of its nation-building efforts, that the state has enacted policies to encourage the growth of a Singaporean national identity. A relatively recent example of this is the National Education or NE programme that was implemented by the Singapore government in 1997 to promote a sense of national identity amongst school-going youth through history education, visits to state institutions and the observance of special events like National Day.

Scholars have noted that both the scale of recent migration and the relative recentness of Singaporean identity discourses have created social anxieties about the resilience of existing identity narratives.[20]

In response to these anxieties one of the strategies employed by the State has been the use of history as a tool to strengthen national identity. Whereas in the preceding decades history had largely been overlooked as an effective tool for citizen socialisation, from the 1980s onwards, the Singapore government began to actively engage in the creation of historical discourse in an attempt to strengthen Singaporean identity. Historian Loh Kah Seng has described the shift in the government's attitudes, focusing on its efforts in the 1990s to utilise history as a means of imparting a stronger sense of citizenship and identification with the country through the crafting of a particular political and economic narrative that it termed the 'Singapore Story'.[21]

Given the enduring anxieties over Singapore's identity, history has also proved to be a useful tool in the attempt to integrate new migrants into the Singaporean social fabric. New migrants—specifically new citizens—are encouraged to integrate into Singaporean society and adopt a Singaporean identity by adopting the values that underpin Singapore's multi-racialism and meritocracy, and by gaining an understanding of and appreciation for Singapore's history.[22] For example, as part of the final stages of the 'Singapore Citizenship Journey', a process for educating new citizens into Singapore's culture and values, The National Integration Council, the People's Association, and the Immigration and Checkpoints Authority organise museum tours for new citizens that include visits to landmarks, monuments, museums and heritage centres to acquaint new citizens with the history of Singaporean communities and Singapore's national history.[23]

This raises a number of questions. How do historical practices shape national identity in the midst of a new wave of migration? And what impact do certain historical narratives about diversity, race and ethnicity potentially have on integration? Gérard Noiriel has discussed the possibility of migration history in France going beyond a mere acknowledgement of the importance of migration in French history, and instead providing millions of French citizens from migrant backgrounds, 'the *possibility* of legitimately locating their personal history, or that of their family, within the "master narrative" of French national history'.[24] Today, historians of Singapore have an opportunity to raise similar questions about how existing history discourses in Singapore continue to shape perceptions, and facilitate the capacity for new migrants to situate themselves within Singapore's history.

Cultural Resources

Public history and heritage resources that celebrate specific cultures, regions and backgrounds that do not fit into traditional models of CMIO are currently limited in Singapore. The presence or absence of certain kinds of cultural resources like ethnic heritage museums can influence public discourse about new citizens from diverse national and ethnic backgrounds. This contributes to a politics of inclusion and exclusion by reinforcing definitions of who authentic Singaporeans are, and whose histories are a legitimate part of the nation's broader history, whilst obscuring the existence and growth of new diasporic communities on the island.[25]

Part of this problem is the way that migration has been historicised and linked to specific communities. There are, for example, no museums or heritage centres in Singapore that are dedicated to migration history, like those that have been established in North America and Australia since the late 1980s. Focusing on museums in Australia, Eureka Henrich has examined how the evolution of museums' practices and philosophies has mirrored broader changes in how migration has been conceptualised in Australian public discourse. Henrich's research showed that museums evolved to represent diverse histories of mobilities in different ways as discourse and policy shifted from a focus on the assimilation of new migrants into a dominant Anglo-Celtic culture, to one that foregrounded a paradigm of multiculturalism in which new migrants were seen to contribute to a changing Australian culture, and finally to an understanding of Australia as a 'Nation of Immigrants'.[26]

Even though Singapore does not have a museum dedicated to migration history, migration is a prominent feature of the overall narrative of Singapore's history in the National Museum's 'Permanent Singapore Gallery'. The gallery showcases the island's history from the late thirteenth century to the contemporary period and features political, social and cultural history approaches that explore various aspects of the island's past. The visitor progresses through the gallery along a linear path that is arranged in a chronological sequence. Migration is a recurring theme in much of the displays and exhibits that cover the pre-war period in particular. The galleries showcase the migration from Chinese, Indian, Malay and other communities through material artefacts, photographs and textual panels that describe the lives of elite 'pioneers' as well as ordinary migrants and members of settled communities. The Second World War and Japanese occupation serve as an interlude before the gallery focuses the attention of the visitor to Singapore's path to decolonisation and nationhood.

From the post-war period onwards, the focus of the panels and displays turns to the political and social milieu in which Singapore gained independence and embarked on a period of nation-building. Much of the focus of these later galleries is on the political and social effort to forge a common national identity amongst the island's diverse ethnic communities in the midst of communal tensions in Singapore and the region. Later, near the very end of the gallery, a panel on Singapore's evolution into a global city focuses on Singapore's economic achievements, and its increasing integration into the global economic system as a cosmopolitan city-state. The increasing numbers of Singaporeans 'living, working and studying overseas and building international collaborations' are also mentioned in this panel.[27] This absence of immigration into Singapore as a theme in *recent history* is significant, as it appears to suggest that Singaporean national identity emerged further in the past, through the common historical experiences of the population under colonialism, occupation and the politics of decolonisation.

Peggy Levitt has pointed out that the question of how new immigrants will fit into contemporary articulations of Singaporean cosmopolitanism has not been sufficiently discussed in the public sphere.[28] Drawing on her recent analysis of the ways in which museums in a number of world cities negotiate and display different kinds of 'cosmopolitics' and display particular vernacular cosmopolitanisms or 'national cosmopolitanisms', I would argue that the National Museum illustrates how contemporary migration has not yet found a place within Singapore's primary national historical narrative, even as that narrative continues to re-articulate regional and global connections in the context of Singapore's economic stake in continued globalisation.[29]

'Old' and 'New' Diasporas

To date, a significant portion of new migrants, particularly naturalised citizens and permanent residents, have been individuals from either China or India, countries to which many Singaporeans have ancestral ties.[30] Singapore, therefore, is uniquely situated as a site of encounter, interaction and contestation between so-called 'old' and 'new' diaspora.[31]

These demographic trends have been influenced by policies that encourage permanent and long-term migration from groups that fit into existing ethnic categories. The Singapore Government first publicly disclosed its policy of maintaining the ethnic distribution of citizens through migration in 1990 in a written response provided by the political secretary to the Deputy Prime Minister. The government was addressing concerns from members of the public about the effects of immigration on the existing ethnic distribution in the country. At the time, it was argued that this policy maintained societal harmony and economic success.[32] There are policy assumptions behind a strategy of augmenting existing ethnic communities with new arrivals and maintaining the demographic distribution of the settled population by race. One of these assumptions is that new migrants will find it easier to assimilate into existing co-ethnic communities because of similarities in culture, language and traditions.

Yet, recent sociological literature suggests that this kind of integration has to a large extent failed to occur. Despite community efforts from new migrants, settled Singaporeans and government organisations like the People's Association and the National Integration Council, separation persists between settled communities and new migrants. The extent and social significance of this issue is reflected in the growing body of academic work by geographers, public policy analysts and sociologists dedicated to identifying, analysing and understanding its contours.[33]

The Indian community—already ethnically, linguistically, culturally and religiously highly diverse—has been singled out by politicians and academics as a prime example of the difficulties in bridging connections between Singapore Indians and so-called 'New Indians', or recent migrants.[34] For new migrants from Indian and Chinese backgrounds, assimilation into pre-existing Singapore-Indian and Singapore-Chinese categories can be eased by certain cultural similarities. However, in terms of historical resources, the commemoration of ethnic heritage has perpetuated certain forms of exclusion in so far as historical narratives reify Indian-Singaporean and Chinese-Singaporean identities by rooting them to particular periods in the past. This is evident in the ways that ethnic heritage centres periodise migration in Singapore's past.

Ethnic heritage centres like the recently opened Indian Heritage Centre play a dual purpose of serving as a space for community activities and cultural events, as well as providing a commemoration of the community's history. Housed on three floors, the museum within the Indian Heritage Centre is the first museum in Southeast Asia to feature the history of the Indian diaspora. It displays India's ancient connections with Southeast Asia through archaeological artefacts. Other displays focus on the religious, political, social and material culture of the 'Indian' community in Singapore from the early nineteenth century to the present day, using a combination of artefacts, textual panels, oral histories, visual displays and augmented reality interfaces.

The Centre has applied to be one of the public institutions that new citizens can choose from whilst completing the 'Singapore Citizenship Journey' component of their naturalisation process, and therefore will likely constitute a new site of integration. It facilitates connections between new and old citizens by providing new citizens with an understanding of the history of the settled community, whilst providing old citizens with an appreciation of their historical and cultural connections with India.

As far as migration and the periodisation of the exhibits go how-ever, after the 1960s, there is no longer a strong emphasis on any sub-sequent migration. Instead, there is a focus on how former migrants contributed to the Singaporean nation-state. On the one hand, rather than this being a conscious curatorial decision, this particular empha-sis can be read as an institutional expression of dominant Singaporean discourses surrounding race, nationality and Indian identity. Indeed the Indian Heritage Centre is not unique in this regard and mirrors not just other institutions like the National Museum, but academic and popular discourses as well.

In the Centre, 'authentic' Indian Singaporean identity is linked to sig-nificant events in the wider national history narrative of Singapore, sig-nalling that Indian Singaporean identity has been established from other historical Indian identities and is now somewhat fixed. The final gallery at the Centre that celebrates the contributions of Indians to the nation-state of Singapore, features a large quotation from Singapore's third president Devan Nair, who like many others of his generation was born outside of Singapore (in this case in Malacca in present day Malaysia).

My generation did not begin as Singaporeans. I myself started out as a Malacca-born British subject of Indian origin. But our children are all Singaporeans. They feel like Singaporeans, comport themselves like Singaporeans, and eat and live like Singaporeans.[35]

Prior to this final gallery, the Indian Heritage Centre celebrates colo-nial migrants from various sub-ethnic groups who played different roles in the early colony. It describes the pre-war journeys of individuals on board ships like the SS *Rajula* that travelled to Singapore from India. It also focuses on transnational connections that were facilitated by migra-tion. It highlights for example the political and social activities of Indian nationalists and Tamil reformers in the Indian community during the Second World War and the post-war period.

Contemporary migration is briefly mentioned in a looped video which plays at the very start of the galleries. The video offers visitors a pre-view by presenting a concise history of Indians in Singapore from the pre-colonial era to the present. At the end of the video, viewers are told that 'new waves of migration continue from the subcontinent bringing fresh influences and energies, adding a new dimension to the Indian community'.

The brief acknowledgement of new migrants in the introductory video suggests that there are also other factors involved in the absence of such narratives in the actual displays and artefacts within the galleries. The Indian Heritage Centre, like other heritage centres in Singapore, is dependent to a large degree on community participation. That is to say that the current exhibits have been in part shaped by material contributions of artefacts and historical information by the Singapore Indian community, as well as its feedback through public consultation exercises. Perhaps then the absence of artefacts relating to more recent migrations can be partially attributed to the fact that the new Indian community has not yet come forward to offer significant input or contributions, whether due to a lack of engagement efforts or the external orientations of migrants themselves. As with other museums that deal with migration elsewhere, perhaps it will be the second generation of migrants who more actively intervene to have their stories of migration and identity woven into the existing narratives to create new ones.

PROBLEMATISING AND RECONCEPTUALISING MIGRATION IN SINGAPORE'S HISTORY: EXAMPLES IN THE INDIAN DIASPORA

There is no direct equivalence between the substance and nature of migrations past and present in Singapore. Post-colonial state formation, contemporary discourses on multiculturalism, the further collapsing of distance through technology, and neo-liberal transformations to human and capital flows have all introduced new contexts. Yet, there are similarities between the conditions of mobility that existed in the transcolonial world of the past and the globalised present. The tendency within existing scholarship to treat immigration before independence and recent immigration in Singapore as separate phenomena diminishes and obscures the continuities that have existed between different eras of migration. Identifying and exploring common themes can perhaps help to shift historical discourses towards narratives that are more inclusive to newcomers.

Some scholars have made connections between past and present migrations. Historians like Sunil Amrith have utilised the theoretical approaches of the 'mobility turn' in migration studies to offer new ways of understanding Singapore's migratory past. In his work on Tamil migration from South India, Amrith argues that different kinds of mobility shaped Singapore's history and continue to shape its present.[36]

Past migration and settlement also highlight themes of belonging and identity that challenge the assumption that similar issues relating to contemporary migration are novel. The erection of national borders, the issuing of passports, and other newly emerging regimes for managing and deciding nationality and citizenship amidst the incremental retreat of the British Empire proved to be a profoundly traumatic experience for many in minority communities in Malaya and Singapore in the post-war period.[37] British foreign office papers and Singapore parliamentary records between the late 1940s and mid 1960s demonstrate the considerable debates that policy proposals underwent before being passed as law. The records and discussions also indicate the differing motivations and priorities of Malay elites, political leaders in Singapore, the British authorities and new nation states like India.

The ensuing discussions led to the introduction of somewhat arbitrary rules for determining who was eligible for citizenship and who was not, including amongst other things the specific length of time a foreign-born individual had to have stayed in Singapore in order to qualify. Newspaper reports and parliamentary records suggest that many were not only confused by the evolving criteria, but found themselves on the wrong side of eligibility laws.

However, rather than being passively subjected to legislation, anecdotal evidence suggests that many tried to navigate the uncertainty of immigration legislation by maximising their mobilities with varying results. Like the 'flexible citizens' described in Aihwa Ong's work on contemporary Chinese migrants who economically rationalise citizenship decisions, oral histories suggest that for many Indians, the final decision to adopt Singaporean citizenship was a fundamentally pragmatic one, an economic decision based on Singapore's prospects vis-à-vis India's.[38] Similar to strategies undertaken by married migrants who qualify for citizenship today, many Indian couples consisted of one individual with Singaporean citizenship and another with Indian citizenship. Thus, as Sunil Amrith has argued, transnational families remained the norm amongst South Indian Tamils throughout much of the 1950s.[39] For many others, Malaya simply was the only home that they knew, which highlights the diverse nature of migration in the past.

Looking to Singapore's twentieth-century colonial history also reveals that tensions and encounters between older and newer migrants and settled communities have a longer lineage than current discourses would suggest. By the early twentieth century, 'Malayan-born' Indians identified with Malaya as home and no longer had strong contemporary cultural connections with India but demonstrated syncretic 'Malayanised' Indian identities. Internal power struggles that took place in the 1930s and 1940s within the Indian Association, one of the most prominent Indian social organisations in Singapore at the time, reveal the tensions between a settled population focused on a future in Malaya and newer arrivals who identified with political developments in India.[40] Rather than being a unique product of contemporary globalisation, manifestations of anxiety, conflict and contestation between rooted populations and recent arrivals occurred well before the construction of the nation-state and national citizenship, as did cooperation between groups.

In the case of Singapore, there are enough commonalities, particularly with regard to the complex ways in which migrants of different eras understood their own identities vis-à-vis those of others, as well as their place in society, to suggest that a comparative exploration of over-arching themes in Singapore's past and present might yield meaningful contributions to our understanding of the island's historical continuities.

Conclusion

Singapore's history has been successfully utilised by state institutions and the public as a means of generating social cohesion and a sense of Singaporean national identity amongst an ethnically plural citizenry. In highlighting a shared history, discourses have also emerged that situate Singapore's identity in fixed ethnic configurations and specific historical periods and social experiences. This has limited the capacity of new citizens to fully situate themselves within Singapore's national identity, as well as furthering the persistence of ideas about authentic and inauthentic citizenship in the public sphere.

As Singaporean society continues to become increasingly diverse, there will be a growing need to produce a more dynamic understanding of migration within the 'Singapore Story' to make representations of the nation's history more inclusive. Historians can facilitate this by critically examining the underlying assumptions and discourses within academic and public histories of migration that are situated within the overarching narrative of Singapore's history. Approaches that examine and acknowledge the continuities in migrations past and present can also open avenues for the enrichment of migration histories with more complex configurations of identity and belonging and the new experiences of Singapore's rapidly diversifying citizenry.

Notes

1. Anoma Pieris, *Hidden Hands and Divided Landscapes: A Penal History of Singapore's Rural Society* (Honolulu: University of Hawaii Press, 2009), 10.
2. Kwa Chong Guan, Derek Heng, and Tan Tai Yong, *Singapore: A 700 Year History: From Early Emporium to World City* (Singapore: National Archives of Singapore, 2009).
3. In the context of its use as an official 'race' category in Singapore, the term 'Indian' is quite expansive and usually refers to anyone whose ancestry can be traced to the colonial territories under direct and indirect British control in the region that is today known as South Asia. For example, the Sindhis, a community that has had a presence in Singapore since the late nineteenth century and were classed as 'Indians', currently remain categorised under this label despite the fact that the province of Sindh currently exists in the nation-state of Pakistan rather than in contemporary India. The Ceylon Tamil community has also been absorbed into the 'Indian' category in Singapore, demonstrating the slipperiness of the term and its contingency on a colonial past.
4. The history of the Eurasian community in Singapore is represented within the Eurasian Heritage Centre. Singapore's Deputy Prime Minister Teo Chee Hean has highlighted the importance of heritage centres in facilitating the growth of a shared national identity. See 'Heritage centres have even bigger role today in building a shared identity: DPM Teo,' *Straits Times*, 29 November 2015, http://www.straitstimes.com/singapore/heritage-centres-have-even-bigger-role-today-in-building-a-shared-identity-dpm-teo.
5. Beng Huat Chua, 'Culture, multiracialism and national identity in Singapore,' in *Trajectories: Inter-Asia Cultural Studies*, ed. Kuan-Hsing Chen (London: Routledge, 1998), 190; and Sharon Siddique, 'Singaporean identity,' in *Management of Success: The Moulding of Modern Singapore*, eds. Kernial Singh Sandhu and Paul Wheatley (Singapore: Institute of South East Asian Studies, 1989), 570.
6. Castro, Carmina, 'Social integration: Regardless of race, language or religion,' *Yahoo News*, 10 May 2016, https://sg.news.yahoo.com/social-integration-regardless-race-language-035515374.html?nhp=1&guccounter=1. At the time of writing, Castro was a member of the NUS Communications and New Media department. The article was written as part of a joint project with NUS and Inconvenient Questions, a socio-political Singaporean website that aimed to provide a forum for citizens to ask questions about government policy.
7. Natalie Oswin and Brenda S.A. Yeoh, 'Introduction: Mobile city Singapore,' *Mobilities* 5, no. 2 (2010): 171.
8. Saw Swee Hock has examined the rapid decline in population that occurred as a result of state attempts to prevent population increase. Saw Swee Hock, *Population Control for Zero Growth in Singapore* (New York: Oxford University Press, 1980).

9. For a detailed explanation of Singapore's foreign labour policies between the 1960s and 1990s, see Weng-Tat Hui, 'Regionalization, economic restructuring and labour migration in Singapore,' *International Migration* 35, no. 1 (1997): 109–30.

10. Vineeta Sinha, *Singapore Chronicles: Indians* (Singapore: Straits Times Press, 2015), 91.

11. Calculations based on figures taken from the Ministry of Labour, Singapore. Figures taken from Chew Soon-Beng and Rosalind Chew, 'Immigration and foreign labour in Singapore,' *ASEAN Economic Bulletin* 12, no. 2 (November 1995): 193.

12. Terence Chong, 'Stepping stone Singapore: The cultural politics of anti-immigrant anxieties,' in *Migration and Integration in Singapore, Policies and Practice*, eds. Yap Mui Teng, Gillian Koh, and Debbie Soon (London: Routledge, 2015), 224–25.

13. Steven Vertovec, *Diversities Old and New: Migration and Socio-Spatial Patterns in New York, Singapore and Johannesburg* (New York: Palgrave Macmillan, 2015), 1–2.

14. *Population in Brief 2015* (Singapore: Department of Statistics, Ministry of Manpower, 2016), 5, https://www.strategygroup.gov.sg/docs/default-source/Population/population-in-brief-2015.pdf. Singapore Permanent Residency provides a pathway to citizenship as well as certain rights privileges, obligations that accompany citizenship. For a more comprehensive description of migrant categories, refer to Brenda S.A. Yeoh and Theodora Lam, 'Immigration and its (dis)contents: The challenges of highly skilled migration in globalizing Singapore,' *American Behavioral Scientist*, 60, no. 5–6 (2016): 641–42.

15. Norman Vasu, Yeap Su Yin, and Chan Wen Ling, eds., *Immigration in Singapore* (Amsterdam: Amsterdam University Press, 2014), 15.

16. Terence Chong, 'Singapore's Population White Paper: Impending integration challenges,' *ISEAS Perspective* 9 (2013): 2.

17. Chong, 'Stepping stone,' 214, 217, 221–23.

18. 'Integrate, not assimilate', *My Paper*, 22 May 2012, http://news.asiaone.com/print/News/Latest%2BNews/Singapore/Story/A1Story20120522-347411.html.

19. Vasu et al., *Immigration in Singapore*, 7–24.

20. Ibid., 10.

21. Loh Kah Seng, 'Within the Singapore Story: The use and narrative of history in Singapore,' *Crossroads: An Interdisciplinary Journal of Southeast Asia Studies* 12, no. 2 (1998), 1–22.

22. Selina Lim, 'Images of the new citizen and permanent resident in Singapore's mainstream news media: Prospects for integration,' in *Migration and Integration in Singapore, Policies and Practice*, eds. Yap Mui Teng, Gillian Koh, and Debbie Soon (London: Routledge, 2015), 200.

23. 'Singapore Citizenship Journey,' National Integration Council, https://www.nationalintegrationcouncil.org.sg/citizenship/singapore-citizenship-journey. Last updated on 21 August 2017.

24. Gérard Noiriel, *The French Melting Pot: Immigration, Citizenship, and National Identity* (Minneapolis: University of Minnesota Press, 1996), xxviii.

25. A Belgian naturalised Singaporean citizen, who participated in a recent study on immigrant integration in Singapore, commented on the under-representation of the culture of new communities in Singapore's newspapers, and said that increased representation would promote greater understanding between different communities. Mathew Mathews and Zhang Jiayi, 'Sentiments on immigrant integration and the role of immigrant associations,' *IPS Exchange Series*, no. 7 (January 2016), 60.

26. Eureka Henrich, 'Museums, history and migration in Australia', *History Compass* 11, no. 10 (2013): 783–800.

27. 'The world in our hinterland...', panel display, Singapore History Gallery, National Museum of Singapore, viewed August 2016.

28. Peggy Levitt, *Artifacts and Allegiances: How Museums Put the Nation and the World on Display* (Oakland: University of California Press, 2015), 103.

29. Ibid., 3–6.

30. Chinese Malaysians comprise the largest segment of new residents (citizens and permanent residents), with Chinese from the People's Republic of China comprising the second largest segment. Chong, 'White Paper,' 2.

31. The terms 'old' and 'new' diasporas have been particularly used by scholars of the Indian Diaspora who wish to make a distinction between Indian migration largely under colonialism and Indian immigration that occurred after the 1960s. See Johannes G. De Kruijf, 'Migrant transnationalism and the internet,' in *Indian Transnationalism Online: New Perspectives on Diaspora*, eds. Ajaya Kumar Sahoo and Johannes G. De Kruijf (Oxon: Routledge, 2016), 3.

32. *Straits Times*, 19 April 1990. Quoted in Beng and Chew, 'Immigration and foreign labour,' 196. Other scholars have discussed the existence of 'preferred races' in Singapore's citizenship policies in the 1990s. See, for example, Allan M. Findlay, Huw Jones, and Gillian M. Davidson, 'Migration transition or migration transformation in the Asian dragon economies?,' *International Journal of Urban and Regional Research* 22, no. 4 (December 1998): 653–54.

33. For a comprehensive introduction to some of these issues, refer Vasu et al., *Immigration in Singapore*.

34. 'GE 2015 analysis', Facebook post by PAP MP Inderjit Singh on 17 September 2015, edited 3.18 pm. Accessed 24 September 2015; Shashi Tharoor qtd. in Asad-ul Iqbal Latif, *India in the Making of Singapore* (Singapore: Singapore Indian Association, 2008), 92; and Latif, *India in the Making of Singapore*, 93.

35. Panel display, Indian Heritage Centre, viewed December 2016.
36. Sunil S. Amrith, 'Reconstructing the "plural society": Asian migration between empire and nation, 1940–1948,' *Past and Present* 210, no. 6 (2011): 237.
37. Sunil Amrith has described the massive displacement which occurred in Asia after the war and the difficulties that those who had formerly led mobile lives as part of labour and merchant diasporas faced in re-establishing their claims and mobilities. Amrith, 'Reconstructing,' 237–47.
38. Aihwa Ong, *Flexible Citizenship: The Cultural Logics of Transnationality* (London: Duke University Press, 1999).
39. Amrith, 'Reconstructing,' 250.
40. John Solomon, *A Subaltern History of the Indian Diaspora in Singapore: Gradual Disappearance of Untouchability* (Oxon: Routledge, 2016), 114–15, 145.

CHAPTER 7

'They Don't Call Us Indian': Indian Muslim Voices and the 1947 India/Pakistan Partition

Anindya Raychaudhuri

In 1947, as British rule over the Indian subcontinent came to an end, the land and its people were divided into two new states, broadly along religious lines. Punjab in the West and Bengal in the East were divided in two. West Punjab, along with Sindh, Baluchistan, North-West Frontier Province, together with East Bengal, formed the new state of Pakistan with a majority Muslim population. This was a state of two halves, separated by hundreds of miles of India, which had a Hindu majority. While the apparent symmetry of a Muslim Pakistan and a Hindu India can be destabilised in many ways—both States were officially secular on independence, and India remains so—there also remains a hegemonic perception of the binary identities of the two people in national-religious terms. In 1971, East and West Pakistan divided again, leading to the independence of Bangladesh, further complicating the nature of religious and national identities in the Indian subcontinent.

A. Raychaudhuri (✉)
University of St Andrews, Fife, Scotland, UK

© The Author(s) 2019   113
E. Henrich and J. M. Simpson (eds.),
History, Historians and the Immigration Debate,
https://doi.org/10.1007/978-3-319-97123-0_7

No single event in the modern history of the Indian subcontinent has had as significant an impact on the everyday life of the various South Asian communities in the region and around the world as decolonisation and partition. In part, this significance comes from the unprecedented levels of violence, certainly in recent South Asian history, which accompanied the act of partition. Inevitably, perhaps, estimates of actual numbers of casualties remain controversial. The most conservative figure of the number of deaths was that suggested by the eyewitness account of British administrator Penderel Moon who, in 1961, wrote that he believed only about 200,000 people were killed in the Punjab.[1] At the other end of the scale, Kavita Daiya is one of a number of South Asian scholars who has put the figure 'at least two million'.[2] Ian Talbot has argued that the number 'is conventionally reckoned at around 1,000,000',[3] though Gyanendra Pandey has questioned the basis for this acceptance on the grounds that 'it appears something of a median'.[4] In short, the exact number will probably be never known. What is generally accepted is that along with the death toll, the partition led to the largest forced migration in human history, with an estimated 18 million people forced to leave their homes forever.[5] In addition, between 100,000[6] and 150,000[7] women were abducted, raped and often forced to convert.[8] The emotional losses were also huge, as people had to leave ancestral homes—communities where they had been living since time immemorial. Most were unable to take any of their property with them; some deliberately chose to leave everything behind because they were convinced they could come back at a future date. Millions of people became destitute overnight. Returning home proved impossible, as conflict between the two states intensified, leading to multiple wars in the past seven decades. Partition was a seismic event that completely transformed public and private life all over the subcontinent.

Since 2011, I have been working on an oral history project on the Indian/Pakistani partition. The project was conceived with the idea that there is a need for a truly inter-disciplinary study of the memorial legacy of partition. In my work, I look at oral history narratives and literature and cinema as examples of cultural texts and argue that in order to have a fuller picture of the ways in which partition is remembered today—individually and collectively, these texts need to be studied together. So far I have interviewed about 160 people across India, Pakistan and the UK.

My ethnographic work took the form of loose, semi-structured interviews. The recruitment process for participants was extremely organic—a mixture of word-of-mouth and personal contacts, official and semi-official approaches to religious and community groups, as well as more formal contact with various academic and non-academic organisations. I have, wherever possible, attempted to make the cohort as diverse as possible but I have not set any selection criteria, beyond a genuine desire on the part of the participant to be interviewed. As such, my interviewees represent a huge range of age, religious, class, national and regional groups.

When trying to locate potential interviewees, then, I would say again and again that I was looking to collect people's memories of 1947, and that I was interested in speaking to anyone who might have something to say about 1947, and who would be happy to speak to me. I formulated this request in oral and written communication—as I contacted individuals (colleagues, friends, family and community leaders) and institutions (temples, mosques, community centres, academic and research institutes, and local history groups) in India, Pakistan and the United Kingdom on a search for potential participants. Interestingly, more often than not, this request was subtly though significantly altered by the person I had initially approached. When being introduced to a third person, I would be described as a researcher who was interested in collecting *refugee* voices of 1947. There seems to be a generally-held, usually unquestioned assumption that the quintessential partition experience—the most authentic source of information of what partition was like to live through, was the migrant populations—those Muslims who left India for Pakistan, and those Hindus and Sikhs who made the reverse journey. As such, the people I was speaking to would more often than not assume that I was trying to record the refugee experience of partition.

This slippage between experiencing partition and experiencing migration during partition is reminiscent of Ravinder Kaur's argument about the important role played by the refugee:

> In the history of India's Partition, the 'refugee' is a central – almost mythical – figure without which the national histories of India and Pakistan can hardly be told. The processes of Partition become particularly palpable when narrated through the lives of ordinary people who experienced violence and homelessness in the course of the boundary making between the two states. Thus, the official narrative of Partition is built around an abstract notion of 'refugee experience' wherein the multitude of refugees is

often articulated as a singular body with a common origin, trajectory and destiny. This archetypal refugee appears as an enigmatic construct – part pitiful, part heroic, though mostly shorn of agency – representing the surface of the human tragedy of Partition, even as it masks the tense undercurrents and distinctive state practices of resettlement.[9]

It is perhaps as a result of this privileging of the refugee experience as the authentic partition experience, that most of the existing oral history scholarship of partition concentrates largely on migrant voices. Pioneering works such as those of Urvashi Butalia, Ritu Menon and Kamla Bhasin, all largely reinforce this trend, which, in turn, has the possibly unintentional but nevertheless unfortunate result of reinforcing the notion of a Muslim Pakistan and a Hindu/Sikh India.[10] It is deeply unfortunate that such large sections of existing oral history scholarship of partition so rarely feature Muslim Indians or non-Muslim Pakistanis, especially in terms of how these perspectives contest nationalised histories of partition, and therefore challenge hegemonic notions of post-partition nationhood.

In this chapter, then, I hope to begin to address this gap in the oral history of partition, by examining oral history narratives, and literary and cinematic texts that articulate specific Indian Muslim identity-positions. Why did some Indian Muslims choose not to migrate to Pakistan? How did they define their own identities in the context of a fundamental re-alignment of religious and national identities? And how have they negotiated this re-alignment in the years since partition? Reading these Indian Muslim voices, I argue, encourages a re-examination of the process of partition migration, as well as giving a greater insight into the post-1947 Indian state and its often brutal oppression and marginalisation of Muslims cloaked under a statist blanket of multi-cultural plurality. Listening to these voices that disrupt the axis along which national and religious identities are supposed to be ordered will, I argue, help to complicate the abstract 'refugee experience' that Ravinder Kaur, among others, has identified as part of the dominant myth of partition.

H.[11] is a Bengali Muslim whose family originated from, and remained in West Bengal. At one point during the violence of partition, however, H. and his family were forced to relocate to Dhaka. They could not settle and, instead, chose to return to their home, where they have carried on living since. The only member of H.'s family who did not leave was his grandfather. When asked why his grandfather chose to remain, H. says:

> He said, 'My mosque is here, I am not going to leave my mosque.' A very old mosque, you can still see it. It had lain abandoned, but grandfather renovated it ... It was overgrown with plants and weeds, but the three domes are still there, unharmed. He has left a lot for the mosque as well.[12]

H. and his family still live in the house that his grandfather refused to leave, two doors from the mosque that proved too strong a bond for him. His grandfather is buried in the courtyard of the mosque, which is still regularly used for prayers. After I interviewed him, he and his family members showed me around this mosque that still means so much to their whole family.

Yasmin's[13] family originate from Uttar Pradesh (UP) in Northern India, and even though her grandfather was a prominent Muslim League politician, his mother, her great-grandmother, refused to accompany her family and move to Pakistan:

> Because his, I think his grandmother stayed there, in West UP near Bareilly. He told a story about her - a tiny little woman smoking *bidis* [traditionally made cigarettes]. I think that was my great-grandmother, my grandfather's mother. Now I'm talking about it a memory comes back to me that she'd refused to go. Somebody said that she'd actually just said 'I'm not going'. You know, that's it – 'this is my home, I'm not going anywhere'.[14]

Yasmin's account of her family is echoed by Muqtada,[15] whose family were prominent supporters of the Muslim League in eastern Uttar Pradesh. In his account, he, too, paints a picture of a mass-movement of which he was a part:

> In '45, '46, I was in Class Eight or Nine – so I was quite old. My father was a big supporter of Pakistan ... We took part as well, we took women to the polls so they could vote. We worked in the camps. All day we used to shout the slogans – plan meetings here and there, plan demonstrations here and there, people used to come to watch the demonstrations and listen to the speeches. Then Pakistan was made.[16]

Muqtada deliberately draws a clear causal link between his and his family's efforts, and the creation of Pakistan. When asked to elaborate his family's involvement, he traces it to his father:

[The Muslim League was] very powerful, very powerful, very powerful, very powerful ... A movement for Pakistan was very strong. It had
entered people's minds. What was good, what was bad – people didn't
always understand. They just thought it was all good. They may have suffered afterwards and realised the negatives but at the time it was all for
the Muslim League. 'We will get Pakistan', 'We will get Hindustan', 'We
will take Pakistan' – these were the slogans ... [My father] was the main
person. We were all involved because of him. Sons only learn from their
father. We were fourteen, fifteen and he was fifty years old.

What is interesting however, is that this strong political commitment is
not, in Muqtada's narration, translatable into any easy nationalist identity. Even though his entire family campaigned for Pakistan, he was the
only one who decided to leave India for a new life in the new country:

He [Muqtada's father] thought, with such a family, we didn't know anyone, no land, no house, for us in our old age, it is difficult to do all this.
We already have a built home here, we have our land here, you can eat
and drink from your home, we spend a little, but vegetables and rice come
from our land. Things were going along as normal. If we left there, there
would be problems for us. We had no particular difficulties here, there
were no riots or anything. Thinking of all this, they hesitated.

Whether or not they believed in the cause of Pakistan, Muqtada, H. and
Yasmin's family-members' affective connection with particular Indian
spaces—a mosque, their home, their land—implicitly re-affirms the
importance of a distinctively Indian and Islamic identity.

A similar gesture can be seen in many literary and cinematic narratives
of partition as well. Sajjad, the protagonist of Kamila Shamsie's *Burnt
Shadows* is born and brought up in Delhi, and expresses an intimate,
almost physical relationship with the city:

But that was September. Now the violence had ended, and though Sajjad
said he knew it would be a different Delhi he'd be returning to, nothing
could change the essential Dilliness of the place. He said it emphasizing
the 'dil' (it was in their first lesson that he'd told her 'dil' meant heart...[17]

Events transpire against him, however, and Sajjad is unable to return
home, a loss that is depicted in shockingly visceral terms:

Hiroko could only watch as her husband drew up his legs and curled over the mattress. She said his name, repeated endearments in English, Urdu, Japanese – but he couldn't hear her above the fluttering of pigeons and the call of the muezzin of Jama Masjid and the cacophony of his brother's arguments and the hubbub of merchants and buyers in Chandni Chowk and the rustling of palm leaves in the monsoons and the laughter of his nephews and nieces and the shouts of the kite-fliers and the burble of fountains in courtyards and the husky voice of the never-seen neighbour singing ghazals before sunrise and his heartbeat, his frantic heartbeat.[18]

In his imaginative reconstruction of Delhi, it emerges as a distinctively Muslim space. Sajjad remembers the 'muezzin'—the man who performs the call to prayer at Delhi's Jama Masjid—one of the largest mosques in India. Ghazal, a poetic form composed of rhyming couplets and a refrain is, in this context, also coded as Muslim. In articulating the right to mourn the loss of Delhi, Sajjad (and, by extension, Shamsie) is recreating the city as an Islamic space, and therefore implicitly undermining the Hindu–Muslim, India–Pakistan dichotomy that lies at the heart of the project of partition.

Sajjad's grief at being separated from the landscape of Delhi is mirrored by Salim Mirza from M. S. Sathyu's 1973 film *Garm Hava* (*Scorching Winds*). When Salim decides that he has to leave his native Agra and move to Pakistan, there is a haunting sequence as Salim, on his own, stands and weeps in front of the Taj Mahal. Interestingly, for both Sajjad and Salim, they are not only mourning the loss of their homes, and the familiar spaces that they are being forced to leave, but they are also mourning the loss of a distinctively Islamic India. The Jama Masjid in Delhi, and the Taj Mahal in Agra were both commissioned by the Mughal Emperor Shah Jahan in the seventeenth century. Through the affective connection that Sajjad and Salim experience with these buildings, Shamsie and Sathyu are reminding us of the multi-century-long history of Islamic India. At a moment when national and religious borders were being forcibly realigned, this poignant depiction of this specifically Indian tradition of Islam cannot but be enormously radical.

While H. and his family, Muqtada's family, and Yasmin's grandmother felt the same pull that Sajjad feels for Delhi, they were able to resist this force and did not migrate. While it is important not to underestimate the horror of actual violence of partition, nor the overwhelming force of fear of potential violence, it is also important to recognise that the decision to (or not to) migrate was made for a wider variety of reasons. If we recognise the complex emotions and judgements that went into deciding to leave one's home or not, we can begin to challenge the abstract myth of refugee-experience, and also to look for signs of agency that the refugee or migrant is often denied.

Habibur[19] and Afroz[20] got married in 1954, and separately describe their family's decisions not to migrate to East Pakistan. Habibur describes East Pakistan as it then was, Bangladesh as it became in 1971, as a place of alienation and disorientation. Unlike many other people I interviewed, Habibur did not recognise the newly created nation-state of Pakistan as immediately a place of belonging based on his own religious identity. Indeed, the disorientation he felt is semantically reflected in his language which is, at times, quite hard to follow:

> I feel for myself, that there is no place in the entire world that is better than my motherland … [In 1947] we got a steamer to Bangladesh, to Khulna. We got off, and then another steamer took us. That was Khulna – we didn't know what was Khulna, and where was anything. I was by myself then, the rest [of my family] were on another steamer. So I thought, 'Come on – let's go and see what there is.' We went to the market, and were told, this is Khulna. I bought 16 bananas for 4 *annas*.[21] I had a 2 rupee note from India, but they said that wouldn't work. Can I change it? You will get one [Pakistani] rupee – we got 16 tandoori *rotis*. Ma was very happy with it – 'Where did you find it?' 'I bought it in Khulna town' – 'That's great, now hide it.' The next day the steamer came to the end of its journey – they said, this is the final stop, if you want to go to Dhaka, you have to take a train from here. We got to Dhaka, but where should we go then? We didn't know anyone. We found a medical institute and went there. We didn't have much money, but bought what food we could. We were there in Dhaka for three months. Then we got some dole, so we could buy rice.[22]

From the bewilderment about place-names, to the confusion about accepted currency—Habibur's account is marked by the uncertainty of being in a foreign country. It is noticeable as well that Habibur's own confusion and fear is mirrored by his mother's insistence that the money be hidden—perhaps a sign of the inherent insecurities of the refugee or migrant. This insecurity is sharply contrasted with his account of the stability of life in his 'motherland', India. It is surely no coincidence that he prefaces this with a simple and heartfelt declaration of love for his country—India—in stark contrast with the new nation that was created specifically for South Asian Muslims like him. This testimony undermines the hegemonic view that pre-existing religious and new national identities could always be simply and uncomplicatedly aligned.

Afroz's family demonstrate a similarly complex response to partition:

> 1946 riots happened straight in front of me. We were on the school bus, and we escaped. Half way, they attacked the bus. The driver was very good, he saved us. We escaped three times. Had Pakistani military not arrived, they would have killed us. There was no question of surviving. Then we thought, let's move to East Pakistan. We had business connections in East Pakistan, in Dhaka. But we weren't getting tickets – then my mother said, 'Let's not go, let's stay here.' My mother didn't want to go, I didn't want to go either, because we had got to know everyone in here (in Kolkata) – there was no family [there]. So we remained here. My father went twice a week for business. He wanted to settle there. All our furniture had been sent. My older sister didn't want to go. Then the business started growing here, so we settled.[23]

Similar to Habibur's account, Afroz's family's confusion is reflected in the syntactical confusion of her own testimony, as she goes back and forth trying to represent the complicated positions various members of her family adopted in relation to the new nation of Pakistan. The Pakistani military appears in her story as a saviour, an emotional connection that is not seen as contradictory with her and her family's identification of Kolkata as their place of home.

For all of the undoubted emotional connection to people and places in India that both Habibur and Afroz demonstrate, it is also true that they both attribute their decision not to migrate, at least in part, to specific economic reasons. Habibur describes how their family were called back to their place of origin in Bankura, West Bengal because the business opportunities there were superior:

> My father's friends from Bankura, wrote to us – what are you doing there? Everything is good here, you can get working. We got back, and started working. Our work was shoe business, shoe materials and shoes. My father's business. Everything was cheap, we could do all our shopping for 12 *annas*.

For me, Habibur and Afroz's emphasis on economic reasons to do with opportunities for business reinforces the gap between the hegemonic narrative of partition that essentialises specific forms of religious identities on the one hand, and the everyday priorities of ordinary people on the other. This is not to suggest that their religious identity is not important to them—it is merely to say that religion was not the only factor determining their reaction to partition.

Habibur and Afroz's account of their families remind me of the Mirza family in *Garm Hava*. The Mirza family too are trying to decide whether to stay in India or move to Pakistan, partly based on the fortunes of their shoe-making business. Salim's entire extended family leaves for Pakistan, but in a moment of political commitment, Salim and his son decide not to leave India, but to stay and fight for their economic and social rights. Through this act of political resistance, Salim and his son are declaring their right to fight for an India which has space for them as Indian Muslims, an India which will allow them to exist as legitimate economic agents.

Similarly, Afroz puts her family's decision to stay in India in economic terms:

If we had gone to Pakistan, it would not have been good. It isn't easy to start a new business. There was an established business here – and my father died very young, that would have been difficult there. He didn't want to go to Pakistan, he said it would take years to establish a new business, and he said 'I don't have so much time'. I don't know why he said that.

Afroz's hesitancy about ascribing specific motivations to her father's response reminds me of the complexities of life after partition, and how many facets of one's identity—religious, regional, professional—could often be in conflict with each other. In any case, however, both Habibur and Afroz are clearly convinced that their families made the right decision in staying in India. 'India is vast', Habibur says, 'a big part of the world', which makes it more attractive for business purposes. Habibur and Afroz are both patriotic Indians, and devout Muslims, but contrary to much of the hegemonic thinking surrounding partition, these identity-formations are only part of their engagement with, and memories of 1947. Through this complex interaction with partition, through the ways in which they implicitly question the assumptions inherent within the decision to partition the country, and through the ways in which they value their present life, and imagine an alternative life had they chosen to migrate, Afroz and Habibur, like so many of my other interviewees, articulate a definite sense of agency—not least in and through their decision in 1947 to migrate or not to migrate.

Perhaps the most remarkable example of agency of this type can be seen in the Bengali novel *Agunpakhi* [*Firebird*], by Bangladeshi novelist Hassan Ajijul Haque. Haque's novel is written in the first person, the unnamed narrator being a poor, uneducated village woman in a Muslim family in West Bengal, on the Indian side of the new border. Her family are actively campaigning and fighting for Pakistan, though she does not understand their logic. One by one, her entire family leaves for Pakistan, but she refuses to join them. When pressed, her response reveals the same agency that is visible in the testimonies quoted above:

> I was thunderstruck. I had never thought to hear anything like this. It's as if my entire world had turned upside down, I leaned against the floor for support. Where will I go? Where will I go? I know where I will end up when I am dead, in my grave. You can see the cemetery on either side of the lake from our new house. I will end up there when I am dead, but I can't imagine where I would go if I left this country. All I was thinking is, someone needs to explain to me why I should go. If they could explain, then I would go wherever they told me. But to say that that country is for the Muslims and this for the Hindus is not enough. That won't work with me anymore.[24]

A large part of the force of Haque's writing is lost in translation—Haque writes entirely in dialect—his narrator's Bengali is not the standard Bengali of the middle-class intellectual, rather it is the colloquial dialect of the uneducated village woman, which is very difficult to translate into English.

What is not lost, however, is the way in which Haque's narrator's refusal to join her family after partition is empowering for her. 'I have never argued like this with my husband'[25] she admits, while explicitly standing up to him when she disagrees with his demand that she join her family across the border:

> I was angry as well, said, all this time I learnt whatever you taught me, said whatever you made me say. But now perhaps I have taught myself a couple of things.[26]

Her decision to stay back is momentous, and while it is not without consequence, it is also the most power she has ever exercised in her life:

> In that place, in that half-light, I looked at him and said, I don't know how, but I said, I am going to stay in this house.
>
> It was like someone had slapped his mouth shut. The first time in my life, I had hit him like that, his face had darkened in that half-light. So much pain there. But for how long? Then in manly anger, he screamed out, Go wherever you want, stay wherever you want, I have swapped this house for another.
>
> Hearing that, I didn't move from there either. I will stay in this house. I will only leave if someone takes me out by my hand.[27]

Her decision to leave her family means she remains alone on the 'wrong' side of the border but she is emphatically not a victim. It may in fact be the most empowering thing that has ever happened to her, as the ending of the novel makes clear:

> No one could explain to me why that country is mine only because I am a Muslim, and this country is not mine. No one could explain to me why I have to go there just because my children have gone there. What will I do if my husband goes there? He is not the same as me, but different. Close to me, part of my soul, but a different person.
>
> When dawn breaks, when it's light, I will sit facing the East. Looking at the Sun, I will stand up again.
>
> I am alone. However, I can pull everyone towards me.
>
> Alone.[28]

Through her rejection of her family's decision to move to Pakistan, Haque's narrator re-inscribes India as an Islamic space.

Like H.'s grandfather, her powerful articulation of the right to live and die in India serves for me as a powerful antidote to the all-too common Hindu nationalist slogan that Indian Muslims should choose between Pakistan and *Kabaristan* [cemetery].[29] This obscene slogan characterises the essence of Hindu nationalism or Hindutva—perhaps the strongest political movement in India since the 1990s, though, as Christophe Jaffrelot has persuasively argued, 'this *ism* is one of the oldest ideological streams in India'.[30] Partha Chatterjee has articulated the all-pervasive nature of this religious-nationalist ideology, arguing that 'The idea of the singularity of national history has inevitably led to a single source of Indian tradition, namely ancient Hindu civilisation'.[31] This hegemonic view of the Indian nation constructs the Indian Muslim as always already extraneous, and dangerous to the body-politic. Dibyesh Anand, for example, has forcefully argued that:

> Hindu nationalism normalizes a politics of fear and hatred by representing it as a defensive reaction to the threats supposedly posed by Muslims to the security of the individual Hindus as well as of the Hindu collective. Hindutva is porno-nationalism in its obsessive preoccupation with the predatory sexuality of the putative Muslim figure and the dangers to the integrity of the Hindu bodies. The proponents of Hindutva mobilize and generate negative stereo-types of Islam and Muslims to legitimize violence against actual Muslims living in India.[32]

As Anand among others has argued, this form of religious-nationalism has resulted in cyclical waves of anti-Muslim violence—Ayodhya in 1992, Gujarat in 2002 and Muzaffarnagar in 2013 to name but a few—which has made the position of Indian Muslims even more precarious. In the words of journalist and commentator Subhash Gatade,

> One can imagine the ramifications of giving primacy to a particular religion or a particular people in a multireligious, multicultural, multilingual nation at the dawn of the 21st century. One can imagine the havoc this can create where such blatant 'majoritarianism' is peddled as 'democracy' in a composite culture like ours ... any impartial, objective student of Indian society and state would agree that the idea of Hindutva and its paraphernalia of numerous organisations posit the biggest threat to the cause of justice and peace in the Indian subcontinent.[33]

In the context of this seemingly irresistible rise in Hindu nationalism, as Muslim men in India are lynched on suspicion of eating beef[34] and Muslim actors prevented from taking part in Hindu performances,[35] these articulations of the validity and legitimacy of a distinctively Islamic India pose a challenge to hegemony that remains powerfully relevant.

There is ample evidence, not least in my oral history interviews, that this challenge is not without its repercussions. In 1947, and since, articulating the right to be Indian and Muslim opens one up to rejection and ridicule. Muhammad,[36] whose family originate from Bihar and who decided not to migrate to Pakistan, sums it up though his father's experience:

> Then I would say in that time I heard from...in my household, that according to the people at that time during the Partition time there was choice to go to Pakistan or stay there. So in our village nobody went, everyone stayed. But my father was working in Calcutta in railways and there somehow he opted to go to East Pakistan – that time it was East Pakistan; Pakistan was divided into West and East. So he opted to see, just before Partition. They were given choice and things. So he went there... which place in East Pakistan I don't know exactly but I think it was Chittagong he used to say those things. But after a month he came back. He didn't like place or people or whatever. He came back; he came back and he stayed in his job. He stayed in his job till he retired from the railways ... But one thing he always...he was always called by his colleagues as a Pakistani. They said, 'You went there, you came back, you are Pakistani.' So that stigma remained on his job, career.[37]

Similarly, when Habibur reflects on the legacies of partition, he outlines how he thinks it was catastrophic for Indian Muslims like himself:

> Partition was bad, absolutely bad – bad then, bad now, bad in the future, it was bad. It was good for some people, bad for others. Like us, for us – we had nowhere left. Even our own country's people say – 'These bastards, they wanted Pakistan. Today they are roaming around freely, but yesterday they wanted Pakistan.' And the others, they wanted Pakistan – they got it and are now in power ... It was a sad thing for Indian Muslims ... they just lost. Even today, people say 'Go, go, just go to Pakistan.' I am Indian in my heart and soul – but people say 'Why are you here? There is Pakistan for you.'

H. makes a similar point when asked if he has ever felt discriminated against for being Muslim:

> I have one thing, something I don't like – that we are still called minority. Why is this? They don't call us Indian, at least if they called us minority Indian, that would be something, but they don't even do that. They just call us minority – this is something I don't like. We are not called Indian.

The accusation that is explicit in Muhammad, Habibur and H.'s testimony cuts to the heart of what seems to me to be the single biggest problem in Indian public life at the moment. I have lost count of the number of times I have encountered friends and family who treat the labels Bengali, Punjabi or Indian, and Muslim as apparently mutually exclusive. Across all aspects of public life, Indian Muslims are repeatedly being asked to choose between their national and religious identity, to the point where a proud articulation of one's Islamic religious identity is in and of itself considered to be treasonous. In this context, there is an urgent demand to ensure that through omissions in our scholarship we do not unintentionally reinforce this pernicious linkage of religion and nationhood. As H. himself said at the end of his interview, 'This, too, is history. What is happening now is history as well. This, too, is being written. People like you and me are writing it'. Voices like these powerfully demonstrate the importance of ensuring that when we write histories, we don't leave huge swathes of people, their voices, stories, and aspirations unrepresented.

NOTES

1. Penderel Moon, *Divide and Quit: An Eyewitness Account of the Partition of India* (Berkeley and Los Angeles: University of California Press, 1962), 293.
2. Kavita Daiya, *Violent Belongings: Partition, Gender, and National Culture in Postcolonial India* (Philadelphia: Temple University Press, 2008), 6.
3. Ian Talbot, 'The 1947 partition of India,' in *The Historiography of Genocide*, ed. Dan Stone (Basingstoke, Hampshire and New York: Palgrave Macmillan, 2008), 420.
4. Gyanendra Pandey, *Remembering Partition* (Cambridge: Cambridge University Press, 2001), 89.
5. Talbot, 'The 1947 partition,' 420.
6. Ibid., 420.
7. Daiya, *Violent Belongings*, 6.
8. See, for example, Urvashi Butalia, *The Other Side of Silence: Voices from the Partition of India* (New Delhi: Penguin Books, 1998); and Ritu Menon and Kamla Bhasin, *Borders and Boundaries: Women in India's Partition* (New Brunswick: Rutgers University Press, 1998).
9. Ravinder Kaur, 'Distinctive citizenship: Refugees, subjects and postcolonial state in India's partition,' *Cultural and Social History* 6, no. 4 (2009): 429.
10. See, for example, Urvashi Butalia, *The Other Side of Silence: Voices from the Partition of India* (London: C. Hurst & Co., 2000); Ritu Menon and Kamla Bhasin, *Borders and Boundaries: Women in India's Partition*

(New Brunswick: Rutgers University Press, 1998); Pippa Virdee, 'Negotiating the past: Journey through Muslim women's experience of partition and resettlement in Pakistan,' *Cultural and Social History*, 6, no. 4 (2009): 467–84; a notable exception in this regard is Vazira Fazila-Yacoobali Zamindar, *The Long Partition and the Making of Modern South Asia: Refugees, Boundaries, Histories* (Oxford: Oxford University Press, 2007).

11. Male, Muslim, Bengali, b.c. 1946 in Bilkuli, West Bengal, India. For those of my interviewees who, like H., have expressed a desire to be anonymous, I use initials instead of a pseudonym as I feel it is important to typographically display their desire for anonymity.

12. Interview with author, originally in Bengali, Bilkuli, West Bengal, India, 8 January 2015

13. Female, Muslim, b. 1977, in London, UK.

14. Interview with author, Egham, Surrey, 13 March 2012.

15. Male, Muslim, b. 1934 in Uttar Pradesh, India.

16. Interview with author, originally in Urdu, Karachi, Pakistan, 11 September 2013.

17. Kamila Shamsie, *Burnt Shadows* (London, Berlin, and New York: Bloomsbury Publishing, 2009), 125.

18. Shamsie, *Burnt Shadows*, 126.

19. Male, Muslim, Bengali, b. 1930 in Bankura, West Bengal, India.

20. Female, Muslim, b. 1934 in Uttar Pradesh, India.

21. Pre-decimal currency, 16 *annas* made 1 rupee.

22. Interview with author, originally in Bengali and Urdu, Kolkata, India, 13 April 2012.

23. Interview with author, originally in Urdu, Kolkata, India, 13 April 2012.

24. Hassan Ajijul Haque, *Agunpakhi* (Kolkata: Dey's Publishing, 2008), 243 [Translations are my own].

25. Ibid., 244.

26. Ibid., 245.

27. Ibid., 247.

28. Ibid., 252.

29. See, for example, Pankaj Mishra, 'Holy lies,' *The Guardian*, 6 April 2002, https://www.theguardian.com/theguardian/2002/apr/06/weekend7. weekend2 or Dean Nelson, 'Fear and loathing in India's Muslim heartland could decide general election,' *The Telegraph*, 5 April 2014, http://www.telegraph.co.uk/news/worldnews/asia/india/10746241/Fear-and-loathing-in-Indias-Muslim-heartland-could-decide-general-election.html.

30. Christophe Jaffrelot, ed., *Hindu Nationalism: A Reader* (Princeton and Oxford: Princeton University Press, 2007), 3.
31. Partha Chatterjee, *The Nation and Its Fragments: Colonial and Postcolonial Histories* (Princeton: Princeton University Press, 1993), 115.
32. Dibyesh Anand, *Hindu Nationalism in India and the Politics of Fear* (New York: Palgrave Macmillan, 2011), 1.
33. Subhash Gatade, *The Saffron Condition: Politics of Repression and Exclusion in Neoliberal India* (Gurgaon: Three Essays Collective, 2011), 31.
34. See, for example, Michael E. Miller, 'A mob in India just dragged a man from his home and beat him to death—For eating beef,' *The Washington Post*, 30 September 2015, https://www.washingtonpost.com/news/ morning-mix/wp/2015/09/30/a-mob-in-india-just-dragged-a-man-from-his-home-and-beat-him-to-death-for-eating-beef/?utm_term=.380802b160dd.
35. See, for example, 'Nawazuddin Siddiqui pulls out of Ramleela event after Shiv Sena protests,' *Hindustan Times*, 7 October 2016, http://www.hindustantimes.com/bollywood/nawazuddin-siddiqui-pulls-out-of-ramleela-event-after-shiv-sena-protests/story-J7IhaXawaXY1UOmnIGqBWO.html.
36. Male, Muslim, b. 1947 in Bihar, India.
37. Interview with author in South Wales, 14 October 2011.

PART IV

Europe

In 'The Role of Immigration in the Making/Unmaking of the French
Working Class (Nineteenth and Twentieth Centuries)', Gérard Noiriel
shows how migration history can be written back into overarching
national narratives and the potential of such an approach to inform our
understanding of contemporary politics. Noiriel reminds us that immigration as we currently understand it is ultimately a modern invention;
a product of laws on nationality and of the nineteenth-century French
state's desire to exert control over people crossing borders. He argues
that international population movement has always been at the heart
of the history of the French working class. Contemporary narratives
suggest that migration is a product of the post-war era, but in the late
nineteenth-century, France was already being described as a 'land of
immigration'. In 1896, the socialist leader Jules Guesde was accused
of representing 'naturalized Belgians' rather than 'real French people'.
Reconnecting with this long history of movement and tensions helps
to understand the dynamics of exclusion at play in twenty-first century
France. Noiriel's analysis, connecting urban violence to social contexts,
offers a powerful rejoinder to those who write of a 'clash of civilisations'.

Margaretha A. van Es's chapter 'Was the Multiculturalism Backlash
Good for Women with a Muslim Background? Perspectives from Five
Minority Women's Organisations in the Netherlands' explores the latter question from a much-neglected vantage point. Van Es looks at the
impact on women from a Muslim background of the rapid changes that
have played out in recent Dutch history, with the rise of populism and

anti-immigration sentiment. Her analysis highlights the extent to which migrant and minority voices are excluded from European debates on migration and culture. She shows how listening to people from migrant and ethnic minority backgrounds can serve to undermine stereotypical representations and has the potential to shift the focus of ongoing debates, widening the scope of questions asked of migrant communities—for instance, about whether wearing a headscarf is a manifestation of a 'free choice'. Again, migrant and minority history is reconnected to the social mainstream, with Van Es pointing out that women's own emancipatory strategies should be given value and that they are relevant to the broader context of gender equality in the Netherlands.

CHAPTER 8

The Role of Immigration in the Making/ Unmaking of the French Working Class (Nineteenth and Twentieth Centuries)

Gérard Noiriel

Immigration has been central to political debates in France since the 1970s. After May 1968, the figure of the 'migrant worker' came to embody the modern proletariat for parties on the far left who were speaking out against assembly line work, slums and racism. But things began to change following the victory of the socialist candidate François Mitterrand in the 1981 presidential election. From then on, the right and the far right took ownership of the immigration 'problem', with a focus on issues around terrorism and security. Against an economic backdrop of industrial decline, the far right started to attract substantial

This chapter was first published in German as G. Noiriel, 'Die Rolle der Einwanderung bei der De-/Konstruktion der Arbeiterklasse in Frankreich (19.-20. Jahrhundert),' in Alexander Mejstrik, Thomas Hübel, and Sigrid Wadauer, eds., *Die Krise des Sozialstaats und die Intellektuellen* (Frankfurt: Campus, 2012). Translated from the original French text by Julian M. Simpson.

G. Noiriel (✉)
École des hautes études en sciences sociales (EHESS), Paris, France

© The Author(s) 2019
E. Henrich and J. M. Simpson (eds.),
History, Historians and the Immigration Debate,
https://doi.org/10.1007/978-3-319-97123-0_8

working-class support by promoting a xenophobic agenda. That is when the general public discovered the dividing lines, related to nationality and/or ethnicity, that run through the 'working class'. However, France differs from the majority of other European countries in that this is not a new phenomenon. Immigration has played a major role in the making/unmaking of the working class since the nineteenth century. This chapter will show that current forms of antagonism and solidarity within the working class can only be properly understood with reference to this history.

Town Workers and Country Workers

At the heart of the history of the French working class resides a major paradox. On one hand, because of the influence of Karl Marx, the French proletariat was presented as the model revolutionary proletariat. And indeed, it played key roles in the revolutions of 1789, 1848 and 1870 (with the Paris Commune). Similarly, in 1936 and in 1968, the working-class movement successfully organised general strikes that brought France to a standstill for several weeks. However, on the other hand, workers' organisations (unions and parties) have historically been weaker in France than in other major industrialised countries. The vast majority of French workers have never joined a trade union or a political party.

Adopting an historical perspective brings to the fore the factors that explain this persistent structural weakness of the French working-class movement. In England, rural flight gathered pace as early as the eighteenth century. Faced with extreme poverty, a large number of agricultural workers had to flee the countryside to find work in factories that were booming, thus making up a 'reserve army of labour' that industrialists could draw upon. As a result, it was possible for an autonomous working class to emerge under the banner of Chartism.[1]

This process, described by Karl Marx in *Capital*, did not take place in France. There was no 'foundational' moment in the history of the working class, because the rural population was not subjected to brutal and large-scale proletarianisation.

Marc Bloch has shown that as early as the Late Middle Ages, the alliance between regal power and the peasantry had enabled the latter to assert its right to land ownership, at the expense of the aristocracy.[2] Thus, a class of small-scale property owners emerged at the very time when it was disappearing in England. The 1789 Revolution gave fresh impetus to this process: the sale of the *Biens Nationaux* (the 'national goods' which belonged to the Church) allowed the peasantry to consolidate its new status. In the nineteenth century, agriculture and crafts remained the two pillars of economic development. But this reality was partially obscured by the huge role played by Paris which was then truly a 'State within the State'. With its own police force, the capital was Europe's foremost working-class city, but it was also where intellectual, cultural and political power resided. This is why a simple revolt in Paris could rapidly turn into a revolution.

Until the late nineteenth century, there was therefore no unified French working class. The town/country divide (Paris/provinces) was reinforced by a cultural divide which separated those who had access to written culture from those who did not. There were therefore two working-class worlds which were poles apart. Artisans in urban areas were carrying forward the traditions of the *Ancient Regime* corporations. This is the elite which Marx calls the 'revolutionary proletariat'. But peasant-workers accounted for the majority of industrial labour at the time. From the eighteenth century, 'proto-industrialisation' led to the development of a textile industry and of small-scale metalworks in the countryside. By engaging in both agricultural and industrial activities and often, in addition to this, migrating on a temporary basis, many rural workers were able to remain in rural areas.

Paris attracted a large number of these seasonal workers as the rapid development of the city created a strong demand for labour in the building sector. One can therefore argue that in the French capital, there were already at the time divisions within the working class that can be attributed to immigration. But the nationality of workers was not at the time of huge importance. The key driver was *local* belonging. It separated workers who were 'settled' (i.e. who resided in the city where they worked) from those who came from further afield. Temporary migrants, who came from rural areas, were 'alien' in the eyes of Parisians and their experience of life was similar to that of the Portuguese or Algerian migrants who came to work in France in the 1960s and 1970s. They did not speak French, lived in slums and were subjected to 'racism'. It is in this context that elites started to produce discourses concerned with security and the 'immigration problem'. But in the mid-nineteenth century, issues concerning migrants were not yet linked to debates about aliens (in the legal sense of the word). The 1848 revolution made it possible for these two groups of working-class people to come together and form a united front.

Under the *Second Empire* (1852–1870), Napoleon III was consumed by the need to prevent another revolution. The first 'identity documents' (internal passports and workers' logbooks) were aimed at shaping the movement of migrants to prevent them from congregating in major cities when economic conditions were poor. The elites also sought to stem the rural exodus through supporting industrial development in the countryside. Economists influenced by Saint-Simon argued for an alternative type of economic development that rejected the English model. They believed that if workers remained anchored in rural areas they would be less volatile than their counterparts in big cities and avoid the negative influence of 'intellectuals'. If a crisis struck, they could work the land. Women, children, and older people unable to work in factories could also rely on agriculture. This model explains an apparent paradox of the *Second Empire*: the fact that it experienced rapid industrialisation at a time when the number of workers recorded in censuses remains stable.[3]

THE INVENTION OF IMMIGRATION

An additional important change took place in the 1880s. At this time, France was a largely rural country. Half of the labour force was working in the agricultural sector (in the UK, this was true of only a quarter of the working population in 1840—France only caught up in...1950). The republican activists who deposed Napoleon III in 1870 drew on the support of small landowners to impose reforms that mainly sought to integrate the working classes into the nation-state. This republican political project was undermined by the first major crisis of capitalism (the 'Great Depression'), which laid waste to a mode of production based on pluriactivity and complementarity between agriculture and industry. The 'Second Industrial Revolution', reliant on the coalmining industry and steel, led to the proliferation of large factories, separated from the rest of the world by high walls. Their internal regulations provided for punishment for lateness, absences, etc. It is at this time that a new working class, entirely dependent on industry and the salaries it offered, took shape in France. Rural flight gathered pace as a result of the economic crisis. Between 1866 and 1896, the urban population increased from 30.5 to 42.1%. In 1931, for the first time, it was higher than the rural population. By then, over 50% of employees were working in companies that had more than 200 staff and 25% were employed by businesses with over 500 staff. Over the course of three decades, 40% of 'independent' workers disappeared.

However, if we compare France to Germany, it is clearly apparent that the process that led to the formation of a French industrial working class was radically different to the one which unfolded on the other side of the Rhine. In Germany, under Bismarck's iron rule, industrialisation was brutally imposed, resulting in a mass rural exodus, the effects of which were 'offset' by a programme of social legislation.

In France, the efforts made by the lower classes to put a stop to proletarisation met with a degree of success. First, the rise of trade unionism in the new industrial areas led to a series of disputes. It is at this time that the image of the industrial worker took shape (typified by the figure of the miner) and was disseminated by the press whose coverage was largely focused on industrial accidents and strikes put down by the military. From then on, it was no longer the Parisian craftsmen who were the driving force behind social conflicts; the proletariat employed by major industries had taken over (it accounted for 35% of those taking part in strikes at the end of the century). These workers had a voice in Parliament: the POF (*Parti Ouvrier Français*, French Workers' Party), which was the first Marxist party to be formed in France. During the 1890s, the POF acquired a solid base in a number of working-class local authorities, particularly in the North. As social conflicts became increasingly politicised, the working class became more homogenous as its leaders tended to speak for all of the group, ignoring the dividing lines that ran through it.

The shared identity of the working class was consolidated by the introduction of the first social laws. The adoption of legal codes relating to social relations and their bureaucratic implementation led to the emergence within the lower classes of groups that had previously been hard to differentiate. At the very moment when the town/countryside divide was becoming a thing of the past, a new split appeared between workers and the petty bourgeoisie involved in commerce and crafts. Up to the Paris Commune, these two groups were very closely linked, but their paths diverged towards the end of the nineteenth century. Workers in heavy industry were increasingly drawn towards socialism, whereas independent small-scale producers leant towards nationalism and antisemitism.

Country dwellers opposed proletarisation through different means. The increasing prevalence of Malthusian behaviours (the 'only child' model) is explained by the desire to avoid sharing out land, which would force the poorest to emigrate to the city. Birth rates collapsed as a result.

France's population stagnated, whereas in other major European countries it was rapidly increasing. Ordinary people in the countryside were also able to use the right to vote that they had been given in 1848 to put pressure on republican elected representatives. They succeeded in getting them to take protectionist measures, which shielded the countryside from the effects of the crisis. The Republic also created a large number of junior civil service jobs (i.e. gendarmes, customs officials, teachers, postal workers) which offered the poorest rural dwellers an alternative to joining the working class. In the final decades of the nineteenth century, the impact of the rural exodus was thus absorbed by the 'service' sector where the number of employees doubled in the space of twenty years.

At the same time, the *Comité Central des Houillères de France* (the Central Committee of the French Coalfields) was complaining that it could not recruit the additional 15,000 miners (10% of the total workforce in the coal industry) it needed to meet orders. French industry started to hire large numbers of foreign workers in order to address the persistent problem of workforce shortages. This led to the appearance within the working class of a new divide, based on nationality. The word 'immigration' gained a prominent place in the French language in the 1880s, as republican governments passed the first major law on French nationality (1889) and introduced the first measures aimed at protecting the national workforce (1893). Up until then, foreigners living in France had not been registered anywhere. They were now required to declare their presence at their place of residence. The mayor or the local police superintendent would in exchange give them a document that can be considered as the precursor of today's identity cards.[4]

At this stage, it was clear that France's industrialisation would require mass immigration. In 1887, the economist Paul Leroy-Beaulieu wrote: 'France is a land of immigration, like Argentina or Australia. On average, 40 to 50,000 foreigners settle here every year'. Although the statistics are not necessarily reliable, censuses provide evidence of this influx of migrants. The number of foreigners living in France, which had already doubled under the *Second Empire*, doubled again between 1872 and 1886 when it reached 1.2 million—a figure that remained broadly stable until 1914. Migration, at the time, was principally the product of people crossing the borders between France and neighbouring countries. The two main nationalities in France at the beginning of the twentieth century were the Belgians, who were mainly to be found in Northern France, and the Italians who were concentrated in the South East.

These changes can also be explained with reference to the sudden recalibration of international relations. At the end of the nineteenth century, a new divide appeared, separating countries of immigration (most of them being 'new': i.e. the USA, Argentina, Australia) and countries of emigration (i.e. the majority of European states). France represented an exception in this context: from being the most populous country in Europe until the early nineteenth century, with high levels of emigration (settlers in Canada and India, Huguenot refugees in England or in German states, aristocratic families who fled France at the time of the Revolution), it became a major destination for immigrants. But unlike those who arrived in the 'new' territories, immigrants who settled in France did not seek to exploit vast swathes of land by imposing their authority on the local populations. In France, the influx of migrants was the result of a chronic shortage of 'proletarians' and the desire of a number of industrialists to put pressure on salaries.

The Contradictory Effects of Immigration on the Making of the French Working Class

The first effect of the influx of immigrants was to accentuate the heterogeneity and instability of the industrial proletariat. In the coalfield areas of Northern and Central France, there was a spectacular decline in the number of workers who 'inherited' their jobs. In Saint-Etienne, for example, in the period from 1875 to 1895, over 70% of miners had a father who was also a miner. By the beginning of the twentieth century, this was true of only a third of them.[5] The economic crisis also greatly exacerbated the tensions among workers of different nationalities. There were violent clashes in several parts of France which resulted in around ten deaths in the 1880s and around fifteen deaths in the 1890s. The number of people taking part in these eruptions of xenophobia varied. In some instances, it was just a case of fights between small groups. However, at times, large sections of the population were involved. Some 1200 workers demonstrated against foreigners in Annonay en 1886. Between 1000 and 1500 people gathered in Caudry (in the *Nord* department) in 1892, and in the same year, several thousand took to the streets in Drocourt. The figures were similar in Aigues-Mortes in 1893. These crowds marched while shouting unambiguous slogans: 'Down with the Italians' or 'Death to the Belgians'. The local population was directly involved in a third of these conflicts. The duration of these events was variable. At times, they were limited to scuffles after a disagreement in a café or at a Saturday night dance. But tensions could escalate, leading to violent turmoil over a period of weeks and strikes demanding the expulsion of foreigners.[6] Movements of this type were common in regions with numerous migrant workers (in the North, the South East and in Lorraine with its iron industry). They mainly affected mines, the building industry and traditional occupations with strong corporatist tendencies (e.g. glass making).

But these clashes did not stop foreign workers from playing an active part in the birth of trade unions. In Belgium, the mining and textile industries developed earlier than in France. As a result, organisations defending employees appeared as early as the mid-nineteenth century. Under the *Second Empire*, Belgian migrants set up the first working-class organisations in the North. They also played a key part in enabling socialism to gain a foothold. In 1896, Baron Beyens, a conservative, accused the POF leader Jules Guesde of being 'the Assembly Member of naturalized Belgians rather than of the real French people of the neighbourhood'.[7]

World War I was the culmination of the institutionalisation of migrations that began three decades earlier. As able-bodied men were at the front, labour shortages dramatically worsened. This resulted in the recruitment of workers not only from European countries allied to France but also from the colonial empire. 440,000 foreign workers and 225,000 colonial workers (over a third of them from Algeria) were hired to work in factories supporting the war effort and in the agricultural sector. But the most important dimension of this development was that in the context of the wartime economy, the state took responsibility for the recruitment of immigrants, in partnership with employers and trade unions. The pre-1914 laissez-faire approach came to an end. Drawing strength from this '*Union Sacrée*' ('Sacred Union'), an alliance that transcended political divides for the purposes of the war effort, the Interior Ministry managed to impose on colonial and foreign workers the new identification techniques (files and identity cards) that it had devised in the late nineteenth century, and that it had previously been unable to roll out as they were seen as an infringement of individual liberties.

Initially described as a necessary response to war, the joint recruitment of immigrants continued after 1918. Spontaneous migratory flows were not on their own able to provide the workers and the family men that France needed in order to rebuild. Responsibility for joint recruitment and the selection and placing of foreign workers was given to bodies that built on the *Union Sacrée* between employers, trade unions and the republican state. The guiding principles of this 'selective' immigration policy were drawn up in the 1920s by academic experts, most of them from the centre left and members of the *Ligue des droits de l'homme* (Human Rights League). The key rule involved keeping out workers from what were then termed 'antagonistic races' (principally the Germans) and 'inferior races' (natives of the colonies).

By the late 1920s, there were more than three million foreigners in France. The country was at the time described by an economist as 'the world's main destination for immigrants'. In 1925, 178,000 foreign workers came to France when only 171,000 entered the United States which had closed its borders in response to pressure from nativist groups. This mass migration was prompted by existing workforce shortages exacerbated by the legacy of the Great War: 1.3 million French people, the majority of them rural and industrial workers in their prime, died at the front. A similar number had been left with disabilities. In 1919, the shortfall in terms of the entire working-class workforce was of the order of ten per cent.

The hardest-hit sectors were heavy industry and agriculture. Paradoxically, although a large proportion of the working-age population was still rural, there were shortages of agricultural workers in the countryside. The extent of the need led to a broadening of recruitment zones. Movement across the borders of neighbouring countries began to play a less important part and longer-distance migration became more prominent. The Italians, who had overtaken the Belgians at the beginning of the century, were the main foreign community and would continue to be the largest immigrant group up to the beginning of the 1960s. Still present in large numbers in the South East, they had also established themselves in Greater Paris and in the East and North of France. But the most notable development during this period was the arrival of migrants from Central and Eastern Europe. Over a period of ten years, 500,000 Poles were recruited, often as families, with their own priests and teachers. The vast majority of them were hired to work in the coalmines of the Nord-Pas-de-Calais region: their role was to help rebuild a corps of miners that had been decimated by war and an exodus towards Greater Paris.

The interwar period was also very important in terms of the right to claim asylum. France became the main global destination for refugees. Hundreds of thousands of Russians fleeing the Bolsheviks, Armenians persecuted by Turkey, and Italian antifascists settled in France in the 1920s. Over the course of the following decade, in spite of the economic crisis, some of the victims of Nazism and Francoist Spain also found refuge in the country.

Recourse to large-scale immigration made it possible for French employers to 'unblock' the industrial labour market, with the help of the state and trade unions representing workers. The principal 'attraction' of foreign workers was that they were not French citizens. They could therefore be subjected to specific constraints. In order to obtain an employment contract, they had to accept the toughest jobs—those that the French did not want to do. The use of identity cards enabled the bureaucracy to channel migratory flows towards those sectors experiencing shortages, which contributed to ever-greater clustering in the labour market and to making the working class more heterogeneous.

The concentration of migrants varied greatly from one sector to the next. Some hardly recruited any foreign workers. The railways were a case in point. They were seen as a strategic area in terms of national security, only recruited French nationals and offered them secure employment. In contrast, migrants were present in large numbers in mining, the building sector and the steel industry. In 1930, foreigners made up 15% of the working class, but 42% of miners and 30% of excavation workers.

Prior to 1914, heavy industry had been a driver of the development of the working class. It is in this context that the making of a group of workers with a strong class identity had reached its most advanced stage. However, the massive destruction wrought by World War I, the loss of scores of workers who died on the battlefields and the fact that many of the workers hired by factories serving the war effort (that were located in the suburbs of Paris and in central France) did not want to return to the regions they hailed from, all help to explain the scale of immigration in the industrial areas of the North and the East. What took place in these regions can be described as involving the actual substitution of one working class for another. This break in the generational chain explains the collapse of the working-class movement.

The professional discrimination that immigrants faced was mirrored spatially. In certain regions of France, particularly the West, foreign workers were few and far between. But in the North, the East and Greater Paris, the first immigrant 'ghettos' appeared. In 1930, in 1700 French local authority areas, the number of foreigners was equal or superior to the number of French people.

There were various types of 'immigrant spaces'. The first was the inner-city slum. In Lille, from the *Second Empire* onwards, in neighbourhoods where traditional small-scale textile industry was based (e.g. Saint-Sauveur), all of the workers were *Lillois* 'by descent'. But in neighbourhoods where the new cotton or flax mills were based (e.g. Wazemmes), the majority of workers were Flemish migrants from Belgium. These workers had their own priests and associations. They formed an 'inward-looking community which is slow to open up to the indigenous population which was itself on its guard, jealous and disdainful'.[8] The same was true of Marseilles, where the *Vieux Port* neighbourhood was home to Neapolitan fishermen; in Toulon where the city centre streets were divided between migrants from Genoa, Naples and the Piedmont; in Valence with its Armenian quarter and in Paris where Jewish workers from Central Europe congregated in the Marais district.[9] In Greater Paris, mass migration also resulted in the expansion of the suburbs. Paris acquired a ring of poor quality housing, home to migrants from a number of countries.

Another consequence of mass migration was the development of another type of space, typical of industrial regions: factory towns (such as Longwy in Lorraine or Lens in the North) made up of workers' housing estates. The population was generally of 20,000 or fewer and the vast majority of those in work were working class. It is in these spaces that the greatest concentrations of migrants were to be found. In some locations, they made up more than 80% of the population. These factory towns were built by companies involved in mining or the production of steel in order to attract workers and offer them a base. In addition to the estates which were reserved for families, there was also shack-like accommodation for single migrants. Foreigners working in agriculture (who accounted for 20% of all migrants recruited in the 1920s) were also frequently offered basic accommodation of this type.

This spatial and professional segregation fed the divisions within the working class following World War I. The '*Union Sacrée*' facilitated the integration of French workers into the nation-state. The class collaboration strategy of the CGT (*Confédération Générale du Travail*, General Labour Confederation) trade union was mirrored politically by the socialist party. Migrant workers, who were not part of this consensual arrangement, found in the PC (*Parti Communiste*, Communist Party) and its trade union the CGTU, an internationalist party willing to defend their interests during the 1920s. It is true that the PC was then but a very small movement. However, the crisis of the 1930s provided it with an opportunity to establish itself in a French political landscape that lurched between the far right and the far left, national revolution or social revolution.

Xenophobia made a comeback after being less prominent in the 1920s. Many letters written by unemployed workers bear witness to rising intolerance. 'You say that the French should not revolt', writes a worker from Lorraine in 1934, 'but they are confronted with what one can see here, while us French starve [along with] our wives and children. If we ask for work, we're told they're not hiring here and next door foreigners are doing 13 or 14 hour shifts, women are working and there's nothing for us (...). No work for us French fuckers but for the others, oh yes, from 5 in the morning until 8 at night. It's a disgrace (...). It makes my blood boil to see what is going on'.[10] This sense of injustice felt by those who believed themselves to be abandoned by the state when they had 'put their lives on the line for France' was behind the resurgence in physical assaults on migrants. A Belgian worker was killed in the North in 1933. The following year, an Italian woodcutter and a Moroccan worker fell victim to this wave of hostility. In 1938, a Polish foreman was killed in a fight.

Hatred was stoked up by the right-wing press. The influx of refugees from Nazi Germany brought antisemitism to the fore once again. 'Not only are the German Jews taking the place of the French' according to the *Petit Bleu* of 7 December 1933, 'but they represent a threat to public health (...). To summarise, Jewish immigration offers nothing to our country. On the contrary, it is a serious danger from a national, political and social point of view'.[11] The *Action Française*, the country's main far-right organisation, complained that the German Jews were being portrayed as 'victims' and questioned the notion that they were persecuted under Hitler: 'When the Jews believe that one of theirs has distinguished himself in some part of the world, all of Jehovah's trumpets sound from the East to the West. If one of them gets kicked in the backside by a Christian in some obscure backwater, the whole universe is turned into a Wailing Wall' (9 December 1933).

Nonetheless, the crisis of the 1930s also led to bridges being built between French and foreign workers. Rising unemployment encouraged immigrants who had not been sent back to their country of origin to keep working for the same company. Many decided to get married or to ask their wives to move to France. The 'feminisation' of the foreign population is apparent in statistics. In 1931, there were fewer than 64 women for every 100 men. By 1936, the figure had risen to 72. As a result, the migrant worker community became more family-orientated and also more willing to make demands. Having ceased to believe they would return home one day, immigrants became involved in trade union activism. French workers, who thought their jobs were safe, were also badly hit by the crisis. The social context was now suited to a political alliance between reformers and revolutionaries in the working-class movement. The *Front Populaire* (Popular Front) was formed and won the parliamentary elections of May–June 1936.

This marked the beginning of a period of intense social and political conflict (which was to last until the end of the 1950s) in which the PCF (*Parti Communiste Français*, French Communist Party) played a leading role. It became the main political party in France after World War II and could count on the support of the vast majority of the children of immigrants who settled in France in the 1920s.

THE COLONIAL TURN

From the 1950s to the 1960s the world economy was booming again and French companies once more had recourse to large-scale immigration. There were two stages to this process. Between 1946 and 1954, France's foreign population showed only a very slight increase. There was even a decline in the number of Belgians, Poles and Spaniards. The number of Italians rose by just 10% (by roughly 50,000). The only spectacular increase was in the number of Algerians which increased tenfold, from 22,000 to over 210,000.

However, the war in Algeria stemmed this flow and led to a shift in recruitment policy. Between 1962 and 1965, immigration rates reached an unprecedented level. Acts of violence perpetrated in Algeria by the French army and the displacement of local populations made the crisis affecting the countryside much worse, with many poor rural dwellers opting to emigrate to France. But the public authorities sought to contain this movement. Between 1962 and 1982, official estimates of the number of Algerians in France show it rose from 350,000 to 800,000. But in relative terms, this rise was much lower than amongst the Portuguese, the group which expanded at the highest rate between 1962 and 1982 (from 90,000 to 760,000). The desire to curtail migration from Algeria was also in evidence in the intensification of efforts to recruit workers from Morocco (whose number rose from 31,000 to more than 440,000 over twenty years) and Tunisia (from 26,000 to 190,000). During the same period, migratory movements from other African countries gathered pace (17,000 people in 1962, 157,000 in 1982).

It was at this point in time that the migrant population in France became much more diverse. It can be divided into two main groups of similar sizes. The first was made up of migrants from the Iberian Peninsula (some from Spain, but most from Portugal) and the second of workers from France's former colonial Empire (North Africa, sub-Saharan Africa and South-East Asia). Migrants from Algeria had a particular status within this second group as a result of the legacies of the colonial war. In addition to Algerian migrant workers, there were two other groups of migrants. The largest one was made up of the former settlers known as '*Pieds Noirs*' (literally 'Black Feet') or 'returnees'. They cannot be classed as immigrants as they had full French citizenship even if this period was one of brutal upheaval for them. The second group was made up of '*Harkis*' (around 90,000 people) who had fought in the French army. They had to flee Algeria and were gathered together in camps where many of them lived out the rest of their lives.

This mass immigration occurred at a time when the rural exodus was rapidly gaining pace. The *banlieues*, the suburban areas of major cities, expanded at a rapid rate, with huge slums forming in an echo of the migrant shacks of the 1920s. At the same time, huge towers capable of accommodating several thousand people were erected for French migrants from the countryside.

This spatial segregation intersected with professional discrimination. The services sector experienced rapid growth and significant numbers of 'white collar' jobs were created. As was the case previously, the majority of French people who were leaving the countryside moved into these new roles and therefore did not become part of the working class. Large-scale recourse to immigration once again offered a solution to the structural shortage of workers. Newcomers were directed towards the less attractive sectors in the labour market (agriculture, construction, car manufacturing). The impact of immigration was therefore felt disproportionately in the working class. In the 1982 census, foreigners accounted for 6.8% of the total population (3.6 million people), but 12.7% of workers. And as was the case previously, migrants were concentrated in the lowest ranks of the workforce. 17 percent of construction workers and a third of unskilled workers in the car manufacturing industry were migrants. In the working population as a whole, over half of all migrants were unskilled workers as compared to one French person out of five.

From the end of the nineteenth century, migrants had been divided into three main categories: foreigners from an independent state, political refugees and colonial natives. In the 1960s, the legal status of migrants became more complex and a new institutional paradigm emerged. On one hand, the Convention relating to the Status of Refugees (adopted by the United Nations in 1951) afforded refugees a legal status, which meant that they had more rights than foreigners. On the other hand, the Treaty of Rome, signed in 1957, marked the beginning of the European project. One of its main consequences was that the rights of citizens of a particular state and those of citizens of other member states gradually converged. The emergence of a 'European citizenship' helps to explain why the divide between 'them' and 'us' increasingly relates to those who are part of this community and those who are not.

The arrival of these new waves of migrants put an end to the process of unification of the working class which had begun in 1936 with the *Front Populaire*, the alliance of left-wing parties that came to power that year. As had been the case with their predecessors, these new migrant workers found themselves marginalised. The Communist Party, which was by then part of the state apparatus, refused to defend their specific interests and as a consequence, far-left organisations tried to take on this role. But the economic crisis that began in the early 1970s led to a resurgence of racism and xenophobia which was further fuelled by the legacies of the war in Algeria. Racist violence reached a peak during the '*été rouge*' ('red summer') of Marseilles in 1973. Eight North African workers were killed during clashes.

IMMIGRATION AND URBAN VIOLENCE IN FRANCE TODAY

Faced with an economic crisis, the authorities put a stop to immigration in the mid-1970s. From this point, only foreigners moving to be reunited with their families and asylum seekers who had obtained refugee status were allowed to settle in France. The predictable impact of these changing circumstances on migration flows is in evidence in official statistics. The foreign population continued to grow slowly between

1975 and 1982 (from 3.4 million to 3.7 million people), then gradually declined to 3.3 million in 1999. The number of Italians and of Spaniards declined steeply during this period, but the most spectacular drop was in the number of Algerians which halved between 1982 and 1999 (from 805,000 to 475,000). In contrast, the number of Moroccans rose (from 441,000 to 506,000) and the most rapid increase was in migrants from sub-Saharan Africa (from 157,000 to 282,000) and Asia (from 289,000 to 410,000).

As had been the case in the 1930s, the crisis encouraged the migrant population to settle and to a degree to put down roots. Slum clearances lead to migrant families being rehoused in '*cités de transit*' ('transition estates') and in HLM (*Habitations à Loyer Modéré*, Rent-Controlled Housing) in the neighbourhoods that the authorities now refer to as ZUS (*Zones Urbaines Sensibles*, Sensitive Urban Areas). As the French workers and employees who were initially housed in these vast projects left to live elsewhere, they became the new ghettos for poor immigrants.

Foreigners were the worst affected by the economic crisis. In 2002, 8.3% of French people were unemployed. The figure for foreigners from non-EU states was 25% (rising to 36% for those aged between 18 and 25). The worst difficulties in terms of employment were to be found in the ZUS (there were 751 of these areas, with 4.7 million residents) where up to half of the population could be affected by unemployment.

These economic and social factors explain the rise in urban violence in France since the 1980s. This violence, in the form, for instance, of clashes between police and young people from estates often makes the front pages of the press. It reached a peak in the autumn of 2005, during urban riots which followed the death of two young people in Clichy-sous-Bois, in Greater Paris. The main difference is that the discrimination described above no longer only affects the first generation of immigrants, but also their children, even though they are French citizens. As these young people often have roots in countries that were previously French colonies, many observers see the violence as being linked to 'racial discrimination'. The right and the left now agree on the need to denounce 'racism'. This shows how those that the sociologist Howard Becker describes as 'moral entrepreneurs' have taken on a central role in French public debates.

From a scholarly perspective, reality appears more complex. It is first of all important to recall that the discrimination that affects this section of working-class youth is a delayed consequence of the immigration process itself. As the foreign workers recruited in the 1960s felt the full force of the economic crisis, unemployment tended to affect their children, because the cycle that enabled the previous generations of migrants to blend into French society was interrupted.

The changed economic climate also resulted in young people from less affluent backgrounds facing much greater competition for jobs. The arrival of large numbers of women on the labour market from the 1950s onwards and the disappearance of a number of jobs that were reliant on physical force made things harder for boys. New roles in the service sector which young people are now invited to apply for demand 'people skills', which does not sit easily with traditional male identities in working-class communities. This 'handicap' is even harder to overcome for those who suffer the worst stigma as the latter makes individuals more prone to violent reactions. Another factor that has led to many young people being kept away from the labour market is the demand for better qualifications. Statistics show that the main cause of unemployment is poor performance at school. Degrees provide some protection from unemployment. But the children of migrant labourers or unskilled workers are the least well equipped to succeed in an education system that is not designed for them.

Those whose parents are from Africa or Eastern Europe are more likely to underachieve at school. This suggests that we need to look beyond a simple opposition between 'European' and 'post-colonial' migrants. Similarly, if one examines the 1999 census, it is clear that the role of ethnicity is not always as clear-cut as sometimes thought. Drawing a comparison between French people of Algerian extraction and those with roots in Portugal reveals that there are many more French people with an Algerian background who have never worked (4700 out of around 118,000 people of working age) than French people with a Portuguese background in the same situation (1500 out of 156,000). But the figures for managers and the professions are suggestive of reverse 'discrimination'. There are 9645 French people of Algerian extraction in these sought-after occupations (8.5%), as opposed to 6415 French people of Portuguese extraction (4.1%). This leads us to conclude that what distinguishes post-colonial migrants is that they are over-represented *both* in the poorest sections of society and among the elites.

These figures confirm that when people find themselves unable to access the jobs market, it is for a number of reasons. Statistical models show that immigration is not 'in itself' a risk factor when it comes to success at school. If many young people leave school without qualifications it is because of the social conditions that immigration is associated with. More than a quarter of young people without qualifications come from single-parent families, with parents who are themselves unskilled and badly affected by unemployment.[12] Another key factor is time spent in France. Those who find themselves in the greatest difficulty are mainly the most recent arrivals. Sociologists now emphasise the contrast between two 'mini-generations' of young people with roots overseas, with different narratives about migration. The children of Algerians were at the heart of the social protests of the 1980s (with the '*beurs*' movement), but those who played a key role in the urban violence of the early 2000s are mostly connected to more recent migratory movements. Moroccan, African and Turkish families are now more numerous than Algerian families. A small proportion of young people from the Caribbean community also find themselves marginalised. Naturally, in this case, we are looking at 'internal' migration as their parents are French citizens, but these young people's lived experiences are at times identical to those of the poorest immigrants.

NOTES

1. E.P. Thompson, *The Making of the English Working Class* (London: Penguin Books, 1964).
2. Marc Bloch, *Les Caractères originaux de l'histoire rurale française* (Paris: Armand Colin, 1932); and *Seigneurie française et manoir anglais* (Paris: Armand Colin, 1960).
3. Gérard Noiriel, *Les ouvriers dans la société française* (Paris: Le Seuil, 1986).
4. Gérard Noiriel, *Le Creuset français: Histoire de l'immigration* (Paris: Le Seuil, 1988).
5. Jean-Paul Burdy, *Le Soleil noir: Un quartier de Saint-Etienne, 1840–1940* (Lyon: Presses Universitaires de Lyon, 1989).
6. See Laurent Dornel, *La France hostile* (Paris: Hachette, 2004).
7. Firmin Lentacker, *La Frontière franco-belge* (Lille: Librarie Giard, 1974).
8. Pierre Pierrard, *La Vie ouvrière à Lille sous le Second Empire* (Lille: Gérard Montfort, 1965).

9. See Maxime Serre, 'Problèmes démographiques d'hier et d'aujourd'hui: note sur l'immigration italienne à Toulon et dans le Var,' *Revue de Géographie Alpine* 40, no. 4 (1952); Anne Sportiello, *Les pêcheurs du Vieux Port* (Marseilles: Jeanne Laffite, 1981); Aznive Keuroghlian, 'Les Arméniens dans la région Rhône-Alpes' (Université de Lyon, Thèse de 3ᵉ cycle, 1977); and Nancy Green, *Les travailleurs immigrés juifs à la Belle Epoque* (Paris: Fayard, 1985).

10. Gérard Noiriel, *Longwy. Immigrés et prolétaires* (Paris: PUF, 1984).

11. Ralph Schor, *L'Antisémitisme en France dans l'entre-deux-guerres* (Brussels: Complexe, 1992).

12. Florence Lefresne, ed., *Les jeunes non qualifiés, Problèmes politiques et sociaux* (Paris: La Documentation Française, 2005).

CHAPTER 9

Was the Multiculturalism Backlash Good for Women with a Muslim Background? Perspectives from Five Minority Women's Organisations in the Netherlands

Margaretha A. van Es

'Is multiculturalism bad for women?' the political philosopher Susan Moller Okin famously asked twenty years ago.[1] Rather than providing a simplistic answer, Okin wanted to initiate a critical debate about possible tensions between feminism and multiculturalism. At that time, Okin noted a strong multiculturalist commitment in Western countries to group rights for minorities, and she warned against letting this commitment overshadow the individual rights of women within minority groups. A lot has happened since Okin asked that question.

Multiculturalism, which was already increasingly condemned in the 1990s, came under fierce attack after the 9/11 attacks in 2001. Scholars describe a 'backlash' or 'crisis' of multiculturalism including a growing chorus of voices condemning multiculturalist policies, an increased

M. A. van Es (✉)
Utrecht University, Utrecht, The Netherlands

© The Author(s) 2019
E. Henrich and J. M. Simpson (eds.),
History, Historians and the Immigration Debate,
https://doi.org/10.1007/978-3-319-97123-0_9

emphasis on national identity and civic integration, a growing critique of Muslim minorities and their religion, and a surge of right-wing populist parties with an anti-immigration agenda.[2] Stereotypical images of Muslim women as oppressed have played an important role in the multiculturalism backlash. Western societies supposedly have to be protected against the 'backward' and 'oppressive' religion of Islam, and Muslim women have to be protected against Muslim men.[3]

The Netherlands, famous for its multicultural tolerance in the 1980s and 1990s, has since experienced a particularly virulent multiculturalism backlash. In her much-cited work on the Dutch integration debate, Baukje Prins describes how politicians such as Pim Fortuyn, Ayaan Hirsi Ali, Rita Verdonk, and later Geert Wilders, accused the Dutch political establishment of political correctness towards Muslim minorities, and of refusing to acknowledge the problems caused by multiculturalist policy-making. The charge sheet included failed integration, youth criminality, homophobia, and—last but not least—the systematic oppression of women. Ayaan Hirsi Ali in particular became known for her radical statements about Islam, which she saw as an inherently patriarchal religion. If Muslim women wanted to emancipate themselves, they had to leave their faith behind. Prins refers to this form of right-wing populism as hyper-realism: a political ideology and rhetorical style where politicians claim to speak on behalf of ordinary people, daring to face the 'facts'.[4]

After Pim Fortuyn was assassinated by an animal-rights activist on 6 May 2002, his party List Pim Fortuyn (LPF) won 26 out of 150 seats in the parliamentary elections few weeks later. The LPF joined a new coalition with the liberal conservatives and Christian democrats. From then onwards, Dutch policy for gender equality became inextricably linked with immigrant integration and vice versa.[5] In 2003, the new Minister of Social Affairs Aart Jan de Geus announced that the emancipation of Dutch women had been accomplished and that future emancipation policy should focus entirely on (Muslim) minority women.[6] The government installed a special committee to stimulate ethnic minority women's social, economic and cultural participation in Dutch society. But the new policy for women's emancipation consisted first and foremost of imposing civic integration courses, restricting marriage migration, and initiating special projects against forced marriages, female genital mutilation, honour killings, and domestic violence within minority families.[7] Despite several changes of government, the policy decisions regarding civic integration and migration control have never been revoked since then.

This reveals the lasting effect of hyper-realism on Dutch policy-making. Besides, after Hirsi Ali left the Netherlands in 2006, the emerging right-wing populist MP Geert Wilders kept addressing gender equality as one out of many 'Dutch' values that have to be protected against the 'Islamisation' of Dutch society. He repeatedly proposed forced assimilation and a ban on the Qur'an, the headscarf and the construction of new mosques.

The developments described here stirred much debate. In contemporary Dutch public discourse, there are two competing ways of representing the multiculturalism backlash and its effect on minority women. Those who are sympathetic to the hyper-realist view tend to argue that a radical break with multiculturalism was necessary to address the disadvantaged position of women in Muslim minority families without being hindered by political correctness. The underlying assumption is that ethnic minority women, especially Muslim women, have many problems that ethnic majority women do not have, and that these problems have previously been ignored or even concealed by minority communities and left-wing politicians alike. On the other hand, critics tend to argue that the hyper-realist approach has not served the interests of minority women, but that a discourse of 'saving Muslim women' has been used to legitimise a restrictive immigration and assimilation policy, and to strengthen national identity as 'emancipated', 'sexually liberated' and 'enlightened' in contrast to a 'backward' and 'misogynistic' Muslim culture. Moreover, the setting apart of Muslim minority women as 'pitiable' and 'oppressed', and the repeated accusation that Islam inherently oppresses women, would cause Muslim women to feel stigmatised, draw back in their own ranks and reject feminism altogether.[8]

Interestingly, almost no research has been conducted on how women with a Muslim background have experienced the multiculturalism backlash, let alone on how it has affected their efforts for women's empowerment.[9] More than fifteen years after the 9/11 attacks and Pim Fortuyn's murder, it is time to weigh things up: was the multiculturalism backlash good for women? There is obviously no simple answer to this question, but one can at least explore the perspectives of women with a Muslim background. In this chapter, I look at how women active in a variety of minority women's organisations in the Netherlands have perceived the recent developments in public debate and in public policy towards Muslim women, and how these developments have affected their organisational work in terms of strengthening women's position in the family and in

Dutch society. I have included five large minority representative organisations set up by and for women with a Muslim background, out of which two are secular and three are Islamic organisations. All of them were established before the turn of the century, and all of them still existed when I carried out my research. They are the Turkish Women's Association in the Netherlands (established in 1975), the Moroccan Women's Association in the Netherlands (1982), the Al Nisa (1982) and Dar al Arqam (1992) foundations, and the Milli Görüş Women's Federation (1999). My analysis is based on archival material from the organisations and on interviews with their (former) leaders, and covers the period 1975–2010.[10] I will first discuss my results regarding the secular organisations and then the Islamic organisations, before I come to my conclusion.

THE PERSPECTIVES OF TWO SECULAR MINORITY WOMEN'S ORGANISATIONS

The Turkish Women's Association in the Netherlands (HTKB) and the Moroccan Women's Association in the Netherlands (MVVN) were established in Amsterdam with the aim to improve the position of Turkish and Moroccan women in the family and in Dutch society. Although the two associations represented women from different countries, they were similar in many ways. In both cases, the original target group consisted of women who came from rural areas and had recently migrated to the Netherlands, had little or no education and did not speak Dutch. The leaders had the same national origins as the target groups, but were relatively resourceful in terms of their educational level and Dutch language skills.[11]

Both the HTKB and MVVN had a progressive, socialist approach. In the beginning, their political struggle mostly targeted the exploitation of women migrant workers on the Dutch labour market, the vulnerable position of migrant women as a result of Dutch rules regarding family migration, and racism in Dutch society. The MVVN also addressed the consequences of the Moroccan family code for Moroccan women living in the Netherlands. Both the HTKB and the MVVN regularly organised and/or participated in public protests. However, the organisations also wanted to change traditional gender roles in the family, encourage women to become engaged in activities outside the home, and enable them to make informed choices regarding sexuality and reproduction. Both organisations offered Dutch language courses, literacy courses in the women's mother tongue, sewing lessons, cultural activities, consultation hours, and information sessions about topics such as health care, workers' rights, migration laws and the Dutch social service system. These initiatives had the additional purpose of bringing women together to let them reflect upon their position in the family and in Dutch society.[12] Hundreds of women took part in their activities. In the 1980s and early 1990s, they were considered the largest organisations run by and for Turkish and Moroccan women in the Netherlands. They received large subsidies from the Amsterdam municipality and also received support from the Dutch government.[13] At that time, the Dutch authorities aimed to encourage the social and economic participation of ethnic minorities through group-level emancipation 'with preservation of identity'. Supporting minority women's organisations was considered to be an important means to strengthen these women's position in Dutch society.[14]

During the 1990s, the HTKB and MVVN went through several changes. In 1995 the HTKB split into two organisations: a local Association of Women of Turkish Origin Living in Amsterdam (ATKB) and a nationwide federation with the acronym HTKF that served as an umbrella for a number of local Turkish women's associations in the Netherlands.[15] From then onwards, the ATKB carried out most of the former HTKB's activities. However, as the constituency grew older, the ATKB's focus shifted gradually from women workers to ageing women and their teenage daughters.[16] The latter also applied to the MVVN.[17] In addition, the MVVN developed into an important centre of expertise regarding the sharia-based Moroccan family code or *Mudawwanah*. For example, the MVVN assisted Moroccan-Dutch women who had divorced their husbands according to Dutch law, but whose divorce was not recognised by the Moroccan authorities because their ex-husband refused to sign the Islamic divorce papers.[18]

After the turn of the century, the multiculturalism backlash had strong consequences for the ATKB and MVVN, the most important one being a growing difficulty to set their own agenda. Perhaps one would expect that the heightened public concern with the emancipation and integration of Muslim minority women caused the authorities to increase financial support for minority women's organisations. Yet, what happened was exactly the opposite. The multiculturalism backlash led to a more selective funding of minority organisations, which at the same time helped budget-cutting.[19] In 2004, the year in which public debate about

Muslim minority women peaked,[20] the Amsterdam municipality decided to stop giving structural funding to several minority women's organisations, including the ATKB and MVVN. This meant that the ATKB and MVVN could no longer afford to hire paid staff or provide extensive training to their volunteers. Both organisations became dependent on a small group of volunteers.[21] As a result, the MVVN, for example, had difficulties maintaining its legal expertise regarding the *Mudawwanah*.[22]

From now on, the organisations could only apply for project funding, and these projects were increasingly designed by the municipality instead of by the organisations themselves.[23] In the case of the ATKB, this meant that the organisation became significantly more often engaged in projects targeting problems within the Turkish-Dutch community that were high on the right-wing populist agenda. For example, in 2004 the ATKB had among others a project against domestic violence,[24] and in 2008, it started a project where Turkish-Dutch volunteers visited isolated women at home to convince them to participate in the association and in Dutch society.[25] The MVVN, on the other hand, feared turning into a 'project agency' for the Dutch authorities and decided to forego many funding opportunities. The MVVN prioritised setting its own agenda, which meant that the organisation had to work with very little means. During the last few years, the MVVN has mostly organised low-budget activities such as lectures, debates and social gatherings.[26] Both the ATKB and MVVN still provide consultation hours, and they try to influence public policy towards minority women through lobbying. But it seems that there is little room left to address hindrances to Turkish-Dutch women's emancipation that are not 'culture-related' but located in Dutch society, such as unemployment or the criminalisation of undocumented residence.[27]

Neither the Amsterdam municipality nor the Dutch government provided the support that the organisations had hoped for. Women on the ATKB and MVVN boards felt that politicians liked to 'break taboos' about minority women's oppression, but no substantial help was given to women in difficult situations.[28] During the first years of the new millennium, the MVVN, for example, tried to raise public awareness of the problems of Moroccan-Dutch women who were 'left behind' by their husbands or fathers during a holiday in Morocco. These women could not return to the Netherlands because their husbands had confiscated their identity documents. Married migrants without an independent residence permit were in a particularly weak position. After having done extensive research, the MVVN proposed to the Dutch government to develop an emergency system allowing victims to get appropriate help from the Dutch embassy. The MVVN also urged the authorities to give married migrants independent residence rights upon arrival in the Netherlands, instead of keeping them legally dependent on their spouse. Integration Minister Rita Verdonk did not take this policy advice on board and only allocated the MVVN a minimum budget to print information booklets for Moroccan-Dutch women.[29]

Another important consequence of the multiculturalism backlash and the growing negative focus on Islam was that the ATKB and MVVN felt forced to position themselves in a polarising debate about Muslim women and their religion—something that they were very keen to avoid. The HTKB/ATKB and MVVN had been secular organisations from the very beginning. The women who led the organisations did not identify as believers or practicing Muslims, and they did not consider religion relevant to their organisational work. Moreover, they wanted to unite women with different religious views in a joint struggle for women's rights.[30] Before the turn of the century, both organisations regularly criticised 'conservative' or 'traditional' attitudes towards women,[31] and the MVVN repeatedly addressed the disadvantaged position of women in the Moroccan family code that was 'based on an interpretation of Islamic law by the *Maliki* school of thought'.[32] Moreover, shortly before the 9/11 attacks in 2001, MVVN spokeswoman Nora Azarkan wrote an opinion piece in the newspaper *Trouw* where she warned against the misogynistic attitudes of many conservative imams in Dutch mosques.[33] However, neither the HTKB/ATKB nor the MVVN worked with an essentialist concept of Islam that was either 'good' or 'bad' for women.

After the 9/11 attacks, when Dutch public debate became characterised by a growing critique of Muslims and Islam, both organisations virtually stopped mentioning Islam. Not only did the women on the groups' boards want to avoid confrontations between religious and non-religious women within their organisation, they also refused to participate in debates that diverted attention from issues that really mattered to them. As long-time ATKB board member Sevgi Göngürmüş says:

> Each time they talk about the headscarf, about religion, but they don't discuss improving the position of women: how and which way? We find this discussion important, and it needs to be discussed in depth. That's why, if there is a debate about religion, we keep ourselves out completely. [...]

Often it is purely about the headscarf. 'Is it a free choice or not?' Well, free choice? What does a 'free choice' actually mean? And why don't we discuss the free choice with regards to the labour market, education, the important role of the wife for men, and legal rights, and unequal payments. And we talk, we are not allowed to talk about that, but we can talk about the headscarf or about clothing.[34]

However, there was yet another reason not to discuss religion. MVVN leader Ikram Chiddi explains that during the last fifteen years, the MVVN board has felt less and less room to make critical statements about issues that are somehow related to Islam, because it fears that such statements will be misused by right-wing populist parties:

> Since the emergence of Wilders, or at least the populists, it has become really complicated for the MVVN to take a position in public debates about social issues. Because so much has changed. Before, if you sent out a press release because ten women complained after the summer holidays that their husbands got married [to a second wife] without their permission, and you said like: 'Morocco must abolish polygamy', you issued a press release, then it was simply like, you got a debate and it was done. Or something like that. Well, now it is of course used for a different political agenda. [...] So that is the tricky part. Because those statements, we are now extra careful with our statements of course. You see the dilemma? [...] We see that people do everything they can to stigmatise that group, or at least the Muslim women [...] But to take part in that, well, that is a choice. And we actually chose to simply not take part in that. [...] Which makes it quite hard at times. Because almost every week or month you get a call from some radio or TV programme. It is always very sensation-oriented. [...] While, originally, when it comes to our foundation we are secular. And we have clear ideas about that. For the rest, whether we are all Muslims or religious doesn't matter at all. [...] But if you for example look at the Moroccan family code, then we do see how Islam is being used. We do see that as part of the problem. We are very clear about that, we are explicit about that. But now, in this period it is very difficult to take a position there. It is just tricky. [...] So, that nice story of a progressive, secular Moroccan women's organisation, that has been adjusted a bit, to put it that way.[35]

In other words, secular organisations that were critical of patriarchal laws and practices in Muslim societies felt forced to under-communicate the possibly negative role of religion because they did not want to contribute to the stigmatisation of Muslim women and Islam. The polarisation of public debate about Islam resulted in there being little room for constructive criticism. The MVVN has always remained highly vocal about Moroccan women's problems, but it did adapt its choice of words. Secular organisations that did not want to contribute to a right-wing populist agenda thus saw their actual freedom of expression becoming more and more limited.

THE PERSPECTIVES OF THREE ISLAMIC WOMEN'S ORGANISATIONS

The foundations Al Nisa and Dar al Arqam and the Milli Görüş Women's Federation are Islamic women's organisations, meaning that the women involved have organised themselves on the basis of their religious identity. Al Nisa and Dar al Arqam were both established by Dutch converts to Islam, but over the years, they acquired a more ethnically diverse constituency, including many Turkish-Dutch and Moroccan-Dutch women.[36] The goal of Al Nisa was originally to give information about Islam in Dutch (mostly through monthly lectures and a monthly magazine) and to provide a platform where Muslim women from all over the Netherlands could share their experiences. Although Al Nisa was not an explicitly feminist organisation, it wanted to enable women to develop their faith in their own way, independently from male-dominated mosque associations.[37] Starting in 1982 in Amsterdam, it rapidly acquired new chapters across the country. Within five years, the foundation's magazine *Al Nisa* had more than 750 subscribers.[38] Dar al Arqam was established in 1992 in Rotterdam with goals and activities similar to those of Al Nisa, but it chose to remain a local organisation. In addition to its monthly meetings with lectures about Islam in Dutch, Dar al Arqam also organised coffee mornings and sewing lessons for Moroccan-Dutch women in the participants' mother-tongue that were funded by the Rotterdam municipality. A few years later, the activities were expanded with Qur'an study groups, Islamic consultation hours, Arabic lessons for converts, youth activities for teenage girls, and Islamic education for children.[39]

The Milli Görüş Women's Federation (MGVF) was established in 1999 as an umbrella organisation for about thirty small women's associations in the northern half of the Netherlands, most of which had already existed for years. Milli Görüş is a transnational religious revival movement founded by the Turkish politician Necmettin Erbakan.

The Milli Görüş Women's Federation is part of the general Milli Görüş North Netherlands Federation, and the local women's associations are each connected to a local Milli Görüş mosque association. Almost all MGVF-affiliated women have Turkish origins, and most activities are in Turkish. The local women's organisations run activities varying from Qur'an reading sessions to museum visits and charity markets, while the MGVF umbrella maintains contact with the press and the Dutch authorities, and coordinates larger projects across the local chapters.[40] The original goal of the Milli Görüş movement was to strengthen the Islamic identity of Turkish migrants in Europe, provide information about Islam and encourage them to live a religious life.[41] However, in 2000, the then leader of the Milli Görüş North Netherlands Federation, Haci Karacaer, introduced 'Integration, Emancipation, Participation and Performance' as the new slogan of his organisation. These four words have always remained the main objectives of the MGVF during the period studied.[42]

The multiculturalism backlash and the growing debate about Islam after the 9/11 attacks have neither caused these organisations to reject feminism, nor to 'break taboos' about the oppression of women in Islam. In fact, all three of them intensified their efforts for women's empowerment. Instead of telling women to leave their faith behind, they explicitly used Islam as a source of inspiration for their efforts. All three organisations had already started working for women's empowerment before the multiculturalism backlash, albeit each in their own way. In Al Nisa, women had since the 1980s encouraged each other to read the Qur'an themselves, instead of blindly following the patriarchal interpretations of male scholars.[43] Dar al Arqam had organised coffee mornings and sewing lessons for Moroccan-Dutch women who otherwise lived fairly isolated lives.[44] The MGVF had adopted the slogan 'Integration, Emancipation, Participation and Performance' already before the 9/11 attacks and before the escalation of the Dutch integration debate. In 2002 it initiated a large project against domestic violence, a year before the Dutch government started its policy programme for the integration and emancipation of minority women.[45] However, as a result of the multiculturalism backlash and the criticisms made of Islam, the organisations became more outward-oriented. They started to address women's emancipation more explicitly, and they began to focus more on particular problems that were a subject of public debate.

Al Nisa became by far the most outward-oriented. Around the turn of the century, a new board had decided to take the foundation in a new direction. Rather than organising social gatherings and providing information about Islam to Muslim women, Al Nisa wanted to represent the interests of Muslim women in the Dutch public sphere. The escalation of the debate about women in Islam after the 9/11 attacks then created an urgent need for an organisation that could give voice to Muslim women. From then onwards Al Nisa's new leader Ceylan Weber—a Dutch convert who had been active in the women's movement for a long time— often wrote opinion pieces, gave interviews and took part in panel debates about Muslim women's emancipation.[46]

Meanwhile, in its magazine, Al Nisa paid more attention than ever before to the position of women in Islam and the compatibility of Islam with feminism. Articles appeared about issues such as domestic violence, female genital mutilation, women's achievements on the labour market, forced marriages, women's rights to active participation in the mosque, 'honour killings', and women's rights to initiate divorce.[47] Some of these articles were written in response to a public debate about that particular issue, other topics were chosen simply because the constituency considered them important. A common thread was that although gendered violence and gender discrimination occurred in Muslim families, these could not be legitimised through Islam. In the Qur'an, men and women were equal before God. If women's rights were violated, this was the result of cultural practices and/or patriarchal readings of sacred texts.

There were clear similarities between the ideas expressed in these articles and Islamic feminism, and many Al Nisa-affiliated women felt inspired by activist scholars such as Fatima Mernissi, Amina Wadud and Asma Barlas.[48] While various forms of feminism have existed in the Muslim world for more than a century, Islamic feminism emerged as a transnational phenomenon from the 1980s onwards. It can be defined as a specific form of feminism that is explicitly embedded within Islamic discourse. Islamic feminists object to the fact that women have historically been largely excluded from interpreting the Qur'an and Hadith. Simultaneously, they object to accusations from non-Muslims that Islam is inherently patriarchal. They point to sacred texts that emphasise gender equality and argue that gender discrimination and gendered violence are incompatible with the Islamic notion of social justice. Central to Islamic feminism is the idea that Islam was originally much more empowering to women than it is as practiced by Muslims today.[49]

The Dar al Arqam board decided not to participate in public debate through the media,[50] but it did begin to focus a lot more on women's emancipation in the organisation's activities. It organised lectures and workshops with titles such as 'Women's Emancipation and Islam' and 'Boys and Girls: Respect for Each Other'.[51] In 2003, Dar al Arqam gave a course entitled 'Qur'an and Women's Rights',[52] and it also began to organise assertiveness training for Muslim women.[53] However, in 2007, the board concluded that these emancipatory activities diverted attention away from the foundation's original goal. It decided to bring back its focus to providing basic information about Islam to Muslim women. Emancipation-related issues kept being addressed, but with lower frequency.[54] The MGVF continued its project against domestic violence. In addition, it started new projects, including assertiveness training for Muslim women, workshops about sexuality and reproduction for teenage girls, and a course to increase women's leadership skills in organisations.[55] The MGVF was particularly good at getting Milli Görüş-affiliated imams and male Milli Görüş members positively involved in their projects.[56] In both organisations, the core message was that domestic violence and other violations of women's rights could not be legitimised through Islam. If Muslim women and girls gained more knowledge about their rights in Islam, this would help to strengthen their position.

The decision of Dar al Arqam and the MGVF to intensify their efforts for women's empowerment can in part be explained through changes in the authorities' funding policies. The story of Dar al Arqam is somewhat similar to that of the ATKB and MVVN. Until 2002, Dar al Arqam received core funding from the Rotterdam municipality, but after that, it could only apply for project funding. This meant that its new activities had to be clearly connected with Muslim women's emancipation and/or integration in order to be eligible for subsidies.[57] Also, the MGVF projects were funded by the local (and sometimes the national) authorities,[58] and the MGVF clearly benefited from the large subsidies that were allocated for projects against 'culture-related' barriers to minority women's emancipation. However, funding policies do not explain everything: Al Nisa never received any funding, but was also more occupied with gender equality than ever before.

From the interviews and the archival material, it appears that there were other, more important reasons why these organisations intensified their efforts for women's empowerment during these years. First, there was a sincere wish among the women who were active in these groups to improve their position and that of other Muslim women. They perceived a discrepancy between Islam as a religion that promotes social justice, and the disadvantaged position that many Muslim women had in their families and in broader society. Many of the women involved felt a growing urge to help other women.[59] Second, specific conditions in public discourse made it almost impossible *not* to address the problems that Muslim women encountered, especially when these problems were perceived as culture-related. Hyper-realism had brought along a new form of political correctness where forced marriages, 'honour killings', female genital mutilation, and other 'Muslim' problems had to be recognised and explicitly condemned; otherwise, one would become accused of denying the existence of these issues.[60] Third, many Muslim women felt stigmatised and excluded by right-wing populist statements about Islam being a 'backward' and 'oppressive' religion that was incompatible with Western values. Through their organisational work, they wanted to challenge the negative image of Islam that they thought had been created by politicians and the mainstream news media. They wanted to show that many pious Muslim women were strongly committed to women's empowerment, and that there was ample room for such a struggle in Islam.[61]

CONCLUSION

This chapter has shown that the multiculturalism backlash has not stopped women with a Muslim background from fighting for women's rights. On the contrary, several of the organisations studied have intensified their efforts for women's emancipation during the first years of the new millennium. However, the post-9/11 developments in public debate and in public policy have put strong pressure on minority women's organisations to position themselves regarding women's rights in Islam. On the one hand, the multiculturalism backlash seems to have boosted Islamic feminism. The negative focus on Islam in Dutch public debate has encouraged women in Islamic organisations to show that their religion was not the cause of women's problems, but the key to the solution. In that sense, one may argue that right-wing populist critics of Islam such as Ayaan Hirsi Ali have unintentionally contributed to the rise of Islamic feminism among Muslim women in the Netherlands. On the other hand, the multiculturalism backlash has made it more difficult for women in secular organisations to formulate constructive criticism against conservative religious attitudes. The growing fear of contributing to a right-wing populist agenda seems to have decreased the actual freedom of speech of those who had already been working for minority women's rights from a secular perspective for several decades.

Several of the organisations studied have also found it more diffi-cult to set their own agenda, as a result of increasingly selective funding policies from the authorities. The intense public debate about Muslim women's oppression has by no means always translated into substan-tial support for women in difficult situations. In some of the organisa-tions studied, the multiculturalism backlash has led to an attention shift towards 'culture-related' problems instead of social, economic and legal barriers to women's emancipation. During the last few years, auster-ity measures have caused funding opportunities for minority women's organisations to diminish even further.

What the multiculturalism backlash has not contributed to is an open debate where women of different ethnic backgrounds and religious beliefs can discuss strategies for women's empowerment on an equal footing. White, ethnic Dutch, secular feminist ideals are still perceived as the norm (regardless of whether these ideals are put into practice). Ethnic and religious minority women can 'at best' adapt to this norm. Their own insights and strategies are seldom seen as valuable for their own emancipation process, let alone for that of Dutch majority women. Dutch society is far from gender equal, and as long as that is the case, a broader public discussion of these questions would be of great benefit to all women living in the Netherlands.

NOTES

1. Although Okin originally published her essay 'Is multiculturalism bad for women?' in the *Boston Review* in October 1997, the most-cited version of her essay is the one published as a chapter in an eponymous book: Susan Moller Okin, 'Is multiculturalism bad for women?,' in *Is Multiculturalism Bad for Women?*, eds. Joshua Cohen, Matthew Howard, and Martha C. Nussbaum (Princeton: Princeton University Press, 1999), 7–25.
2. Steven Vertovec and Susanne Wessendorf, *The Multiculturalism Backlash: European Discourses, Policies and Practices* (London: Routledge, 2010); Alana Lentin, Gary Younge, and Gavan Titley, *The Crises of Multiculturalism: Racism in a Neoliberal Age* (London: Zed Books, 2011).
3. Sherene Razack, 'Imperilled Muslim women, dangerous Muslim men and civilised Europeans: Legal and social responses to forced marriages,' *Feminist Legal Studies* 12, no. 2 (2004): 129–74; Moira Dustin, *Gender Equality, Cultural Diversity: European Comparisons and Lessons* (London: Nuffield Foundation, 2006); Tjitske Akkerman and Anniken Hagelund, '"Women and children first!' Anti-immigration parties and gender in Norway and the Netherlands,' *Patterns of Prejudice* 41, no. 2 (2007): 197–214.

4. Baukje Prins, *Voorbij de Onschuld: Het Debat over Integratie in Nederland* (Amsterdam: Van Gennep, 2004); Baukje Prins and Sawitri Saharso, 'From toleration to repression: The Dutch backlash against multiculturalism,' in *The Multiculturalism Backlash*, eds. Vertovec and Wessendorf 72–91.

5. Conny Roggeband and Mieke Verloo, 'Dutch women are liberated, migrant women are a problem: The evolution of policy frames on gender and migration in the Netherlands, 1995–2005,' *Social Policy and Administration* 41, no. 3 (2007): 271–88; Marguerite van den Berg and Willem Schinkel, 'Women from the catacombs of the city: Gender notions in Dutch culturist discourse,' *Innovation* 22, no. 4 (2009): 393–410.

6. 'De Geus Wil Portefeuille Emancipatie Opheffen,' *De Volkskrant*, 15 November 2003; 'De Geus: Post Emancipatie is Overbodig,' *NRC Handelsblad*, 17 November 2003.

7. Roggeband and Verloo, 'Dutch women are liberated,' 271–88; van den Berg and Schinkel, 'Women from the catacombs of the city,' 393–410.

8. Halleh Ghorashi, 'Ayaan Hirsi Ali: Daring or dogmatic? Debates on multiculturalism and emancipation in the Netherlands,' *Focaal: European Journal of Anthropology*, 42 (2003): 163–72; Roggeband and Verloo, 'Dutch women are liberated,' 271–88; Anna Korteweg and Gökçe Yurdakul, 'Islam, gender, and immigrant integration: Boundary drawing in discourses on honour killing in the Netherlands and Germany,' *Ethnic and Racial Studies* 32, no. 2 (2009): 218–38; Van den Berg and Schinkel, 'Women from the catacombs,' 393–410; Halleh Ghorashi, 'From absolute invisibility to extreme visibility: Emancipation trajectory of migrant women in the Netherlands,' *Feminist Review* 94, no. 1 (2010): 75–92; Sarah Bracke, 'From "saving women" to "saving gays": Rescue narratives and their discontinuities,' *European Journal of Women's Studies* 19, no. 2 (2012): 237–52.

9. Valuable exceptions are a study by Yolanda van Tilborgh on Muslim women's perceptions of Ayaan Hirsi Ali, and a study by Conny Roggeband on how migrant women's organisations in the Netherlands deal with contradictory government policy frames that simultaneously position migrant women as agents of integration and as passive victims of failed integration. Yolanda van Tilborgh, *Wij Zijn Nederland: Moslima's over Ayaan Hirsi Ali* (Amsterdam: Van Gennep, 2006); Conny Roggeband, 'The victim-agent dilemma: How migrant women's organizations in the Netherlands deal with a contradictory policy frame,' *Signs* 35, no. 4 (2010): 943–67.

10. The research material has been collected as part of a larger, comparative-historical analysis of the dynamics between stereotyping and self-representation of women with a Muslim background in the Netherlands

and Norway between 1975 and 2010: Margaretha A. van Es, *Stereotypes and Self-Representations of Women with a Muslim Background: The Stigma of Being Oppressed* (London: Palgrave Macmillan, 2016). The interviews took place in Spring 2013. All respondents signed an information-consent form before participating in the research project, and all were given the opportunity to check their quotes.

11. International Institute of Social History (IISH), Archive HTKB, File 7, 'HTKB: Turkse Vrouwen Vereniging in Nederland' (1984), 3–4; Atria Institute for Gender Equality and Women's History (Atria), File: NED7 1992, 'Marokkaanse Vrouwen Vereniging Nederland: 10 Jaar 1982–1991' (1992), 2–3; Khadija Arib, *Couscous Op Zondag* (Amsterdam: Balans, 2009), 138–39.

12. 'Wij Zijn Niet Alleen Een Hulpverleningsorganisatie,' *Turkse Vrouwenkrant*, May/June 1982, 10–11; ISSH, Archive HTKB, File 165, 'Werkplan 1983 SMV/MVVN' (1982); IISH, Archive HTKB, File 7, 'HTKB: Turkse Vrouwen Vereniging in Nederland' (1984), 3–4; IISH, Archive HTKB, File 167, 'Evaluatie 1986–1987' (1987); IISH, Archive HTKB, File 2: 'Evaluatie 1989/1990' (1990); Atria, File: NED7 1992, 'Marokkaanse Vrouwen Vereniging Nederland: 10 Jaar 1982–1991' (1992), 2–3; Atria, File: J 144, 'Jaarverslag Marokkaanse Vrouwen Vereniging Nederland 1991' (1992); Atria, File: J 144, 'Jaarverslag Marokkaanse Vrouwen Vereniging Nederland 1993–1994' (1994); Atria, File: J 144, 'Jaarverslag Marokkaanse Vrouwen Vereniging Nederland 1994–1995' (1995).

13. IISH, Archive HTKB, File 164, 'Subsidieaanvraag bij de Gemeente Amsterdam 1980' (1979); IISH, Archive HTKB, File 2, 'Concept Beleidsplan HTKB 1991' (1991); Atria, File: J 144, 'Jaarverslag Marokkaanse Vrouwen Vereniging Nederland 1991' (1992), 12.

14. Dutch Parliament, Kamerstuk 16012–21, *Nota Minderhedenbeleid* (1982–1983): 107, 123–32.

15. IISH, Archive HTKB, File 147, 'Naamswijziging van HTKB naar ATKB' (1995).

16. Sevgi Güngörmüş and Emel Can—ATKB (interviewed together on 19 April 2013).

17. Ikram Chiddi—MVVN (interviewed on 4 June 2013).

18. Atria, File: NED 31 1999—C, 'Conferenctie "De Mudawwanah"' (1999).

19. Justus Uitermark and Frank van Steenbergen, 'Postmulticulturalisme en Stedelijk Burgerschap: Over de Neoliberale Transformatie van het Amsterdamse Integratiebeleid,' *Sociologie* 2, no. 3 (2006): 265–87.

20. Van Es, *Stereotypes and Self-Representations*, 52–53.

21. Sevgi Güngörmüş and Emel Can—ATKB (interviewed together on 19 April 2013); Ikram Chiddi—MVVN (interviewed on 4 June 2013).
22. Ikram Chiddi—MVVN (interviewed on 4 June 2013).
23. Sevgi Güngörmüş and Emel Can—ATKB (interviewed together on 19 April 2013); Ikram Chiddi—MVVN (interviewed on 4 June 2013).
24. ATKB, Annual Report ATKB 2004, 3–16.
25. ATKB, Annual Report ATKB 2008, 6–17.
26. Ikram Chiddi—MVVN (interviewed on 4 June 2013).
27. Sevgi Güngörmüş and Emel Can—ATKB (interviewed together on 19 April 2013); Ikram Chiddi—MVVN (interviewed on 4 June 2013).
28. Ibid.
29. Landelijke Werkgroep Mudawwanah, 'Achtergebleven of Achtergelaten?' (Booklet, 2005); Ikram Chiddi—MVVN (interviewed on 4 June 2013).
30. Sevgi Güngörmüş and Emel Can—ATKB (interviewed together on 19 April 2013); Ikram Chiddi—MVVN (interviewed on 4 June 2013).
31. See, for example, IISH, Archive HTKB, File 242, 'Buitenlandse Vrouwen Kongres op 27 september in Amsterdam,' (1981), 3–4; 'Wij Zijn Niet Alleen Een Hulpverleningsorganisatie,' *Turkse Vrouwenkrant*, May/ June 1982, 10–11; Atria, File: J 144, 'Jaarverslag Marokkaanse Vrouwen Vereniging Nederland 1991' (1992).
32. Atria, File: NED 31 1999–C, 'Conferentie "De Mudawwanah"' (1999). See also, Stichting Landelijke Werkgroep Mudawwanah, 'Mudawwanah: Informatie over het Marokkaanse Familierecht voor Hulpverleners in Nederland' (Booklet, 2004), 9.
33. 'Wat imam vrouwen aandoet wordt te vaak vergeten,' *Trouw*, 22 May 2001, 5.
34. Sevgi Güngörmüş—ATKB (interviewed with Emel Can on 19 April 2013).
35. Ikram Chiddi—MVVN (interviewed on 4 June 2013).
36. Khadija Withagen—Dar al Arqam (interviewed on 17 April 2013); Leyla Çakir—Al Nisa (interviewed on 22 April 2013).
37. 'Al Nisa—Een Terugblik', *Al Nisa*, September/October 1987, 1–3; '10 Jaar Al Nisa—Verleden, Heden en Toekomst,' *Al Nisa*, June 1992, 20; Farhat Khan-Poos—Al Nisa (interviewed on 2 May 2013).
38. 'Abonnementeninformatie', *Al Nisa*, August/September 1987, 1.
39. Khadija Withagen—Dar al Arqam (interviewed on 17 April 2013); Salima Roelse—Dar al Arqam (interviewed on 9 May 2013).
40. Nesrin Altuntaş, Kevser Aktaş, and Saliha Meray—MGVF (interviewed together on 5 June 2013).
41. Thijl Sunier, *Islam in Beweging: Turkse Jongeren en Islamitische Organisaties* (Amsterdam: Het Spinhuis, 1996), 53–55.

42. MGVF, Annual Report MGVF 2008–2009, 3.

43. Farhat Khan-Poos—Al Nisa (interviewed on 2 May 2013).

44. Salima Roelse—Dar al Arqam (interviewed on 9 May 2013).

45. Roggeband, 'The victim-agent dilemma,' 952.

46. Ceylan Weber—Al Nisa (interviewed on 20 June 2013).

47. 'Geweld Tegen Vrouwen in Relaties,' *Al Nisa*, March 2002, 6–18; 'Krachtige Moslimvrouwen? Jazeker!,' *Al Nisa*, September 2002, 7–16; 'In het Web van Tradities: Vrouwen over Meisjesbesnijdenis,' *Al Nisa*, September 2005, 22–26; 'Uithuwelijking en Islam,' *Al Nisa*, January 2006, 6–13; 'Ik Eis Mijn Plek,' *Al Nisa*, June 2006, 20–21; 'Echtscheiding Op Initiatief van de Vrouw: Een Door God Gegeven Recht,' *Al Nisa*, January 2007, 21–23; 'Eergerelateerd Geweld in Nederland,' *Al Nisa*, April 2007, 6–13.

48. Ceylan Weber—Al Nisa (interviewed on 20 June 2013).

49. Miriam Cooke, 'Multiple critique: Islamic feminist rhetorical strategies,' *Nepantla: Views from South* 1, no. 1 (2000): 91–110.

50. Khadija Withagen—Dar al Arqam (interviewed on 17 April 2013); Salima Roelse—Dar al Arqam (interviewed on 9 May 2013).

51. Dar al Arqam, Annual Report Dar al Arqam 2003; Dar al Arqam, 'Jongens en Meisjes: Respect voor Elkaar' (Flyer, 2003).

52. Dar al Arqam, Minutes of the Board Meeting on 11 July 2002.

53. Dar al Arqam, Work Plan 2003–2004; Dar al Arqam, Work Plan 2004–2005.

54. Khadija Withagen—Dar al Arqam (interviewed on 17 April 2013); Salima Roelse—Dar al Arqam (interviewed on 9 May 2013).

55. MGVF, Annual Report MGVF 2008–2009.

56. Nesrin Altuntaş, Kevser Aktaş, and Saliha Meray—MGVF (interviewed together on 5 June 2013).

57. Khadija Withagen—Dar al Arqam (interviewed on 17 April 2013).

58. MGVF, Annual Report MGVF 2008–2009; Nesrin Altuntaş, Kevser Aktaş, and Saliha Meray—MGVF (interviewed together on 5 June 2013).

59. See, for example, 'Geweld tegen Vrouwen in Relaties,' *Al Nisa*, 6–18 March 2002.

60. Prins, *Voorbij de Onschuld*; Prins and Saharso, 'From Toleration to Repression,' 72–91.

61. Nesrin Altuntaş, Kevser Aktaş, and Saliha Meray—MGVF (interviewed together on 5 June 2013); Ceylan Weber—Al Nisa (interviewed on 20 June 2013).

PART V

Global Perspectives

The final section of this book offers a global view of migration. It would be paradoxical in a volume like this one to simply limit ourselves to geographical regions—they are no less of an artificial creation that the national borders that, we argue, have played too important a role in shaping historical enquiry. The following three chapters show how thinking about migration through national borders can reshape our understanding of the modern world.

The first contribution, Julian M. Simpson's 'Migrant Doctors and the "Frontiers of Medicine" in Westernised Healthcare Systems' looks at the work of migrants as a defining feature of global healthcare, pointing to how population movement is closely connected to the way the world economy functions. As in other parts of the economy, migrants in medicine are disproportionately represented in roles that are constructed as undesirable. Any productive discussion about migratory movements needs to incorporate an understanding of the social and economic function of migrants in modern economies.

In 'The Right to Asylum: A Hidden History', Klaus Neumann argues that revisiting the history of the right to asylum (claimed by individuals) and the right of asylum (as bestowed by states) can bring to the fore different ways of thinking about present responses to movements of refugees. Neumann suggests that a productive way forward can be found in a renewed focus on the rights and needs of refugees—and by paying less heed to emotional responses and presumed impacts (positive or otherwise) on nation-states.

Finally, in the concluding chapter, Donna Gabaccia asks 'Will the Twenty-First Century World Embrace Immigration History?'. She offers a reminder that scholarly work is also the product of the social and cultural environment that it is produced in. This book has aimed to show how migration history can contribute to our understanding of the world. It is worth remembering that this will only happen if and when there is a climate that allows a global body of work to develop. This means that the process whereby history can inform policy and public debate is two-way: scholars can seek to make their work relevant but ultimately for their work to make a difference, there will need to be a shift in policy-makers' attitudes towards immigration and its role in national narratives. Starting these conversations, and taking our place in public debates, is, however, ultimately an optimistic and potentially transformative action.

CHAPTER 10

Migrant Doctors and the 'Frontiers of Medicine' in Westernised Healthcare Systems

Julian M. Simpson

Drawing on the emerging historical scholarship and using data from the much wider social science literature, this chapter argues that the migration of doctors should be conceptualised as taking place not just across borders, but in a transnational space within which international medical graduates circulate. Migration is not a marginal phenomenon in this context, nor one that can be treated in isolation. It is at the heart of what Westernised healthcare is: a system of delivery of treatment that socialises doctors in a particular way and leads them to value their professional status and middle-class lifestyles. They also afford higher status to certain types of clinical interventions. Migrant doctors are as a result often found in the 'frontier' zones of Westernised medicine: the spaces that have historically been low status for socio-professional reasons. Recognising the specific positions that migrants have taken on in medicine can in turn help to stimulate a wider discussion about the roles that migrants have

J. M. Simpson (✉)
Lancaster, Lancashire, UK

© The Author(s) 2019
E. Henrich and J. M. Simpson (eds.),
History, Historians and the Immigration Debate,
https://doi.org/10.1007/978-3-319-97123-0_10

played over time in Western societies and a consequent reassessment of their position in national historical and political narratives.

The international migration of doctors is a large-scale phenomenon that underpins healthcare systems around the world. Many countries export significant numbers of doctors, import a large proportion of their medical workforce or find themselves in the position of doing both. Over 220,000 foreign-born doctors are, for instance, practising in the US[1]—a number which is roughly equivalent to the entire population of Baton Rouge, the capital of the state of Louisiana.

This movement can hardly be said to have gone unnoticed and a vast social science literature addresses it. However, to echo the points that Donna Gabaccia makes in her contribution to this book, discussions about 'brain drain' (or increasingly 'brain circulation' in recognition of return migration and consecutive migrations) and the global movement of medical graduates tend to be ahistorical and shaped by methodological nationalism.[2] There has been too little focus on what can be learnt from a historically informed reflection on the roles played by medical migrants in a global context. What we therefore lack is a sense of the structural impact that migrants have had globally, over time, on Westernized medical systems as a result of the fact that they have historically been over-represented in particular sections of them. Moreover, not only do medical migrants frequently find themselves in less desirable roles and geographical areas, but they also shy away from taking on such roles in the countries they leave behind. It is not just that migrants work in the less popular jobs, but that globally, there is a tendency for these jobs to be avoided even if this results in doctors leaving their country of birth and training. If one considers this phenomenon over time and from a global perspective, it appears as a central dimension of Westernised healthcare systems—defined as systems of healthcare delivery either located in the West or fundamentally shaped by Western biomedical values. Understanding the development of healthcare thus involves not just thinking in time, but rethinking medical labour markets as being quintessentially transnational.[3]

Recent historical research suggests that it is helpful to draw on the notion of 'dirty work' in medicine when analysing the movement of doctors and their role in the shaping of Westernised healthcare systems at a global level.[4] It helps to understand how particular types of work can be constructed as undesirable in the context of Western medical culture. Naturally, not all migrant doctors can be considered to be part of what Parvati Raghuram calls a 'reserve army of medical labour'.[5] Some occupy privileged positions in prestigious institutions. What I want to discuss here, however, is not individual trajectories, but historical continuities and parallels in the deployment of a significant proportion of the medical migrant workforce across time and space and the questions they should lead to us to ask of Western medical culture in particular and attitudes towards immigration in the global North more generally. In essence, this history points to a tension between materially affluent countries needing significant numbers of workers to fulfil specific roles whilst remaining wedded to notions of stable and homogenous national communities.

I start by outlining in more detail the nature and global scale of medical migration before describing the patterns that characterise it. I conclude by discussing what meaning we might attach to this movement—both as far as the culture of medicine is concerned and more broadly when it comes to writing the history of migration—and how it might be relevant to our engagement with policies and discourses concerned with immigration.

Medical Migration, Historical Context and Global Impact

The study of the history of medical migration is not a niche preoccupation: the movement of doctors has become a significant feature of Westernised healthcare systems and by extension of life (and death) in the twenty first century. A better understanding of its historical and global dimensions can therefore significantly contribute to contemporary thinking when it comes to debates on immigration.

A professed ability to treat the sick has always made it possible for individuals to move and build lives elsewhere. This is true of contemporary practitioners of biomedicine as it was of Greek doctors in Ancient Rome and is of African traditional healers in Paris or Montreal today. Moreover, the culture of Western science and medicine has long been international. As Alfonso Mejia of the World Health Organisation's Division of Health Manpower Development put it in an article on the migration of physicians and nurses in the *International Journal of Epidemiology* in 1978: 'Learned men have always travelled abroad seeking a more congenial intellectual milieu to realise their full potential.'[6] In this context, a medical degree is akin to a visa that enables its holder to cross borders at will, or certainly with a freedom denied the vast majority of the citizens of the world.

Empire was instrumental in reinforcing the global nature of Western medicine as an element of the dominant culture exported by colonial powers.[7] The movement of doctors formed a key part of this process. Within the British sphere of influence, graduates of Scottish medical schools who settled in different parts of the world were particularly influential as imperial agents.[8] Colonial Ireland exported significant numbers of its medical graduates: around fifty per cent of them were practising abroad, for instance, as the nineteenth century gave way to the twentieth.[9] From the nineteenth century onwards, colonial subjects, be they from the West Indies or the Indian subcontinent, were also leaving their place of birth to study medicine—either because of the lack of local opportunities for training or because of the prestige associated with qualifications obtained in the imperial metropole.[10] Over time, this led to what Roger Jeffery has described in the context of the Indian subcontinent as the institutionalisation of medical dependency: the establishment of medical systems whose values were formed by imperial powers and whose priorities were aligned with those of the West rather than local contexts.[11] Current migratory flows offer echoes of these legacies. Countries formerly part of the British Empire (such as Australia, Canada, the US and indeed the UK itself) are some of the biggest importers of medical labour. India remains one of the world's principal exporters of doctors,[12] many of whom build careers in the United Kingdom. Nor are these imperial legacies limited to the British context: Algerian doctors are an important source of medical labour in France.[13]

The influence of other forms of political and cultural domination is also in evidence. One of the other main groups of migrant doctors in France is made up of physicians who qualified in Romania,[14] a member of the *Organisation Internationale de la Francophonie* (the international body that promotes French culture and the international use of the French language). Germany, for its part, attracts migrant doctors principally from Austria, Poland, Russia, Ukraine, the Czech Republic and Slovakia—countries which are all within its traditional sphere of influence. More prosaically, the fact that English has become the dominant international language also favours the movement of doctors towards high-income Anglophone countries. The current cross-border movement of doctors, to be properly understood, requires to be placed in its historical context, even if it naturally takes on distinctive and complex contemporary forms—financial considerations and changes to the nature of global travel have, for instance, played a part in the professional trajectories of clinicians. The international culture of medicine and established historical patterns and cultural links have nevertheless made it possible for countries to draw on a migrant workforce to meet the needs of their healthcare systems.

This pattern has been an important dimension of the development of Westernized medical systems over the course of the past fifty years. In the 1970s, the World Health Organisation estimated that at least 140,000 medics were based in countries other than those of which they were nationals or in which they were either born and/or had trained—a number which equated to 6% of the world's physicians.[15] Three countries accounted for over three quarters of these doctors: the USA (approximately 68,000 in 1972), the UK (21,000 in 1970) and Canada (9000 in 1971).[16] Other major destinations for migrant doctors included the Federal Republic of Germany (6000 in 1971) and Australia (4000 in 1972).[17]

International comparisons can, of course, be misleading as official statistics have in some cases minimised the importance of medical migration. In Switzerland, for example, it is estimated that around 4000 migrant doctors employed as assistants in hospitals are not counted.[18] In France, the CNOM (*Conseil National de l'Ordre des Médecins*, The National Council for the Medical Profession) stated in 2013 that a large number of foreign doctors found themselves working in hospitals, where they were helping to fill vacant posts, without appearing on the official medical register.[19]

What is beyond doubt is that even if medical migration has in the past tended to be particularly high in affluent Anglophone countries, it is now a quasi-universal and large-scale phenomenon, giving rise to the emergence of what might be described as a global healthcare system.[20] Migration from China and Eastern European countries has grown and countries such as Japan have begun to import greater numbers of medical graduates.[21] The beneficiaries of these flows are still mainly affluent OECD countries, but countries such as Turkey, Mexico and Greece have also been importing increasing numbers of doctors and migration to the Gulf States has grown in importance since the 1960s.[22] The *International Migration Outlook 2015* report published by the OECD, the Organisation for Economic Co-operation and Development, an international organisation that brings together thirty-five of the world's most affluent countries, provides a telling insight into the scale of con-temporary medical migration. On average, one fifth of doctors in OECD countries are foreign-born. Medical migrants now account for over half of all physicians in Australia and New Zealand, just under half in Israel, around a third in the UK and Canada, approximately 30% in Sweden, a quarter of the US physician workforce and around one fifth of doctors in Norway, France and Slovenia.[23]

This movement is not simply about migration from less materially wealthy to more affluent countries. There are, for instance, over 19,000 overseas doctors in Germany and approximately the same number of German practitioners based abroad.[24] In 2005, according to research published in the *New England Journal of Medicine*, physicians from the United Kingdom were the largest group of migrant doctors in Canada and Australia and physicians from Canada were the fifth largest group of international medical graduates in the US.[25] Much of this movement is, however, from the global South to the global North: according to the same study, just under 60,000 Indian doctors were working in the US, the UK, Canada and Australia and there were 1589 Jamaican doctors practising in these countries as compared to 2253 working in Jamaica itself.[26]

These doctors are important to the medical systems in which they operate (and those that they leave behind), of course, but their num-bers are also significant in absolute terms: they form a relatively high proportion of the migrant population in a number of countries in the global North. If migrants in general tend to be marginalised by histori-ans as noted by Henrich and Simpson,[27] the invisibility of middle-class migrants in accounts of the past is arguably even more striking.

THE TRIAD OF MEDICAL 'DIRTY WORK'

However, these numbers merely give a partial sense of the importance of the international movement of doctors and only form part of the argu-ment for the need to take their impact into consideration when writing accounts of the development of Westernised healthcare systems. As Oscar Gish and Martin Godfrey have pointed out, what is particularly interest-ing about medical migration is not so much the phenomenon in and of itself, but what it tells us about particular healthcare systems in specific social and political contexts.[28] Whilst this has been noted by some social scientists, historians have by and large paid little attention to the issue of how the specific nature of the labour provided by migrants has been at the heart of the development of healthcare in Westernised delivery systems. If we think of a healthcare system as a building, taking migrants out of the equation is not akin to removing the top one or two floors. Because they play such specific roles, it would be more like removing a number of walls, resulting in the sustainability of the edifice itself being under threat.

Whilst we do not have a global database charting precisely where international medical graduates have worked and the posts that they fill, and whilst variations undoubtedly have occurred and continue to occur across time and space, there is a significant amount of evidence, which I will outline in this section, that testifies to the fact that their labour is frequently 'special' rather than 'additional' labour.[29] In other words, as is often the case in other sectors of the economy, medical migrants have tended to be disproportionately represented in roles that involve doing the 'dirty work' of medicine in the sociological sense—i.e. performing functions that are seen as undesirable and as not fully meeting the aspirations of locally trained doctors.[30] Dirty work in this context, as I will show, broadly takes three forms: working in particular medical specialties that are viewed as less prestigious, occupying junior positions in the medical hierarchy, and being based in particular geographical areas (namely areas that are less materially affluent, far from major centres of population or both).

In a sense, this is not particularly surprising. As in other sectors of the economy, opportunities for outsiders arise because those who have the advantages of local networks and cultural capital have not taken them up. The movement of doctors takes place within a global context shaped by Western medicine and a social and professional ethos that values particular interventions and urban middle-class lifestyles. Time-limited and complex interventions that involve younger patients and focused on the upper part of the body are viewed as more prestigious than those involving chronic conditions and older patients.[31] Healthcare professionals are also over-represented in urban and wealthy areas and there is a resultant global shortage of clinicians in rural communities.[32] Maintaining a global perspective thus enables us to resist any temptation to see migrant doctors who end up doing 'dirty work' in the global North as heroic: they have in fact left behind countries where there is also abundant medical 'dirty work' to be done. Indeed, these common values are so influential and widely shared by the medical profession in Westernised medical systems that they have allowed the emergence of a Cuban counter-model which trains large numbers of doctors who work with less affluent and rural populations both in Cuba and internationally.[33] As the title of a book about them suggests, they go 'where no other doctor has gone before'[34]—to areas such as rural Zimbabwe or the materially deprived north-east of Brazil.[35]

Whilst the global history of this movement is still emergent, its relevance to our understanding of the broader history of healthcare and its potential to speak to contemporary debates about immigration are already apparent. When read in conjunction with a body of social science evidence dating back to the 1960s, the historical evidence points unambiguously to the centrality of medical migration to the provision of healthcare in Westernised systems, particularly when it comes to what can be termed the 'frontiers of medicine': low-status specialties and populations and geographical areas that are unattractive to doctors. An additional dimension of this phenomenon is the concentration of migrant doctors in junior roles which are also perceived as less prestigious.

Historical research conducted in the UK in the past decade provides ample evidence that they were both providing 'special' labour and, as a result, having a profound effect on the development of the National Health Service (NHS) following its establishment in 1948.[36] The triad of dirty work (unpopular specialties/unfavoured geographical locations/lower rungs of the profession) is clearly in evidence when it comes to the history of the NHS. Unpopular medical fields such as psychiatry, geriatrics and general practice have traditionally relied on migrants and offered them a career path.[37] Within those specialties, there were, however, significant variations in the concentration of migrant labour depending on geographical location. In general practice, for instance, the number of South Asian-trained GPs working in health authorities ranged from around 1% in more affluent/rural areas to a third and in some cases over 50% in urban/less affluent areas.[38] Migrant doctors were represented in much greater numbers in junior roles: in 1974, they held 50% of senior house officer posts and 60% of registrar posts (i.e. junior positions) as opposed to 16% of all consultant (i.e. senior) posts.[39]

Oral history research into the role of South Asian migrant doctors in the UK has also placed them at the centre of the history of the development of the specialty of geriatrics. As one South Asian doctor put it,

'The local boys wouldn't touch it [the discipline] with a bargepole' and geriatrics was able to emerge as a specialised field as a result of the willingness of thousands of junior doctors from the Indian subcontinent to specialise in the field.[40] Twenty-two per cent of senior geriatricians appointed between 1964 and 2001 in the NHS had trained outside the UK—as compared to 14.1% of all senior positions.[41] As a result, South Asian-trained doctors played what can be termed a constitutive role in the NHS, not only providing essential labour, but also influencing practice by, for instance, establishing new geriatrics departments and being involved in the work of the British Geriatric Society.[42]

Research into the historical roles of migrant doctors in Canada highlights not only parallels, but also differences with the British model. Less affluent provinces such as Newfoundland and Saskatchewan, with low-density populations and where doctors' incomes were lower, were the most active recruiters of migrant doctors in the post-war period.[43] These migrant doctors were notably deployed in primary care in rural areas away from major conurbations, and in the words of John Clarke and David Wright, 'helped to fill the holes in the emerging system of universal health care.'[44] In contrast to the strong patterns of clustering found in the UK, for instance in cities such as Manchester,[45] the historical evidence from Canada shows, however, that once migrant doctors were in the country, many of them were able to move to more affluent areas and practise there, including in more prestigious and well-remunerated specialties.[46] The effect of the triad of dirty work is nevertheless still in evidence: it was due to the shortages in particular parts of Canada that migrants were able to obtain their first opportunities and they played an important part in the development of care in rural parts of the country.

Additional fragmentary historical evidence bears witness to the fact that other migrant doctors found themselves working at the frontiers of medicine. Paul Weindling, in his work on doctors who came to the British Isles as refugees from Nazism, notes that psychiatry and pharmacology were two of the 'accommodating' specialties that provided openings for them.[47] He also reports that a number of refugee physicians ended up in under-supplied territories such as Newfoundland or in locations such as Shanghai, Hong Kong and Burma, which were strategically vulnerable and all succumbed to Japanese occupation during World War II.[48] John Weaver's account of the flight of medical refugees to Australia and New Zealand in the 1930s and 1940s provides evidence of doctors working as 'unregistered' practitioners, one of them describing himself as the only doctor in the neighbourhood (he was based in Fletcher Street in the working-class Sydney district of Bondi).[49]

As this history develops and encompasses the functions of different types of migrant doctors in different contexts at different points in time, it will undoubtedly give us a greater understanding of their varied professional trajectories. International medical graduates make up a hugely diverse group and it would be surprising if the experiences of white Anglophone migrants in Canada or New Zealand did not differ in some respects from those of non-white doctors in the UK whose careers were profoundly shaped by racism.[50] This perhaps serves to explain why there has been a debate amongst social scientists about the extent to which medical migrants help to address imbalances in the distribution of doctors.[51]

J. Ross Barnett, in a study of international medical graduates in New Zealand in the 1970s, concluded that the distribution of migrant doctors was likely to be influenced by the overall doctor supply and the level of competition they faced from local graduates.[52] He also noted that in Auckland, the country's largest city, the majority of the redistributive effect of medical migration on the availability of general practitioners in less affluent areas could be attributed to the presence of large numbers of graduates from Asian medical schools.[53] If its precise nature will only be determined by future research, the impact of migrant doctors on specific types of care is, however, evidenced by a vast body of social science literature that places international medical graduates squarely at the centre of the development of healthcare provision—in the sense that they are clearly indispensable to the delivery of certain types of care in particular areas.

Aboriginal medical services in rural parts of Australia thus rely heavily on overseas-trained doctors.[54] A study of non-EU migrant doctors in Ireland found that they believed that they had been recruited to fill junior hospital doctor 'service' posts, unpopular with local graduates because of the limited opportunities that they offer for career progression.[55] The authors noted that reliance on these doctors to fill such posts persisted, although Ireland was theoretically training enough doctors to staff its health service.[56] Saudi Arabia is greatly dependent on medical migrants who in 1997 made up 81% of the total number of doctors in the country.[57] All of these doctors were on temporary contracts, although in some cases they had been in the country for a number of decades.[58] Indian doctors working in Riyadh reported facing discrimination when it came to promotion and pay—in the view of the majority of respondents this was because of ethnic differences.[59]

There is also a significant amount of evidence that points to the 'special' nature of the labour provided by migrant doctors in the US, the world's largest importer of medical labour. Between 2003 and 2015, international medical graduates accounted for 1.5% of matched residents (i.e. doctors offered a specialist postgraduate training position) in radiation oncology, 2.7% of matched residents in plastic surgery and 6.7% of matched residents in neurosurgery.[60] The equivalent figures for psychiatry, family medicine and internal medicine were 26, 35.7 and 37.1%, respectively.[61] A study of medical migrants in Michigan published in 1978 had already concluded that the state was dependent on their labour, in particular when it came to provision in psychiatry and to the staffing of inner-city hospitals in the industrial city of Detroit and its surrounding area.[62] A study of migrant doctors in Maryland in the same year concluded that migrant doctors 'serve population segments and fill specialty slots not served and filled by USMGs [US medical graduates]', even though distribution varied from one area to the next.[63] It also noted that concentrations of migrant graduates in less affluent areas could be masked in statistics when aggregated with figures for low income areas served by a prestigious university hospital (which would be more attractive to US graduates).[64] A US-wide study of 'alien doctors' also published in the late 1970s came to a similar conclusion: 'the presence of FMGs [foreign medical graduates] camouflages the decision-making effects of USMGs. If there were no FMGs and the existing system of allocating USMGs remained unchanged, states such as New York, Illinois, New Jersey and Michigan would have critically large numbers of vacant positions'.[65]

Memoirs and accounts of life in particular hospitals add to this picture. Diana Dosie, a nurse interviewed for Sydney Lewis' oral history of Cook County hospital in Chicago, a public hospital where many patients are poor and/or without access to private healthcare, reported that amongst the hospital staff, there were 'a lot of foreign doctors, Black doctors, Indian doctors.'[66] Abraham Verghese, in his memoir of work in deprived areas and city hospitals in the US, recalled that in one hospital there were so many South Asian practitioners that those who had the common surname Patel were referred to by their name and specialty—i.e. 'pulmonary Patel' or 'urology Patel'.[67]

Conclusion

There have historically been gaps in Western and Westernized medical systems between the requirements of delivery and the socio-professional aspirations of doctors. Recourse to migration has traditionally offered a way of addressing these gaps. The history of healthcare provision in Westernized healthcare systems is therefore to a great extent also the history of the migration of doctors—and by extension the migration of other healthcare professionals. They have played important roles at the frontiers of medicine. Establishing the precise nature of these roles, how they have varied from one country and one era to the next, would shed significant new light on the development of global healthcare—not least because this history is also the history of a global flight from care. At the heart of this history of migration is a history of absences: those of the medical graduates who did not take on the roles filled by migrants and those of the migrants themselves who chose to build careers in other countries rather than find work in their countries of origin.

Focusing on the ways in which medical migrants have contributed to the development of healthcare provision also points to the fact that it is possible to write histories of migration that dismantle the barriers between population movement and national narratives, thus contributing to the task outlined in the chapters by Henrich and Simpson and by Lucassen of moving 'beyond the apocalypse' to bring migration history into the historical and political mainstream.[68] In fact, focusing on the labour market in general offers a way of doing this. If migrants do the 'dirty work' of medicine, the same, of course, is true in other sectors of modern economies. By studying the history of migrants and work, we cast our gaze towards their interactions with the mainstream, rather than what defines them as outsiders. Such an approach can serve to highlight the contradiction between political discourses emphasising national identity and the need to control borders and the requirements of national labour markets that have long been dependent on international recruitment.

This is not simply of relevance in the context of so-called 'highly skilled' migrants such as doctors. Migrant women, for instance, play an important part in providing low-paid caring services in the UK.[69] Recognising the specific nature of the work done by migrants and its historical significance can thus contribute to a reflection around different imagined communities that locate migrants within national narratives.

Leo Lucassen's point about historians' tendency to focus excessively on the 'problematic' migrants that attract the attention of governments is particularly relevant in this context.[70] If conflict and difference make for interesting subject matter, engaging with the professional impact of migrants over time offers an alternative perspective on migration that can serve to place it at the heart of accounts of national development, rather than on the margins. Migration has come to be constructed as a problem in the global North. It is time we reached a better understanding of the ways it has served to offer solutions to economic and social dilemmas. This in turn, would usefully inform our thinking about future approaches to migration policy.

NOTES

1. OECD, *International Migration Outlook 2015* (Paris: OECD Publishing, 2015), 113.
2. Donna Gabaccia, this volume.
3. Parvati Raghuram, 'Reconceptualising UK's transnational medical labour market,' in *The International Migration of Health Workers*, ed. John Connell (New York and London: Routledge, 2012), 182–98.
4. Julian M. Simpson, Stephanie J. Snow, and Aneez Esmail, 'Providing "special" types of labour and exerting agency: How migrant doctors have shaped the United Kingdom's National Health Service,' in *Doctors Beyond Borders: The Transnational Migration of Physicians in the Twentieth Century*, eds. Laurence Monnais and David Wright (Toronto: University of Toronto Press, 2016), 208–29; and Julian M. Simpson, *Migrant Architects of the NHS: South Asian Doctors and the Reinvention of British General Practice (1940s–1980s)* (Manchester: Manchester University Press, 2018).
5. Raghuram, 'Reconceptualising,' 194–95.
6. Alfonso Mejia, 'Migration of physicians and nurses: A world wide picture,' *International Journal of Epidemiology 7*, no. 3 (1978): 207.
7. Pratik Chakrabarti, *Medicine and Empire 1600–1960* (Basingstoke and New York: Palgrave Macmillan, 2013).
8. Laurence Monnais and David Wright, 'Introduction,' in *Doctors Beyond Borders*, eds. Monnais and Wright, 6.
9. Monnais and Wright, 'Introduction,' in *Doctors Beyond Borders*, eds. Monnais and Wright, 6.
10. Raghuram, 'Reconceptualising,' 185–86; and Juanita de Barros 'Imperial connections and Caribbean Medicine, 1900–1938,' in *Doctors Beyond Borders*, eds. Monnais and Wright, 20–41.

11. Roger Jeffery, 'Recognizing India's doctors: The institutionalisation of medical dependency, 1918–39,' *Modern Asian Studies* 13, no. 2 (1979): 301–26.

12. OECD, *International Migration*, 129.

13. OECD, *International Migration*, 125.

14. OECD, *International Migration*, 125.

15. Mejia, 'Migration of physicians,' 208.

16. Mejia, 'Migration of physicians,' 208.

17. Mejia, 'Migration of physicians,' 208.

18. OECD, *International Migration*, 117.

19. *Le Figaro*, 'De plus en plus de médecins étrangers en France,' 4 June 2013, http://sante.lefigaro.fr/actualite/2013/06/04/20705-plus-plus-medecins-etrangers-france.

20. John Connell, 'Toward a global health care system?,' in *The International Migration of Health Workers*, ed. John Connell (London and New York: Routledge, 2012), 1–29.

21. Connell 'Global health care system,' 1.

22. OECD, *International Migration*, 108; and Connell 'Global health care system,' 5.

23. OECD, *International Migration*, 111.

24. T. Kopetsch, 'The migration of doctors to and from Germany,' *Journal of Public Health* 17 (2009): 34, 37.

25. Fitzhugh Mullan, 'The metrics of the physician brain drain,' *The New England Journal of Medicine* 353 (2005): 1814.

26. Mullan, 'Physician brain drain,' 1814.

27. Eureka Henrich and Julian M. Simpson, 'From the margins of history to the political mainstream: Putting migration history centre stage,' this volume.

28. Oscar Gish and Martin Godfrey, 'A reappraisal of the "Brain Drain"—with special reference to the medical profession,' *Social Science and Medicine* 130 (1979): 1.

29. Stephen Castles and Mark J. Miller, *The Age of Migration: International Population Movements in the Modern World*, 4th ed. (Basingstoke: Palgrave, 2009), 242.

30. Julian M. Simpson, 'Where are UK trained doctors? The migrant care law and its implications for the NHS,' *BMJ* 361, k2336 (2018). On the notion of 'dirty work' see E.C. Hughes, *Men and Their Work* (Westport, CT: Greenwood, 1958); and R. Simpson, N. Slutskaya, P. Lewis, and H. Höpfl, eds., *Dirty Work: Concepts and Identities* (Palgrave, 2012 [ebook]), http://www.palgrave.com/br/book/9780230277137.

31. Dag Album and Steinar Westin, 'Do diseases have a prestige hierarchy? A survey among physicians and medical students,' *Social Science and Medicine* 66 (2008): 182; and Marie Norredam and Dag Album,

'Prestige and its significance for medical specialties and diseases,' *Scandinavian Journal of Public Health* 35 (2007): 655–61.

32. N.W. Wilson, I.D. Couper, E. De Vries, S. Reid, T. Fish, and B.J. Marais, 'A critical review of interventions to redress the inequitable distribution of healthcare professionals to rural and remote areas', *Rural and Remote Health* 9, no. 1060 (2009); Hannah Bradby, 'A review of research and policy documents on the international migration of physicians and nurses,' Max Planck Institute for the study of religious and ethnic diversity, MMG Working Paper 13–07, http://www.mmg.mpg.de/fileadmin/user_upload/documents/wp/WP_13-07_Bradby_A-Review-of-Research.pdf.

33. Steve Brouwer, *Revolutionary Doctors: How Venezuela and Cuba Are Changing the World's Conception of Health Care* (New York: Monthly Review Press, 2011); and Robert Huish, *Where No Doctor Has Gone Before: Cuba's Place in the Global Health Landscape* (Waterloo, ON: Wilfred Laurier University Press, 2013).

34. Huish, *Where no Doctor Has Gone Before.*

35. Abel Chikanda, 'The migration of health professionals from Zimbabwe,' in *The International Migration of Health Workers*, ed. Connell, 125; and *The Guardian*, 'Plan to hire 6000 Cuban doctors attacked,' 8 May 2013: 18.

36. Simpson et al., 'Special types of labour'.

37. Simpson et al., 'Special types of labour,' 216.

38. Simpson et al., 'Special types of labour,' 216.

39. Simpson et al., 'Special types of labour,' 216.

40. Joanna Bornat, Parvati Raghuram, and Leroi Henry, '"Without racism there would be no geriatrics": South Asian overseas-trained doctors and the development of geriatric medicine in the United Kingdom 1950–2000,' in *Doctors Beyond Borders*, eds. Monnais and Wright, 189.

41. Joanna Bornat, Leroi Henry, and Parvati Raghuram, 'The making of careers and the making of a discipline: Luck and chance in migrant careers in geriatric medicine,' *Journal of Vocational Behaviour* 78 (2011): 344.

42. Bornat et al., 'The making of careers,' 343–44.

43. Sasha Mullally and David Wright, 'La Grande Séduction? The immigration of foreign-trained physicians to Canada, c. 1954–76,' *Journal of Canadian Studies* 41, no. 3 (2007): 69.

44. John Clarke and David Wright, 'Too many doctors? Foreign medical graduates and the debate over health care accessibility in Canada, c. 1976–1991,' *Canadian Bulletin of Medical History* 30, no. 1 (2013): 182.

45. Emma L. Jones and Stephanie J. Snow, *Against the Odds: Black and Minority Ethnic Clinicians and Manchester, 1948 to 2009* (Lancaster: Carnegie, 2010).

46. Mullally and Wright, 'La Grande Séduction?,' 69; David Wright and Sasha Mullally, '"Not everyone can be a Gandhi": South Asian-trained doctors

immigrating to Canada, c. 1961–1971,' *Ethnicity and Health* 12, no. 4 (2016) [online].

47. Paul Weindling, 'Medical refugees and the modernisation of British medicine, 1930–1960,' *Social History of Medicine* 22, no. 3 (2009): 505.

48. Paul Weindling, 'Medical Refugees in Britain and the wider world 1930–1960: Introduction,' *Social History of Medicine* 22, no. 3 (2009): 455–56.

49. John Weaver, 'Pathways of perseverance: Medical refugee flights to Australia and New Zealand, 1933–1945,' in *Doctors Beyond Borders*, eds. Monnais and Wright, 57.

50. Bornat et al., '"Without racism"'; Simpson, *Migrant Architects*; and Simpson et al., 'Special types of labour'.

51. J. Ross Barnett, 'Foreign medical graduates in New Zealand 1973–79: A test of the "exacerbation hypothesis",' *Social Science and Medicine* 26, no. 10 (1988): 1049–60; and Vivek Verma, Chirag Shah, Tim Lautenschlaeger, Chi Lin, Sushil Beriwal, Weining Zhen, Minesh P. Mehta, and Anthony L. Zietman, 'International medical graduates in radiation oncology: Historical trends and comparison with other medical specialties,' *International Journal of Radiation Oncology Biology Physics* 95, no. 4 (2016): 1106.

52. Barnett, 'Foreign medical graduates,' 1058.

53. Barnett, 'Foreign medical graduates,' 1057–58.

54. Marisa T. Gilles, John Wakerman, and Angela Durey, '"If it wasn't for OTDs, there would be no AMS": Overseas-trained doctors working in rural and remote Aboriginal health settings,' *Australian Health Review* 32, no. 4 (2008): 655–63.

55. Niamh Humphries, Ella Tyrell, Sara McAleese, Posy Bidwell, Steve Thomas, Charles Normand, and Ruairi Brugha, 'A cycle of brain gain, waste and drain—A qualitative study of non-EU migrant doctors in Ireland,' *Human Resources for Health* 11, no. 63 (2013) [online].

56. Humphries et al., 'A cycle of brain gain'.

57. S.I. Alkhudairy, 'International labour migration to Saudi Arabia: A case study of the experiences of medical doctors in Riyadh' (PhD thesis, University of Essex, 2001), 8.

58. Alkhudairy, 'International labour migration,' 8.

59. Alkhudairy, 'International labour migration,' 141–42, 152.

60. Verma et al., 'International medical graduates,' 1105.

61. Verma et al., International medical graduates,' 1105.

62. Irene Butter, George Wright, and Diane Tasca, 'FMGs in Michigan: A case of dependence,' *Inquiry* 15, no. 1 (1978): 53.

63. Robert M. Politzer, James S. Morrow, and Ruth K. Sudia, 'Foreign-trained physicians in American medicine: A case study,' *Medical Care* 16, no. 8 (1978): 626.

64. Politzer et al., 'Foreign-trained physicians in American medicine,' 626.
65. Rosemary Stevens, Louis Wolf Goodman, and Stephen S. Mick, *The Alien Doctors: Foreign Medical Graduates in American Hospitals* (New York: Wiley, 1978), 265.
66. Sydney Lewis, *Hospital: An Oral History of Cook County Hospital* (New York: The New Press, 1994), 17.
67. A. Verghese, *My Own Country: A Doctor's Story of a Town and Its People in the Age of AIDS* (Phoenix: London, 1995 [1994]), 12.
68. Henrich and Simpson, 'From the margins of history'; and Leo Lucassen, this volume.
69. Linda McDowell, *Working Lives: Gender, Migration and Employment in Britain 1945–2007* (Chichester: Wiley-Blackwell, 2013), 215.
70. Lucassen, this volume.

CHAPTER 11

The Right to Asylum: A Hidden History

Klaus Neumann

The 25-page New York Declaration for Refugees and Migrants, which was prepared for the September 2016 United Nations Summit for Refugees and Migrants, makes only two brief references to asylum. The assembled heads of state committed to address the irregular movement of people 'without prejudice to the right to seek asylum' and 'reaffirm[ed] respect for the institution of asylum and the right to seek asylum'.[1] This lack of attention to the concept of asylum is arguably curious, given that the 'unprecedented level of human mobility',[2] including the large movements of forcibly displaced people, which the summit was trying to

Research for this chapter was supported by Australian Research Council (ARC) discovery grants. I benefited greatly from discussions I had with Savitri Taylor, who has been collaborating with me on a project about the history of the right to asylum.

K. Neumann (✉)
Hamburger Stiftung zur Förderung von Wissenschaft und Kultur, Hamburg, Germany

K. Neumann
Contemporary Histories Research Group, Deakin University, Melbourne, VIC, Australia

© The Author(s) 2019
E. Henrich and J. M. Simpson (eds.),
History, Historians and the Immigration Debate,
https://doi.org/10.1007/978-3-319-97123-0_11

address, is marked not least by a significant increase in the number of persons seeking asylum, particularly in the industrialised world.

The wording of these references is also ambiguous. What does it mean to reaffirm one's respect for the right to seek asylum, without, however, endorsing that right itself? Which previous affirmations of that right did the authors of the declaration have in mind? And given that there is no reference to a right to enjoy, let alone be granted asylum, does the statement refer primarily to the rights of those seeking asylum, or to the rights of nation-states willing and able to grant such requests?

In this chapter, I explore the rise and decline of the right to grant asylum (to which I refer as the 'right of asylum') and the right to seek, enjoy and be granted asylum (the 'right to asylum'). I also discuss references to the history of these rights in public debate. I do so by drawing on examples from Australia, a country that over the past 70 years has been prominently involved in international discussions about the rights of refugees and other migrants, and the concomitant rights and obligations of nation-states, but which has also always been particularly insistent on its prerogative as a sovereign nation to control access to its territory.

CONSTRUCTING A GENEALOGY OF THE RIGHT TO ASYLUM IN 2006 AND 1935

Australia's controversial post-2001 extraterritorial processing and detention regime is often associated with the unauthorised arrival of people from the Middle East and Central and South Asia who tried to seek asylum in Australia after travelling there by boat from Indonesia. Despite its comparative geographical isolation, however, Australia has also been a country of first asylum, particularly for refugees from Indonesia or territories occupied by it. Many of them have been West Papuans, inhabitants of the former Dutch colony of West New Guinea (today's Papua), which was seized by Indonesia in 1962, and formally incorporated into Indonesia in 1969.[3] In January 2006, 43 West Papuans landed on the coast of Queensland, close to the northeastern tip of Australia. They had travelled by canoe from the southern coast of Indonesian Papua. Upon arrival, they sought asylum. The Australian immigration authorities arranged for their transfer to Christmas Island (an Australian territory in the Indian Ocean, which lies more than 1500 kilometres from the Australian mainland), where their claims were processed. None was granted asylum as such, although technically this would have been possible, as I explain below. All but one were deemed to be refugees and issued protection visas; the remaining member of the party was granted protection after a successful appeal to the Refugee Review Tribunal.

One day after the first 42 protection visas had been approved, the Indonesian government recalled its ambassador. It was outraged that the group had been allowed to remain in Australia. It considered the asylum requests a ploy to rally support for West Papuan independence, and anticipated that members of the group would use Australia as a launching pad for a campaign against the status quo in Papua. The government in Jakarta was also concerned that others would follow the example of the 43 and try to similarly embarrass their country of citizenship.

The Liberal–National government of John Howard sympathised with the Indonesian position and in May 2006 introduced legislation to 'excise' the Australian mainland from the migration zone.[4] The exemption would have allowed the authorities to remove future so-called unauthorised arrivals who landed on the Australian mainland, to the Republic of Nauru where their protection claims would be processed, and where they would not have recourse to Australia's legal system. The legislation would have addressed a discrepancy, as unauthorised boat arrivals reaching Australian territorial waters and islands, but not the mainland, were already detained and had their claims processed outside Australia.[5] Unlike asylum seekers for whom Indonesia was a transit country and who embarked on their boat journey in Java in the hope of reaching Christmas Island or Ashmore Reef, West Papuans leaving from the south coast of Indonesian Papua had a realistic chance of making landfall on the mainland. The legislation was therefore widely perceived as an attempt to target West Papuans in particular: their asylum claims could embarrass the Australian government, which has long recognised Papua as an integral part of Indonesia.

The public debate over the *Migration Amendment (Designated Unauthorised Arrivals) Bill*[6] was significant for two reasons. It resulted in a rare defeat for the government, which was forced to withdraw the bill after two of its own crossed the floor in the House of Representatives and a Liberal Party senator announced she would vote against the legislation in the Senate where the government had only a wafer-thin majority. And it marked the last time when the government's attempt to legislate for harsher asylum-seeker policies did not have the overwhelming support of the Australian public.

Much like other recent controversies related to Australia's response to refugees and asylum seekers, the 2006 debate over the government's asylum-seeker policy was remarkable also because its contributors regularly invoked the past to support their claims, but, in doing so, fashioned selective and often misleading histories.[7] The 1951 Refugee Convention and its 1967 Protocol featured prominently in them, because they were thought to be the most, if not only relevant international legal instruments by which Australia was bound in its response to persons seeking asylum.[8]

Contributors to the debate in the House of Representatives on 9 and 10 August 2006 advanced two myths of origin. Three Australian Labor Party parliamentarians claimed, to use the words of the shadow minister for immigration, Tony Burke, that the 1951 Convention 'was put in place because Jewish people fled Germany and no country would take them'.[9] A fourth Labor member, former justice minister Duncan Kerr, suggested that '[t]he refugee convention came about so that countries [accommodating refugees] would be able to say, "This is not an act of hostility towards our neighbour but a recognition of an obligation"'.[10]

Only one speaker invoked a different tradition, without mentioning the 1951 Convention. Petro Georgiou, a backbencher of the governing Liberal Party who crossed the floor to oppose what he considered to be 'the most profoundly disturbing piece of legislation I have encountered since becoming a member of parliament', said: 'The act of taking in a stranger in need is an ancient and universal virtue. ... [T]hroughout history mankind has ... brought succour to the uprooted. ... [T]he giving of sanctuary has become one of the noblest traditions of human nature'.[11] However, while Georgiou demanded that 'if victims of persecution come to our door and ask for asylum we should not turn them away', he seemed to invoke notions of hospitality, rather than the concept of political asylum when he referred to the 'giving of sanctuary'. In fact, in the two-day debate in the House of Representatives, none of the speakers used the term 'political asylum'. None referred to asylum as a right, rather than a privilege granted by a nation-state, although some speakers shared Kerr's view that Australia had an obligation towards people who sought its protection. Finally, all contributors to the debate assumed that the granting of asylum meant recognition as a refugee in the terms of Article 1 of the 1951 Refugee Convention and entailed the granting of a protection visa.

More than seventy years earlier, the House of Representatives had debated an earlier attempt to amend migration legislation to allow Australia to keep out aliens on political grounds. In 1934, the government had been ultimately unsuccessful first in preventing the landing of the Czech journalist Egon Erwin Kisch and the New Zealand anti-war activist Gerald Griffin, and then in effecting their deportation, although both men had failed a dictation test, the instrument used by Australia to exclude unwanted prospective migrants.[12] The following year, the government of Joseph Lyons therefore tried to 'cure' what it considered to be 'certain defects of the *Immigration Restriction Act*' that had been exploited by Kisch and Griffin.[13] In the House of Representatives, the Labor politician Maurice Blackburn, who had successfully represented Kisch before the High Court, railed against that bill. In doing so he invoked the tradition of democracies granting political asylum to aliens who had been persecuted in their home countries. 'The right of asylum has been one of the great contributions that England has made to the cause of the freedom of Europe', Blackburn said. 'The free institutions and free democracy have been developed in Europe to a great degree, because England was the asylum to which political refugees could come'.[14]

This is not the place to analyse the 1935 and 2006 bills, but to draw attention to the histories invoked in two cases in which the Australian government was accused of having drafted legislation designed to bar the entry of non-citizens who had been persecuted for their political stance abroad and/or who could be expected to use Australia as a base from which to campaign against a foreign government.

THE RIGHT *TO* ASYLUM VERSUS THE RIGHT *OF* ASYLUM

Neither Blackburn in 1935 nor any of the speakers during the debate over the migration amendment legislation in 2006 thought that non-citizens (or aliens)[15] might have the right to enter Australia. None mentioned a right *to* asylum. In the 2006 parliamentary debate, the only references to asylum seekers' rights were to their right to appeal a negative determination and have their cases reviewed. Only one speaker used the term 'human rights'; Labor politician Sharon Grierson claimed that the proposed legislation was 'inhumane because it says that Australia does not have any human rights obligations other than the remote processing of people seeking asylum', only to then equate the government's stance with 'a lack of compassion'.[16]

Both in 1935 and in 2006, contributors to the debate assumed that it was Australia's prerogative 'to decide who comes to this country, and the circumstances in which they come', to cite Prime Minister John Howard's famous—albeit not particularly original—line which defined the 2001 federal election campaign.[17] This assumption has been shared across party lines. When in 1935 Eric Harrison, a member of the governing United Australia Party, said that 'Australia has the right to say who shall enter the country and who shall not', Blackburn in fact interjected to register his agreement: 'We have the right to exclude aliens'.[18] His interjection highlighted one aspect of Australia's presumed right. It is this aspect that resonated with voters in 2001. The debate over the 2006 migration amendment legislation focused on the other aspect, namely Australia's presumed right to admit non-citizens.

A nation-state's right to grant admission to non-citizens is usually contested only in instances in which it decides to admit to its territory or to one of its diplomatic missions a person who has been expelled from, or has fled, another country—in which deciding 'who comes to this country' means exercising the right of nation-states to grant asylum to individuals.[19] The existence of such a right *of* asylum was implied in Blackburn's reference to Britain's contribution to the cause of freedom. In 2006, the Australian Labor Party's Duncan Kerr was more explicit; he incorrectly claimed that according to the 1951 Refugee Convention, if one nation-state granted asylum to citizens of another nation-state, the latter must not interpret this as an unfriendly act.

The 1951 Refugee Convention mentions the institution of asylum only in its preamble and does not refer to asylum seekers. The discussions during the drafting process strongly suggest that its architects were primarily concerned with refugee resettlement. The right of nation-states to grant asylum is spelled out most clearly in the 1967 United Nations Declaration on Territorial Asylum, which recognises 'that the grant of asylum by a State to persons entitled to invoke article 14 of the Universal Declaration of Human Rights (UDHR) is a peaceful and humanitarian act and that, as such, it cannot be regarded as unfriendly by any other State'.[20] The Universal Declaration's Article 14 (1) defines a right to seek and enjoy asylum ('Everyone has the right to seek and to enjoy in other countries asylum from persecution.'). The right *of* asylum has also been formulated in regional treaties. For example, according to Article 2 of the 1954 Caracas Convention on Diplomatic Asylum, which was ratified by 14 Latin American states, 'Every State has the right to grant asylum; but it is not obligated to do so or to state its reasons for refusing it.'[21]

Much like the 1954 Caracas Convention, Article 14 (1) of the 1948 UDHR does not postulate a right to be granted asylum, and its critics have therefore pointed out that the right enshrined in Article 14 does not amount to much. Such criticism was particularly strong in the immediate aftermath of the discussions about the UDHR and during the 1950s.[22] For example, in 1950 the renowned international lawyer Hersch Lauterpacht commented that the formula in the UDHR was 'artificial to the point of flippancy' and that it would have been 'more consistent with the dignity' of the Universal Declaration if Article 14 had been left out altogether.[23]

However, although the right to grant asylum does not rest on the idea that a person is entitled to be granted asylum, it nevertheless presumes that the grantee is eligible to be granted asylum. While the UDHR is somewhat vague about the criteria by which somebody might be qualified, it is specific about the grounds according to which a person would be disqualified from seeking and enjoying asylum. According to Article 14 (2), 'This right may not be invoked in the case of prosecutions genuinely arising from non-political crimes or from acts contrary to the purposes and principles of the United Nations.' I would like to suggest that by specifying grounds for ineligibility, Article 14 (2) underlines the fact that the rights spelled out in Article 14 (1) can only be invoked once certain qualifying conditions have been met.

The right of asylum is thus circumscribed by the grounds that prompt a person to seek asylum. According to the UDHR, she must have suffered persecution. According to Article 1 of the 1954 Caracas Convention, diplomatic asylum could only be granted 'to persons being sought for political reasons or for political offenses'. The 1967 Declaration references the UDHR, but adds further grounds for a claimant's eligibility; its Article 1 reads: 'Asylum granted by a State, in the exercise of its sovereignty, to persons entitled to invoke article 14 of the UDHR, including persons struggling against colonialism, shall be respected by all other States'. Both the 1967 Declaration's right to grant asylum and the UDHR's right to seek and enjoy asylum are premised on the circumstances that qualify a person for asylum, such as persecution. They are not defined in terms of the asylee's needs; for example, being stateless or having been made stateless is not a sufficient reason for the granting of asylum.

The earliest legal instrument in the modern era that mentions the right of asylum, the French Constitution of 1793, states: '*[Le peuple français] donne asile aux étrangers bannis de leur patrie pour la cause de la liberté. – Il le refuse aux tyrans*'. ('The French people will grant asylum to foreigners banished from their native land for their commitment to

freedom. They will deny it to tyrants.')[24] For the authors of the 1793
Constitution, the preparedness to grant asylum distinguished the French
people from others. Unlike the nations that banished its citizens, France
embraced the cause of freedom. The ability to exercise the right of asylum is thus not only testament to a country's relative autonomy (because
it does not let itself be pressured into extraditing asylees to tyrannical
regimes), but in the eyes of its citizens, it can also be a marker of its
moral superiority. According to Kisch's supporter Maurice Blackburn,
the institution of asylum was evidence that Britain was a 'free democracy'. 'When we boast of British freedom and British institutions it is of
things like this that we think', he argued in 1935.

Similarly, opponents of the 2006 migration amendment legislation
appealed to Australians' patriotism by arguing that Australia should not
let its policies be dictated by a foreign government, and that its ability
to offer protection to people fleeing persecution marked it as superior
to a country that persecuted some of its citizens on account of their
politics. People asking for asylum as well as their supporters might jus-
tify their claim by drawing attention to asylees' rights; but they often
put forward arguments that cannot be easily supported by international
or domestic human rights law: people seeking asylum might say that
they endured great suffering and are desperate to find a sanctuary, or
they might point out that the leaders of the nation-state to whom they
appeal could safely ignore the sensitivities of the rulers whose territory
they have fled, or they could cite a nation's self-identification as a cham-
pion of human rights and freedom.

The widely accepted right of asylum and, even more so, the (comparatively weak) right to seek and enjoy asylum that is enshrined in the
UDHR contain traces of the human right to be granted asylum even
when the latter is not mentioned. The sovereign right of the nation-
state, rather than merely contradicting the human right of the person
who suffers persecution, is closely related to it. This may appear to be
an issue that falls into the domain of political philosophy; yet, it is also
of much interest to the historian because of the empirical entanglements
of these rights in the past, and because of a long and complex genealogy
of attempts to reconcile the interests of the sovereign nation-state with
individuals' human rights. In the following, I therefore turn to the past
and provide a very brief history of these attempts, beginning with the
1948 Universal Declaration.

CHASING A RIGHT TO ASYLUM: FROM THE 1948 UDHR TO THE 1977 GENEVA CONFERENCE

The draft of the UDHR that had been prepared by the Human Rights Commission at its third session in May and June 1948 included two relevant articles: Articles 11 (2)—'Everyone has the right to leave any country, including his own'—and 12 (1): 'Everyone has the right to seek and be granted, in other countries, asylum from persecution'.[25] Between 30 September and 7 December 1948, the Third Committee of the United Nations General Assembly discussed and amended the draft over the course of 81 meetings. The Soviet Union and its allies objected strongly to the articles enshrining the freedom of movement and a right to asylum.[26] Other delegations also felt that the Human Rights Commission had gone too far.

The leader of the Australian delegation, Australia's ambassador to the Soviet Union, Alan Watt, later wrote that everyone on the Third Committee 'knew perfectly well' that the Universal Declaration 'purported only to embody a set of agreed principles' which would only become binding if they were subsequently enshrined in a covenant, which countries then needed to ratify to commit to the obligations it imposed.[27] The Australian delegation nevertheless argued that '[a]s for the right of asylum, each State must be free to decide the form in which that right, having been proclaimed in the declaration, should be applied', and supported a proposal by the delegation of Saudi Arabia to limit the right to asylum by deleting the words 'and be granted'.[28]

By the time the General Assembly voted on the Universal Declaration on 10 December 1948, draft Article 11 had become Article 14. Among the civil and political rights that were covered by Articles 3–21, Article 14 represents an anomaly, particularly in light of the discussions during the drafting process. Rather than granting a political right to individuals, it effectively curtails individuals' rights in the interest of the nation-state's sovereign rights. Besides, the Universal Declaration was just that: a *declaration* that imposed no legally binding obligations, rather than a covenant.

From the early 1950s, attempts resumed to devise an internationally binding instrument that would guarantee the rights of and to asylum.[29] They centred initially on attempts to include a right to asylum in the International Covenant on Civil and Political Rights (CCPR). These attempts failed. The 1966 CCPR mirrors Articles 3–21 of the UDHR with only one exception: that of Article 14.

In 1957, France submitted a draft declaration on the right to asylum to the thirteenth session of the Commission on Human Rights. Its Article 1 read: 'All members of the international community, represented by the United Nations, shall grant asylum to those persons who seek it'.[30] In assigning the responsibility for granting asylum to the United Nations, this draft tried to circumvent the problem that nation-states were reluctant to agree to an instrument that would oblige them individually to grant asylum. For others, this compromise was still unacceptable; the Australian negotiator, for example, thought that the French proposal amounted to a 'substantial inroad on national sovereignty'.[31]

The discussions in the Commission on Human Rights gave birth to the 1967 Declaration on Territorial Asylum, which made explicit the right of the state to grant asylum, without affirming the individual's right to be granted asylum. While the 1967 Declaration was readily adopted by the UN General Assembly, its status as a declaration (rather than a covenant or a convention) meant that member states did not have to feel bound by it. Therefore Australia, for example, which had misgivings about the 1967 Declaration and had in 1959 abstained from a resolution that paved the way for the drafting of such a declaration, saw no reason not to vote in its favour.

At the level of the United Nations, another effort to formulate the right to asylum commenced in 1971, when the Carnegie Foundation convened a symposium at Bellagio to prepare a draft convention on territorial asylum. As had happened in 1948 with the UDHR, first drafts of a proposed convention on asylum were promising, but got watered down when governments objected for fear that their sovereignty would be impeded. In early 1977, the UN convened a conference of plenipotentiaries to discuss a draft that had been prepared by a group of experts.[32] The conference discussed only four articles and ended without an agreement. The legal scholar Enrico Lapenna, who had been one of the key contributors to the post-1971 discussions, commented: 'Consideration of man himself and his right to asylum was absent throughout the Conference'.[33]

This is not to say that claims regarding the right to asylum were thereby finally put to rest. The right to asylum survived in domestic law. For example, since 1949 the Federal Republic of Germany has guaranteed the right to be granted asylum from persecution in its Constitution.[34] Although the right to asylum is not explicitly mentioned in the European Convention of Human Rights (ECHR), European Court of Human Rights case law drawing on Article 3 of the ECHR has in many instances affirmed the rights of asylum seekers and moved European law incrementally closer to the recognition of a right to asylum.[35] The evidence from the 2006 debate on the *Migration Amendment (Designated Unauthorised Arrivals) Bill* in Australia suggests that elsewhere, even the possibility of a right to asylum soon sank into oblivion.

International Human Rights Law Versus International Refugee Law

Revisiting the history of the right to seek, enjoy and be granted asylum draws attention to the fact that since the end of the Second World War, two distinct international legal traditions have informed the response to refugees and asylum seekers, although in many countries, including Australia, only one is publicly remembered today. One tradition is represented by the 1951 Refugee Convention, which built on the International Refugee Organization's Constitution and earlier instruments developed in the context of the League of Nations, and which in turn became more significant as the office of the United Nations High Commissioner for Refugees gradually gained more clout. The historical context that informed the drafting of the 1951 Convention was the presence of large numbers of Displaced Persons (DPs) in Europe and their resettlement in countries such as the United States and Australia, rather than the refugee crisis of the late 1930s. In the immediate aftermath of the Second World War, refugee situations outside Europe, such as the displacement of Palestinians or the exodus of refugees caused by the partition of India barely registered with the drafters of the Convention. Not only was the 1951 Convention designed for a very specific group of displaced people, it was also a product of the Cold War and largely the result of a Western initiative.

The other tradition has a much longer genealogy, which reaches back to the pre-modern era. A right of and to asylum was known by the Greek city states, in parts of medieval Europe as well as in some non-Western societies. In Europe, the right declined in the early modern era, only to rise to prominence again when enlightened or democratic governments attempted to establish their credentials by granting asylum to people fleeing persecution or tyranny. In Britain, whose tradition Maurice Blackburn held up as a shining example in 1935, the right to asylum was codified in the 1905 *Aliens Act*.[36]

In the immediate aftermath of the Second World War—not least because of the experiences of the late 1930s, which speakers at the 2006 debate about the *Migration Amendment Bill* wrongly held responsible for the genesis of the 1951 Convention—the right to be granted asylum became almost enshrined in a covenant (with the Australian government being among those who initially favoured a binding and enforceable covenant over a declaration). By the time the text was put before the General Assembly, only the right to seek and enjoy asylum remained. Nevertheless, unlike the 1951 Refugee Convention, the 1948 UDHR 'was in no sense a Cold War document', as Jay Winter and Antoine Prost observe in their biography of one of its key architects, René Cassin.[37] The Universal Declaration could claim to have the support of the world community. Attempts to make up for the shortcomings of Article 14 of the UDHR continued until 1977 with the failed Geneva conference of plenipotentiaries.

Today, the vigorous and extensive discussions that began soon after the end of the Second World War during the drafting of the UDHR and ended 30 years later during the Geneva conference are barely remembered. Reading the New York Declaration for Refugees and Migrants, one could be forgiven for thinking that they never took place. However, even in Australia, which does not have a bill of rights and no domestic laws that guarantee a right to asylum, and where the right to asylum is rarely mentioned in public debate, it took a while to forget that the non-refoulement provision of the 1951 Refugee Convention was the outcome of discussions that were distinct from those about the right to asylum. Separate policies regarding refugee protection and asylum remain in place; this is a legacy of the two distinct traditions: one pertaining to international refugee law, and one pertaining to international human rights law.

The Australian government first formulated an asylum policy in 1956 in anticipation of asylum requests during the Melbourne Olympic Games—21 years before it developed a comprehensive refugee and asylum seeker policy.[38] Even after the latter, it retained the option of granting asylum, although it rarely exercised that option. The last time this option came to the fore in public debate was in 2005 when the Chinese diplomat Chen Yonglin explicitly sought asylum instead of applying for a protection visa.[39] Even today, the government has the option to grant non-citizens a subclass 800 'territorial asylum' visa (which entitles its holder to permanent residency without a waiting period), rather than a protection visa.[40]

The parallel histories of the 1951 Refugee Convention (and the making of international refugee law) and Article 14 of the UDHR (and the making of international human rights law) suggest that the contradiction between the human rights of asylum seekers and the sovereignty of the nation-state does not need to be insurmountable. In 1957, the French negotiators in the Human Rights Commission recognised that nation-states would not be prepared to relinquish control over the admission of non-citizens. The solution they suggested may still be the only feasible solution today: namely that while refugees have the right to be admitted to the territory of a state other than their own, the nation-state admitting them would then act on behalf of the international community. This also means that the right to be admitted would not infer an entitlement to permanent residence in a particular country.

A revisiting of the history of the right to asylum is particularly useful in countries such as Australia in which a rights-based discourse is comparatively weak.[41] Such a history focuses attention on the needs and rights of non-citizens (and, particularly, on the rights that are derived from the circumstances prompting people to seek asylum). It turns attention away from the emotional dividends to be gained by supporting refugees, and from the presumed effects the admission of refugees has on the nation-state (such as economic losses or gains).

It is no accident that the 2006 debate about the *Migration Amendment Bill* invoked the 1951 Refugee Convention rather than the UDHR. The Convention has been closely associated with the resettlement of refugees. Australia has formally resettled more refugees than most other countries; this effort, and the supposedly quintessential Australian generosity that has underwritten it, have become a matter of patriotic pride and are regularly cited in discussions about the government's response to asylum seekers. In 2006, proponents and opponents of the proposed legislation identified strongly with that tradition and sought to link the response to West Papuan refugees to it (either by arguing that the bill was justified by Australia's otherwise generous response or by suggesting that the law would sully a proud record).

Finally, a focus on the *rights* of irregular migrants, including people arriving by boat without a valid visa to seek asylum, can serve to question the reliance on emotional responses. Again, this is particularly relevant in Australia, where it is possible to equate the withholding of human rights with a lack of compassion (as Sharon Grierson did during the 2006 debate). While some of those objecting to the admission of so-called boat people are motivated by fear, many Australians who favour the admission of more refugees and asylum seekers draw on the fickle emotion of compassion. In both cases, the focus is on how Australians feel about strangers seeking their protection, rather than on the needs and rights of these strangers.

In many respects, the development of the right to be granted asylum is a dead end of history. Such dead ends are easily overlooked when viewing the past through the lens of the present, which privileges only pasts that are obviously constitutive of the present. Dead ends of history allow us to imagine futures that are more than endlessly reproduced versions of the present. The ability to imagine such futures is particularly important when considering the seemingly intractable issues of increasing human mobility and the large-scale movement of forcibly displaced people.

NOTES

1. UN General Assembly, Resolution adopted by the General Assembly on 19 September 2016: New York Declaration for Refugees and Migrants, 3 October 2016, UN doc. A/RES/71/1, Articles 27 and 67.
2. UN General Assembly, Resolution adopted by the General Assembly on 19 September 2016, Article 3.
3. Klaus Neumann and Savitri Taylor, 'Australia, Indonesia and West Papuan refugees, 1962–2009,' *International Relations of the Asia-Pacific* 10, no. 1 (2010): 1–31.
4. Rowan Day, 'West Papua and the Australia–Indonesia relationship: A case study in diplomatic difficulty,' *Australian Journal of International Affairs* 69, no. 6 (2015): 670–91. In 2001, Australia had excised several islands from the migration zone, with the consequence that asylum seekers arriving on these islands without a valid visa were prevented from applying for one. 'Excising' the mainland from the migration zone did not mean that the mainland would no longer be part of that zone, but rather that non-citizens arriving by boat and without a valid visa on the mainland could be denied the rights available to other non-citizens. In 2013, the Australian parliament passed legislation similar to the one proposed in 2006, which had the effect of 'excising' the entire mainland from the migration zone. See Michelle Foster and Jason Pobjoy, 'A failed case of legal exceptionalism? Refugee status determination in Australia's "excised" territory,' *International Journal of Refugee Law* 23, no. 4 (2011): 583–631; and Anthea Vogl, 'Over the borderline: A critical inquiry into the geography of territorial excision and the securitisation of the Australian border,' *UNSW Law Journal* 38, no. 1 (2015): 114–45.

5. Tania Penovic and Azadeh Dastyari, 'Boatloads of incongruity: The evolution of Australia's offshore processing regime,' *Australian Journal of Human Rights* 13, no. 1 (2007): 33–62.

6. Sue Harris Rimmer, 'Migration Amendment (Designated Unauthorised Arrivals) Bill 2006,' *Bills Digest*, 22 May 2006, no. 138 (2005–2006), http://www.aph.gov.au/binaries/library/pubs/bd/2005-06/06bd138.pdf. Accessed 13 September 2016.

7. Elsewhere, I have written about the use of history in the debate over the *Migration Amendment Bill 2006*, such as references to Australians' supposedly long-standing compassionate response to refugees and Australia's supposedly traditional generosity towards them, and the silence regarding previous instances in which West Papuans had sought Australia's protection. Klaus Neumann, 'Oblivious to the obvious? Australian asylum-seeker policies and the use of the past,' in *Does History Matter? Making and Debating Citizenship, Immigration and Refugee Policy in Australia and New Zealand*, eds. Klaus Neumann and Gwenda Tavan (Canberra: ANU E Press, 2009), 56–61. The bill was the subject of a lengthy debate in the House of Representatives; earlier, it had been scrutinised in a Senate inquiry. For the report, see Senate—Legal and Constitutional Committee, 'Provisions of the Migration Amendment (Designated Unauthorised Arrivals) Bill 2006,' June 2006, http://www.aph.gov.au/Parliamentary_Business/Committees/Senate/Legal_and_Constitutional_Affairs/Completed_inquiries/2004-07/migration_unauthorised_arrivals/report/index. Accessed 13 September 2016.

8. Australia acceded to the 1951 Refugee Convention in 1954, and signed the 1967 Protocol in 1973. Some speakers also referred to the 1989 Convention on the Rights of the Child, to which Australia had acceded in 1990, and to the 1966 International Covenant on Civil and Political Rights, to which Australia had acceded in 1980.

9. Anthony Burke, *Commonwealth Parliamentary Debates* (hereafter: *CPD*), Representatives, 9 August 2006, 20; see also Anthony Albanese, *CPD*, Representatives, 10 August 2006, 35; and Christopher Bowen, *CPD*, Representatives, 10 August 2006, 15.

10. Duncan Kerr, *CPD*, Representatives, 9 August 2006, 118.

11. Petro Georgiou, *CPD*, Representatives, 9 August 2006, 42, 44.

12. Egon Erwin Kisch, *Landung in Australien* (Amsterdam: Allert de Lange, 1937); Peter Monteath, 'The Kisch case revisited,' *Journal of Australian Studies* 16, no. 34 (1992): 69–81; Nicholas Hasluck, *The Legal Labyrinth: The Kisch Case and Other Reflections on Law and Literature* (Claremont: Freshwater Bay Press, 2003); Heidi Zogbaum, *Kisch in Australia: The Untold Story* (Melbourne: Scribe Publications, 2004); and Glenn Nicholls, *Deported: A History of Forced Departures from Australia*

(Sydney: UNSW Press, 2007), 65–69. Prospective immigrants could be required to write a 50-word text in any European language that was dictated to them by a Customs official. Those who failed that test could be barred from Australia. Kisch, who was fluent in many European languages, had been given a test in Scottish Gaelic—by a Customs officer who himself was unable to speak that language. Between 1909 and 1958, when the dictation test was abolished, nobody given that test passed it. See also Alexander T. Yarwood, 'The dictation test—Historical survey,' *Australian Quarterly* 30, no. 2 (1958): 19–29.

13. William Morris Hughes, *CPD*, Representatives, 10 April 1935, 1211.

14. Maurice Blackburn, *CPD*, Representatives, 10 April 1935, 1218.

15. There was no Australian citizenship prior to the *Australian Citizenship Act 1948*. Australian residents were either British subjects or aliens.

16. Sharon Grierson, *CPD*, Representatives, 9 August 2006, 135.

17. John Howard, Speech to launch 2001 election campaign, 28 October 2001, http://museumvictoria.com.au/immigrationmuseum/discovery-centre/identity/videos/politics-videos/john-howards-2001-election-campaign-policy-launch-speech. Accessed 14 September 2016. It is often assumed that Howard coined this line. However, Australian politicians have used variations of it since at least the 1930s; see, for example, Klaus Neumann, *Across the Seas: Australia's Response to Refugees: A History* (Collingwood: Black Inc., 2015), 28.

18. Eric Fairweather Harrison and Maurice Blackburn, *CPD*, Representatives, 10 April 1935, 1223.

19. The scholarship on the right of asylum is rich and substantial. The following are useful entry points: Roman Boed, 'The state of the right of asylum in international law,' *Duke Journal of Comparative and International Law* 5, no. 1 (1994): 1–33; Atle Grahl-Madsen, *Territorial Asylum* (Stockholm: Almqvist & Wiksell International, 1980); Otto Kirchheimer, 'Asylum,' *American Political Science Review* 53, no. 4 (1959): 985–1016; Felice Morgenstern, 'The right of asylum,' *British Yearbook of International Law* 26 (1949): 327–57; M.G. Kaladharan Nayar, 'The right of asylum in international law: Its status and prospects,' *St. Louis University Law Journal* 17 (1972–1973): 17–46; Richard Plender and Nuala Mole, 'Beyond the Geneva Convention: Constructing a de facto right of asylum from International Human Rights instruments,' in *Refugee Rights and Realities: Evolving International Concepts and Regimes*, eds. Frances Nicholson and Patrick Twomey (Cambridge: Cambridge University Press, 1999), 81–105; and P. Weis, 'Territorial asylum,' *Indian Yearbook of International Law* 6 (1966): 173–94.

20. UN General Assembly, Declaration on Territorial Asylum, 14 December 1967, UN doc. A/RES/2321(XXII).

21. Well before others took an interest in the rights of and to asylum, Latin American states played a prominent role in promoting international instruments governing issues of asylum. See, for example, Argentine Republic, Ministry for Foreign Affairs and Worship, *Project of Convention on the Right of Asylum* (Buenos Aires, 1937).

22. See, for example, Manuel R. García-Mora, *International Law and Asylum as a Human Right* (Washington: Public Affairs Press, 1956).

23. H. Lauterpacht, *International Law and Human Rights* (London: Stevens & Sons, 1950), 422.

24. Constitution of 24 June 1793, Article 120, http://www.conseil-constitu-tionnel.fr/conseil-constitutionnel/francais/la-constitution/les-constitu-tions-de-la-france/constitution-du-24-juin-1793.5084.html. Accessed 13 September 2016.

25. United Nations Economic and Social Council, 'Report of the third session of the Commission on Human Rights, Lake Success, 28 May to 18 June 1948,' Annex A: Draft International Declaration of Human Rights, 28 June 1948, UN Doc. E/800.

26. Mary Ann Glendon, *A World Made New: Eleanor Roosevelt and the Universal Declaration of Human Rights* (New York: Random House, 2001), 92.

27. Alan Watt, *Australian Diplomat: Memoirs of Sir Alan Watt* (Sydney: Angus and Robertson in Association with the Australian Institute of International Affairs, 1972), 137.

28. Minutes of the 121st Meeting of the Third Committee, 3 November 1948, UN Doc. A/C.3/SR121; Annemarie Devereux, *Australia and the Birth of the International Bill of Human Rights 1946–1966* (Annandale: Federation Press, 2005), 70.

29. P. Weis, 'The United Nations Declaration on Territorial Asylum,' *Canadian Yearbook of International Law* 7 (1969): 95–97.

30. United Nations Economic and Social Council, Commission on Human Rights, Thirteenth Session, 'France: Draft Declaration on the Right of Asylum,' 12 April 1957, UN doc. E/CN.4/L.454.

31. H.F.E. Whitlam, 'Additional Paragraph to Paper on Asylum,' 26 December 1958, National Archives of Australia: A1838, 929/6/1 PART 1. For the drafting of the United Nations Declaration on Territorial Asylum, see Savitri Taylor, and Klaus Neumann, 'What anniversary? Fifty years of the 1967 Declaration on Territorial Asylum: A case study of the making of international refugee and human rights law,' *International Journal of Refugee Law* 30, no. 1 (2018): 8–30.

32. P. Weis, 'The draft United Nations Convention on Territorial Asylum,' *British International Yearbook on International Law* 50, no. 1 (1979): 151–71.

33. Enrico Lapenna, 'Territorial asylum—development from 1961 to 1977: Comments on the Conference of Plenipotentiaries (Geneva, January 10–February 4 1977),' *AWR-Bulletin* 16[25], no. 1–2 (1978): 4.

34. See, for example, Hanna-Mari Kivistö, 'Asylum as an individual right in the 1949 West German *Grundgesetz*,' *Contributions to the History of Concepts* 9, no. 1 (2014): 60–73; and Hélène Lambert, Francesco Messineo, and Paul Tiedemann, 'Comparative perspectives of constitutional asylum in France, Italy, and Germany: *Requiescat in Pace?*,' *Refugee Survey Quarterly* 27, no. 3 (2008): 16–32.

35. Nuala Mole and Catherine Meredith, *Asylum and the European Convention on Human Rights* (Strasbourg: Council of Europe Publishing, 2010).

36. Alison Bashford and Jane McAdam, 'The right to asylum: Britain's 1905 Aliens Act and the evolution of refugee law,' *Law and History Review* 32, no. 2 (2014): 309–50.

37. Jay Winter and Antoine Prost, *René Cassin and Human Rights: From the Great War to the Universal Declaration* (Cambridge: Cambridge University Press, 2013), 237.

38. Klaus Neumann, *Refuge Australia: Australia's Humanitarian Record* (Sydney: UNSW Press, 2004), 52–64.

39. Senate—Foreign Affairs, Defence and Trade References Committee, 'Mr Chen Yonglin's Request for Political Asylum,' September 2005, http://www.aph.gov.au/Parliamentary_Business/Committees/Senate/Foreign_Affairs_Defence_and_Trade/Completed_inquiries/2004-07/asylum/report01/index. Accessed 13 September 2016.

40. Australian Government, 'Guide to Social Security Law, Version 1.224: 9.2.11.12—Visa Subclass 800 Territorial Asylum,' 15 August 2016, http://guides.dss.gov.au/guide-social-security-law/9/2/11/10. Accessed 13 September 2016.

41. Elsewhere, I have written in more detail about the benefits of such a history for Australia, and about the need for a rights-based discourse. See, for example, Klaus Neumann, 'Rights versus compassion,' *Inside Story*, 3 June 2009, http://insidestory.org.au/rights-versus-compassion. Accessed 16 September 2016; Klaus Neumann, 'Whatever happened to the right of asylum?,' *Inside Story*, 16 December 2010, http://insidestory.org.au/whatever-happened-to-the-right-of-asylum. Accessed 16 September 2016.

CHAPTER 12

Will the Twenty-First Century World Embrace Immigration History?

Donna Gabaccia

Immigration History is a scholarly field with a distinguished, if still debated, genealogy. Yet, a survey of immigration historiography today would produce a decidedly spotty map. As an autonomous field of study, Immigration History—with its own professional societies, pedagogical resources and archives—scarcely exists outside the former British settler colonies, the United States, Canada, and Australia. Historiographies on immigration are much more common; in France, Britain, Israel, Singapore, Argentina and Brazil, there is no separate field called Immigration History, but historians frequently analyse immigration within national histories.[1] Such national histories insert immigration into diverse stories of nation-building.[2] Still, in most countries of today's world, neither Immigration History nor immigration historiography exists, and past population movements are assumed to have been insignificant.

In sharp contrast, many countries around the world are now creating knowledge about recent mobility, written from an ahistorical social science perspective that typically portrays a rupture between a more sedentary past and the emergence of an increasingly mobile world

D. Gabaccia (✉)
University of Toronto, Toronto, ON, Canada

© The Author(s) 2019
E. Henrich and J. M. Simpson (Eds.),
History, Historians and the Immigration Debate,
https://doi.org/10.1007/978-3-319-97123-0_12

after 1945 or 1970.[3] Contemporary political debates also commonly portray immigration as a recent and unprecedented development—one that threatens national solidarity in unprecedented ways. If recent globalisation has produced high mobility, then Immigration History might finally flourish around the world in the twenty-first century, as future historians of immigration begin to interpret their past—which is, of course, our own mobile present.

But that may not be the most likely development. This essay offers a sceptical assessment for the future of immigration scholarship in the world at large. According to world historians, today's migrations are in fact neither new nor unprecedented.[4] The sedentary past is a myth, they assert: almost every corner of the globe has at times experienced, but then forgotten, significant movements of people, sometimes because nation-building seeks origins in a past characterized by homogeneous, sedentary groups. Forgetting has been as important in nation-building as remembering, as Ernest Renan argued over a century ago.[5]

Ultimately, the future of Immigration History and immigration historiography will be determined by processes of nation-building that are ongoing everywhere in today's world. Nation-building, as the imagining of a national community, typically seeks a relevant or useable past. But only occasionally do histories of immigration provide that past.[6] Both historical scholarship and nation-building rest on a shifting foundation of changing 'terminologies of mobility'—literally the words and categories that confront and categorise people at every border they cross. Terminologies of mobility can be identified and traced in print culture, whether through historiography, library and archival collections, or newspapers. Attention to terminologies of mobility shows that historically, most mobile people did not cross borders as 'immigrants', as they did in the countries that dot our imaginary map of immigration historiography. Today, too, people travelling the world are more likely to cross borders as refugees, temporary labour migrants, asylum seekers, or tourists, rather than as immigrants. By examining the historical origins of immigration historiography in the United States and contrasting it to a country with many foreigners, but few immigrants, this essay suggests that Immigration History's twenty-first century future could remain fraught and uncertain.

CONTEXTUALIZING THE PAST: THE ORIGINS
OF IMMIGRATION HISTORY

Immigration History first appeared in the midst of twentieth-century debates about immigration restriction that were as intense as any occurring in today's world. An analysis of the field's origins pinpoints factors that rendered its travel unlikely. Moments of debates about immigration constituted important moments of American nation-building, and immigration became a key terminology of mobility in both scholarship and the national imaginary.[7] But while Immigration History provided a relevant past for Americans, the 'Nation of Immigrants' imaginary was of limited usefulness, even in other countries with sizeable immigrations.[8] Historians who rejected methodological nationalism and uncovered alternative genealogies for immigration historiography helped call attention to the salience of terminology itself. Rather than focus exclusively on 'immigration', their cross-national work required them to identify and work with a broader array of terminologies for mobile people. These terminologies in turn suggest that a country can experience and even acknowledge considerable border-crossing through scholarship without producing a scholarly field of Immigration History or making immigration the key to nation-building.

At least since the 1960s, historians of the United States have credited Oscar Handlin, author of the Pulitzer-prize-winning *The Uprooted: The Epic Story of the Great Migrations* (1951), as the founder of the scholarly field of Immigration History. Handlin's opening statement—'Once I thought to write a history of the immigrants in America. Then I discovered that the immigrants *were* American History'—is oft cited, perhaps because it clearly established a relationship between Immigration History and American nation-building, in the form of a problematic equation of immigrants and the American nation.[9] Americans have understood immigrants to be persons migrating voluntarily in order to settle, live, work and attain citizenship. If immigrants truly *were* American History, then American History had no place for the descendants of slaves or the continent's indigenous peoples, whose mobility was that of slave trade, Bering-Straits crossings or foraging and hunting as ways of life, not immigration.

Soon after Oscar Handlin's death in 2011, the *Journal of American Ethnic History (JAEH)*—the organ of the Immigration and Ethnic History Society—compiled a special issue exploring the life and intellectual legacy of the Harvard historian.[10] In an essay on Handlin's dissertation (which became *Boston's Immigrants,* published in 1941), Tyler Anbinder provided an early biography of Handlin, the son of Jewish immigrants from Ukraine, that placed him squarely within the urban, northeastern immigrant communities that he studied; Anbinder was reluctant to accept Handlin's insistence that his intellectual interests had little to do with his personal biography.[11]

Since the JAEH issue accepted Handlin's status as the founder of American Immigration History, it dated the field's emergence to the years between 1934 (when Handlin began graduate study) and the 1960s when he wrote about ethnicity and post-war cities. Handlin's formative years coincided with the sharp declines in immigration accompanying new restrictive laws and the Great Depression. Yet, immigration remained a hotly debated topic in the 1930s and 1940s. The rise of fascist antisemitism in Germany and the collapse of the world into war in the 1930s and 1940s created millions of refugees who pounded at the closed doors of the United States. Published in 1951, Handlin's *The Uprooted* coincided with the intensification of the Cold War—a period when racial discrimination in American immigration and Jim Crow policies tarnished the country's reputation. Handlin's focus on immigrant alienation giving way to the assimilation of the second generation bolstered the country's reputation for successfully integrating outsiders, but marginalized other forms of mobility from the slave trade to the African American great migration.

Three *JAEH* essays specifically addressed the implications of the Cold War for the field's subsequent development. Mae Ngai showed how 1950s' immigration reformers seized on Handlin's work as a useable past as they sought to eliminate the discriminatory National Origins Quotas.[12] Reflecting on Handlin's 1959 book on African Americans and Puerto Ricans in New York City, Lorrin Thomas concluded that 'Handlin did perhaps a little better and probably not much worse than the majority of white liberal intellectuals of his time'.[13] But in a third contribution, Touré Reed offered a far blunter assessment, concluding that Handlin's characterization of Blacks as the last of the urban immigrants was quite simply incorrect. Black Americans were not newcomers waiting in a neutral ethnic queue for full assimilation into a plural nation; they had long histories in New York and in the United States.[14] Reed suggested that Handlin too easily dismissed African Americans' continued segregation and poverty as products of culturally determined 'deficiencies of the disadvantaged' rather than as the predictable result of structural inequalities and racism. Cold War liberalism's denial of the special burdens of race faced by non-white Americans so tainted Immigration History that it could not provide an attractive model for nation-building in post-colonial countries of the Third World.

The association of Immigration History with American nation-building posed other problems, as historians began to recognize in the 1990s as they engaged with critiques of 'methodological nationalism'.[15] Methodological nationalism had encouraged the examination and interpretation of historical phenomena exclusively within the boundaries of individual nation-states. In the United States, it privileged the study of immigration to the exclusion of analysis of emigration, forced and involuntary migrations, colonisation and internal migrations. Methodological nationalism naturalised immigration, helping to make it the only relevant terminology of American mobility.

As the *JAEH* prepared its special issue, historians whose professional and personal lives repeatedly traversed the borders of Germany, Canada and the United States prepared an alternative genealogy for their scholarly field. In four essays published together in 2015 in the new *Journal of Global Migration History (JGMH)*, Henry Yu[16] and Claudia Roelsch[17] examined early social science research on the Pacific Coast, while Dirk Hoerder turned his eyes eastwards to the students of anthropologist Franz Boas at Columbia University.[18] Donna Gabaccia described early immigration histories written at Midwestern land grant universities, notably at the University of Minnesota.[19]

Collectively, the *JGMH* articles emphasized the interdisciplinary and transnational roots of American immigration historiography, uncovering alternative terminologies of mobility such as return, exclusion and emigration. Yu and Roelsch focused on approaches pioneered on the Pacific coast as students of the Chicago School of Sociology took up the study of Asian immigrants. Hoerder described early historians of immigrants and the African slave trade, Caroline Ware and Frank Tannenbaum, engaging in discussions of traveling culture ('transculturalism') and human migrations with Boas's anthropologist colleagues in the United States,

Caribbean and Brazil. In Minnesota, historians returned to immigrants' homelands to do research, encountering both historians of emigration and folklorists studying immigrants' peasant origins; Theodore Blegen later incorporated their insights when he wrote of 'grass roots history' and 'history from the bottom up'.[20]

Hoerder and Gabaccia pushed the origins of the scholarly field back in time to the peak years of racist and nativist hostility to American immigrants during the first three decades of the twentieth century. On the east coast, Franz Boas—himself a German-Jewish immigrant—became one of the earliest and most outspoken European-origin critics of American racism and racialised American nation-building.[21] Even in the upper Midwest—where historians mainly analysed European-origin immigrants—George Stephenson penned the first American immigration history that problematised anti-Asian prejudice and devoted full chapters to Asian-origin immigrants.[22]

Finally, the four *JGMH* articles described immigration scholars as committed to transforming American communities distorted by nativism and racism. Yu described Chicago-trained scholars developing what he labelled 'collaborative methods of knowledge production' with community members. Like Yu, Hoerder emphasized how the students of Boas absorbed an approach to research that demanded 'a genuine respect' for the people studied. In Minnesota, Theodore Blegen engaged ethnic communities in developing archives that preserved immigrants' words in their own languages. Many of these early scholars originated in the communities they studied. Unlike Handlin they accepted that personal experience shaped their intellectual work; by acknowledging and maintaining community ties, these researchers began to imagine an American nation unmarred by racial exclusions and freed from Immigration History's focus on assimilation as key to nation-building.

The *JGMH* articles described scholarship framed by the terminologies of mobility increasingly preferred within World History—transcultural movement, migration, emigration, mobility—rather than focusing exclusively on immigration and assimilation. Dirk Hoerder and Christiane Harzig had already sketched the changing relationship of migration and scholarly innovation in their book *What is Migration History?*[23] The two historians described the invention of the 'state sciences' (*Staatswissenschaften*—economics, law, demography) as a response to eighteenth-century states' growing awareness of urbanisation and its implications for governance and national solidarity. In the new nations of the Americas, debates over the so-called proletarian mass migrations of the nineteenth and early twentieth centuries nurtured the scholarly innovations in Sociology and History described in the *JAEH* and *JGMH* articles.[24] Hoerder and Harzig also identified a third moment of innovation as social scientists studied colonisation and internal migrations from northern China to Manchuria. While all these cases linked demography, scholarship and nation-building, only in the Americas did immigration (rather than urbanisation, colonisation or internal movement) provide the key to nation-building.

The birth of Immigration History took place under quite specific American circumstances and at quite specific moments in American nation-building, suggesting that, historically, Immigration History and immigration historiography first flourished as post-colonial settler colonies confronted new labour migrations and imagined their nations in new ways.[25] The fact that the historiography of France also features immigration as an element in its nation-building suggests further that immigration historiography could develop in a variety of contexts and serve a variety of nation-building projects. Still, for those contemplating the future, it is also important to examine historiography in places that have denied, forgotten, or rejected mobility as an element in nation-building. Switzerland provides a good example of how alternative terminologies of mobility shaped both scholarship and modes of nation-building that were more often exclusionary than inclusionary.[26]

SWITZERLAND: A 'NON-IMMIGRATION IMMIGRATION LAND'

As the German sociologist—and son of Polish immigrants—Hans-Joachim Hoffman-Nowotny struggled to explain Switzerland to scholars familiar mainly with American or French scholarship, he described the country as a 'non-immigration immigration land'.[27] To understand this label, one must know that immigration was never the preferred terminology for mobility in Switzerland; historically, there have been many foreigners living in Switzerland, but the Swiss, for well over a century, have never aspired to incorporate them as citizens.[28] While Swiss scholars neither forgot nor denied their country's long history of border-crossings, Swiss historiography on mobility did not provide a useable past that could define Swiss citizenship or provide a foundation for social solidarity. It is important to examine the terminologies of mobility in Switzerland precisely because, in today's world, there are many non-immigration immigration lands.

Even if one accepts the usefulness of comparison, juxtaposing the United States and Switzerland may seem a paradoxical choice, like the proverbial comparison of apples with oranges. The United States (at 324 million residents) and Switzerland (with only 8 million) are obviously very different in size and geopolitical power. The United States is a global power with a history of nation-building shaped by conquest, settler colonialism and slavery as well as by immigration. Switzerland instead values its neutrality and—as a culturally plural confederation with four official languages and populations adhering to Catholicism and a considerable array of Protestant churches—it cultivates within its mountain fastness a sense of difference and separation from its German, French and Italian neighbours.[29]

What the United States and Switzerland share is a century-long history of significant border-crossing by people in search of waged work. Both countries also prominently feature democratic governance in their national imaginaries. Switzerland prides itself on being the world's only direct democracy.[30] Both countries have enjoyed high standards of living and, today, both number among the economically most developed countries of the world. Switzerland and the United States are not quite as different as apples and oranges. They can be compared.

But how to do it? Demographers turn to quantitative methods. When faced with the challenge of cross-national comparison, the United Nations in the 1970s chose to calculate the percentages in each country of persons born outside its borders.[31] Using that measure, about 15% of Switzerland's resident population in 1910 had been born elsewhere; the comparable figure for the United States was 14%. Today, 14% of the American population is again foreign-born; the figure for Switzerland is a more impressive 28%.

Comparing terminologies of mobility results in a more complex comparison of the two countries. I contrast here the American terminology of immigration with evidence on alternative terminologies in Swiss print culture as represented in SwissBib, a digital portal and meta-catalogue of holdings in the Swiss National Library and university libraries in Switzerland.[32] SwissBib documents Switzerland's long-term scholarly and governmental interest in mobility. But until very recently, the Swiss rarely included immigration within its terminologies of mobility, especially when writing in German, the majority language.

The earliest discussions of mobility in Switzerland in SwissBib appeared during the sixteenth-century Wars of Religion. Almost all were written in German: French language publications appeared in seventeenth-century SwissBib listings, and Italian-language publications followed in the nineteenth century. Early modern French- and German-language writings in Switzerland documented awareness of emigration as departure from Switzerland, but did not create immigration as a terminology for entry into Switzerland. Before 1789, SwissBib contains dozens of references to German language publications from Zurich about *Auswanderung* (emigration); the authors of these works labelled persons leaving Switzerland not as emigrants (*Auswanderer*), but as travellers, movers or settlers (*Niedergelassen*).[33] French-language publications took up the theme of departure at the time of the French revolution, but focused on *émigrés*. The term *réfugié*, which had been used as a terminology of mobility at least since the Huguenots fled France in the years between 1562 and 1598, did not appear in SwissBib, but is documented for early Swiss publications held in other archives.[34]

The earliest German-language treatments of *Auswanderung* portrayed it as a challenge to state authority. Zurich, for example, issued prohibitions against emigration to Spain, Germany, North America and Carolina in 1652, 1657, 1734, 1739 and 1770. A 1770 publication from Zurich even referred to emigration as an epidemic illness (*Auswanderungs Seuche*).[35] Well before 1800, mobility seemed more problematic to German-speaking than French-speaking Swiss and it was the loss of Swiss population, not the arrival of *émigrés* or *réfugiés* that sparked worried concern.

Rather than analysing immigration, early French- and German-language publications instead focused on foreignness and on foreigners in Switzerland. German-language publications described the arrival of foreign trade goods, foreign plants, foreign animals, and foreign persons, but rarely did they specifically identify the *Fremder* (the foreigner) as an historical subject or identify any person as an *Auslaender* (the most frequently used German term today for foreigner). German-language entries in SwissBib most often assessed foreignness negatively. Foreign settlement in Switzerland was termed *Annahme* (hiring) rather than *Einwanderung* (immigration); reports focused on foreign military recruits, foreign Catholics, foreign women and foreign workers. The city of Zurich even briefly prohibited the renting of rooms to foreign persons in the 1780s and 1790s.[36] Once again, French-language publications struck a different note. They were more likely to focus on the foreigners (*étrangers*) themselves and they also painted more positive portraits of foreigners as friends (*amis-étrangers*), co-religionists, or fellow republicans.[37]

In 1848, when foreigners comprised 6% of its population, Switzerland emerged from a period of civil war in its current confederated form, initiating a century of intensive economic development, industrialisation and nation-building around a new constitution (based on the American one) and direct democracy exercised by citizen voters.[38] By 1910, the proportion of foreigners in Switzerland had reached 15%, slightly surpassing the United States. Between 1848 and 1920, almost no German-, French- or Italian-language works in SwissBib described the entry of more than 500,000 foreign-born persons into Switzerland as immigration. Discussions of *Einwanderung, immigration* and *immigrazione* instead analysed countries in the Americas or France and its colonies. The uses of the terms *immigré, immigrati,* and *immigrante* were both few in number and, again, focused almost exclusively on immigrants in the Americas or in France.

Instead of immigrants, it was foreigners who lived and worked in Switzerland in large numbers in 1910. Most came from nearby Italy, Germany and France. The Swiss rarely wrote of foreigners as a collectivity—as *Fremden, étrangers,* or *stranieri*—but rather, as representatives of particular nationalities; foreigners were Italians, Germans, French, or Austrians. The Swiss also sometimes invented lightly stigmatizing terminologies for foreigners who overwhelmingly spoke the same languages as the native Swiss. For example, Italian workers were called *regnicoli* to highlight their backward status as subjects of monarchy, unlike modern, Italian-speaking Swiss voters.[39]

The Swiss anticipated that foreigners and *émigrés* alike would return to their countries of origin. They provided for naturalisation of foreigners, but after 1870, most foreigners had to submit naturalisation applications for approval by cantonal referenda or popular vote. For the Swiss, as for many other Europeans, nationality emerged from blood ties that could not so easily be altered; the children of foreigners in Switzerland remained foreigners (as they do still today). Like most countries in Europe (and unlike the former settler colonies of the Americas), Switzerland's citizenship was founded on the assumptions of *jus sanguinis*, the 'right of blood' which privileged ethnic belonging.[40] Nevertheless, the Swiss linkage of *jus sanguinis* and citizenship was a distinctive one, for it rooted Swiss citizens to a specific canton and not to the Swiss confederation.

The best evidence that Swiss terminologies of mobility excluded mobile border-crossers from the culturally plural and democratic male Swiss citizenry emerged around 1900 during a widespread and vehement debate about the *Ueberfremdung* ('over-foreignization') of Switzerland.[41] Sometimes also referred to as exploring the *Fremdenfrage* (foreigner question),[42] these debates very much resembled the nativist, xenophobic and racist discussions of immigration occurring in the United States in the same years. In both countries, immigrants or foreigners were imagined as threats to democracy. Switzerland responded by creating demanding new procedures for obtaining short-term work and residence permits and the submission of foreigners to heightened police surveillance. With new procedures in place, the portion of foreign-born residents in Switzerland dwindled to 5% in 1940 (a figure also achieved in the United States through immigration restriction).

Elsewhere in German-speaking Europe, terms such as *Auslaendischearbeitskraefte* (foreign manpower) or, under Fascism, *Fremdarbeiter* (foreign worker), and, in the post-war period, *Gastarbeiter* (guest worker) similarly announced Germany's preference for the temporary employment of foreigners.[43] But the Swiss again made distinctive terminological choices; they drew not on the terminologies of Germany, but on Swiss French-language terms for migrant labourer. The use of temporary, seasonal workers (*travailleur saisonnier*) in construction and agriculture is in evidence in SwissBib from the turn of the century. Beginning in 1931, with a new law on the *Aufenthalt und Niederlassung von Auslaender* (Law on the Residence and Settlement of Foreigners)[44] the Swiss sought to transform foreigners seeking work into *saisonniers* ('seasonals') and *frontalieri* (daily commuters, often from Italy).[45] Ultimately, the Swiss response to over-foreignisation was a system of circulating workers on temporary contracts, with limited rights to settle or unify their families and thus almost no opportunity to begin the decidedly arduous path to naturalisation. Although provisions for settlement and family unification became more generous after the 1960s, debates about over-foreignisation continued, even as the Swiss economy began to draw more professional and highly skilled workers.[46] Naturalisation rates in Switzerland remained predictably lower than in nations of immigrants such as the United States and Canada.[47]

As the proportion of the Swiss population that was foreign-born continued to rise between 1968 and 1987, citizens introduced repeated referenda—some successful, some not—to adjust or limit the employment of foreigners. After that date, however, the terminologies of mobility evoked in Swiss political debates began to shift. Referenda calling for limitations on *Einwanderung* (immigration) first took place in 1988, 1996 and 1997, followed by a proposal to diminish *Zuwanderung* in 2000. In 2014, a successful referendum, passed by a narrow majority, required an end or 'stop' to what was termed a *Masseneinwanderung* (*immigration en masse*, or *immigrazione di massa*)—mass immigration. The success of the 2014 anti-immigration referendum threatened to upend Switzerland's hundreds of bilateral treaties with the European Union, a deeply upsetting possibility for those opposed to the stop. This matter remains unresolved.[48] Scholarly analysis of opinion polls and voting behaviour showed that rural, German-speaking cantons overwhelming desired restriction, whereas French- and Italian-speaking Swiss, along with German-speaking urbanites, were sympathetic to immigration.[49]

If a new Immigration History or immigration historiography is to be created in Switzerland, it will likely be the result of a search for a more useable past by these segments of Swiss society. Still, any positive new national imaginary that could rest on the transformation of foreigners into immigrants and Swiss citizens would require sweeping away not only century-old terminologies of mobility but also the negative associations that the term immigration has acquired through its associations with referenda fuelled by xenophobia and focused on restriction. In the United States, too, immigration had been associated with restriction for much of the nineteenth century before it provided the analytical framing for Immigration History and became the foundation for the imagination of the United States as a nation of immigrants.[50] It is not impossible that Switzerland, too, could move in a new direction. For the study of immigration to flourish more widely in the twenty-first century, however, changes in terminology would have to occur in many countries, and not just in Switzerland.

Conclusion

The prospects for Immigration History and a more expansive twenty-first century mapping of immigration historiographies are decidedly mixed, especially when the cases of Switzerland and the United States are examined within global perspective. Slightly over 3% of the inhabitants of today's world (around 232 million) live outside the countries where they were born, which seems an impressive number until one realises the proportion has scarcely changed since 1960 and may be slightly lower than it was a century ago.[51]

According to United Nations statistics, the largest absolute numbers of migrants—26% of the world's total—live in just three historical nations of immigrants—Canada, the United States and Australia. Another 47 million, or 20% live in the (pre-Brexit) European Union.[52] Despite vehement and often ugly hostility and violence towards immigrants, refugees, asylum seekers and undocumented workers in both groups of countries, Immigration History is likely to survive in the nations of immigrants while historiographies of immigration are likely to continue to expand in Europe. Germany now not only acknowledges its history of recruiting foreign workers but also more often calls today's workers immigrants and has changed its policies to allow for easier naturalisation.[53] In much of Europe, however, *jus sanguinis* and a preference for the terminology of migration—which includes the possibility of foreigners returning to their home countries—rather than immigration will probably limit the number of European countries that appear on any future mapping of immigration historiography.

Although the largest countries of the world—those with populations of over 100 million—each have relatively small proportions of residents born abroad, their absolute numbers (37.6 million, excluding immigrants residing in the United States) constitute an additional 16% of global totals. In this group, again with the United States excluded, only Russia exceeds the worldwide average of 3% foreign born, and in that case, many foreigners enumerated by census-takers are not immigrants at all, but sedentary national minorities transformed juridically by the collapse of the Soviet Union. Many extremely large countries are post-colonial nations where scholarly terminologies of mobility foster scholarship on emigration, refugees, diasporas, displacement, and urbanisation more than on immigration. It is unlikely that Immigration History will become important in twentieth-century China, India, Indonesia, Pakistan, Nigeria, Bangladesh, the Philippines or Ethiopia. Only Mexico and Brazil have seen the recent growth of modest immigration historiographies.

A final grouping includes ten countries with the world's highest proportions of resident foreign-born persons. Together they are home to almost 35 million foreign-born residents, or 15% of global totals. Included in the group are Singapore (43% foreign born) and Hong Kong (39% foreign born). Some scholars categorise these global cities as former British settler colonies, although both today also employ large numbers of foreign domestic servants and service workers on temporary contracts. Both also welcome significant numbers of highly mobile professionals and businesspersons who are understood to be 'expats' rather than immigrants.[54] Jordan (40% foreign born) is another a small country in this group; it is home to exceptionally large populations of refugees, living in refugee camps without access to naturalisation. Singapore has produced an immigration historiography.[55] It is unlikely that Hong Kong or Jordan will follow suit.

The remaining seven countries very much resemble Switzerland. Indeed, Switzerland appears among this grouping, although it has the lowest proportion of foreign-born residents in the group. Ranked well above Switzerland are the United Arab Emirates (83% foreign born), Qatar (74% foreign born), Kuwait (60% foreign born), Bahrain (55% foreign born), Saudi Arabia (31% foreign born). These are all relatively small (with the exception of Saudi Arabia), oil-exporting countries that are heavily dependent on foreigners who work on temporary, short-term labour contracts in domestic service, construction and the oil industry. All are wealthy, all are uninterested in incorporating foreigners as subjects, all operate under the principles of *jus sanguinis*, and all sharply limit opportunities for naturalisation. It is extremely unlikely that these countries will become new centres of either Immigration History or flourishing immigration historiographies in the twenty-first century.

NOTES

1. *The Encyclopedia of Global Human Migrations* (Oxford: Wiley-Blackwell, 2013); Robin Cohen, ed., *The Cambridge Survey of World Migration* (Cambridge: Cambridge University Press, 1995).
2. Andrew Markus and Moshe Semyonov, *Immigration and Nation Building: Australia and Israel Compared* (Cheltenham: Edward Elgar, 2010); Alan Simmons, *Immigration and Canada: Global and Transnational Perspectives* (Toronto: Canadian Scholars Press, 2010).
3. See the first four editions of Stephen Castles and Mark J. Miller, *The Age of Migration: International Population Movements in the Modern World* (Basingstoke: Palgrave Macmillan, 2009).
4. Dirk Hoerder, *Cultures in Contact: World Migrations in the Second Millennium* (Durham: Duke University Press, 2002); Adam McKeown, 'Global Migration: 1846–1940,' *Journal of World History* 15, no. 2 (June 2004): 155–89; and Patrick Manning with Tiffany Trimmer, *Migration in World History*, 2nd ed. (New York: Routledge, 2012).
5. Ernest Renan, 'What is a nation?', Text of a Conference Delivered at the Sorbonne on 11 March 1882, in Ernest Renan, *Qu'est-ce qu'une nation?* (Paris: Presses-Pocket, 1992).
6. As Benedict Anderson argued many years ago, *Imagined Communities: Reflections on the Origin and Spread of Nationalism* (London: Verso, 1983).
7. Aristide R. Zolberg, *Nation by Design: Immigration Policy in the Fashioning of America* (Cambridge, MA: Harvard University Press, 2006).
8. Gabaccia, 'Nations of immigrants: Do words matter?,' *The Pluralist* 5, no. 3 (2010): 5–31.
9. Oscar Handlin, *The Uprooted: The Epic Story of the Great Migrations That Made the American People* (Boston: Little, Brown, 1951), 3.
10. John J. Bukowczyk, 'Oscar Handlin's America,' *Journal of American Ethnic History* 32, no. 3 (Spring 2013): 7–18.
11. Tyler Anbinder, 'Boston's immigrants and the making of American immigration history,' ibid., 19–25; Hasia Diner, 'Oscar Handlin: A Jewish Historian,' ibid., 3–61.
12. Mae Ngai, 'Oscar Handlin and immigration policy reform in the 1950s and 1960s,' ibid., 62–67.
13. Lorrin Thomas, 'Oscar Handlin, *The Newcomers: Negroes and Puerto Ricans in a Changing Metropolis*,' ibid., 46–52, quoted material, 46.
14. Touré Read, 'Oscar Handlin and the problem of ethnic pluralism and African American civil rights,' ibid., 37–45, esp. 40, 44.

15. Nina Glick Schiller and Andreas Wimmer, 'Methodological nationalism and beyond: Nation-state building, migration and the social sciences,' *Global Networks* 2, no. 4 (2002): 301–34.
16. Henry Yu, 'Revising a lost potential of the Chicago School of Sociology? A century of studies of trans-Pacific migrations,' *Journal of Global Migration History* 1–2 (2015): 215–41.
17. Claudia Roelsch, 'The social distance scale, Emory S. Bogardus and Californian Interwar Migration Research Offside the Chicago School,' ibid., 200–14.
18. Dirk Hoerder, 'A genuine respect for the people,' ibid., 136–70.
19. Donna Gabaccia, 'The Minnesota School and immigration history at Midwestern Land Grant Universities, 1890–2005,' ibid., 171–99.
20. Theodore C. Blegen, *Grass Roots History* (Minneapolis: University of Minnesota, 1947).
21. Franz Boas, 'The instability of human types,' *Papers on Interracial Problems Communicated to the First Universal Races Congress Held at the University of London, 26–29 July 1911*, Gustav Spiller, ed. (Boston: Ginn, 1912), 99–103.
22. George M. Stephenson, *A History of American Immigration, 1820–1924* (Boston: Ginn, 1924).
23. Dirk Hoerder and Christiane Harzig, *What Is Migration History?* (Cambridge: Polity Press, 2009), 54–55.
24. Walter Willcox, 'Part I: Proletarian mass migrations, XIXth and XXth centuries,' in *International Migration Statistics*, eds. Walter Willcox and Imre Ferenczi, 2 vol. (New York: National Bureau of Economics Research, 1929).
25. Christopher Lloyd and Jacob Metzer, 'Settler colonization and societies in world history: Patterns and concepts,' in *Settler Economies in World History*, eds. Christopher Lloyd, Jacob Metzer, and Richard Sutch (Leiden: Brill, 2013) include Singapore among the world's settler colonies.
26. Marc Helbling and Nenad Stojanović, 'Switzerland: A nation-state or a multi-national state?,' Special Issue, *Nations and Nationalism* 17, no. 4 (2011): 712–17.
27. Hans-Joachim Hoffman-Nowotny, 'Switzerland: A non-immigration immigration country,' *Cambridge Survey of World Migration*, 302–307.
28. Thus, when writing in English Swiss scholars often adopt American and French terminologies, see Marc Vuilleumier, *Immigrants and Refugees in Switzerland: An Outline History* (Zurich: Pro Helvetia, Arts Council of Switzerland, 1989).
29. Sixty per cent of the Swiss speak German, 20% French and 6.6% Italian.

30. Kris W. Kobach, *The Referendum: Direct Democracy in Switzerland* (Aldershot: Dartmouth Publishing, 1993).
31. Katharine Donato and Donna Gabaccia, *Gender and International Migration: From the Slavery Era to the Global Age* (New York: Russell Sage Foundation Press, 2015), Chapter 5.
32. http://www.swissbib.org/wiki/index.php?title=Welcome. Accessed 30 August 2016.
33. See published works of Johann Jakob Simler (1716–1788), an important collector and scholar in Zurich.
34. See Henri Lancelot-Voisin de La Popelinière, *La vraye et entière histoire des troubles et choses memorables advenue tant en France qu'en Flandres* (Basel: pour Barthélemy Germain, 1579).
35. Hirten-Brief Sr. Hochwurden Herrn Antistes Ulrichs an die Pfarrer auf der Landschaft des Cantons Zurich wegen der Auswanderungs Seuche in Preussich-Pommern, 27 November 1770.
36. *Verordnung wegen Durchfuhrung fremder Recroutes in Ihr Ghaden Landen* (Bern: Hochobrigkeitliche Druckerei, 177); *Verordnung wegen Annahme fremder Weibspersonen in hiesiges Burgerrecht* (Basel: n.p., 1773). *Publication wegen Beherbergung fremder Personen* (Basel: n.p., 1779).
37. 'Lettre écrite de Genève par un citoien à un des ses amis étranger le 22 aout 1735,' Lausanne, chez Zimmerli, 1735.
38. Dominik Hangartner and Jens Hainmueller 'Does direct democracy hurt immigrant minorities? Evidence from naturalization decisions in Switzerland,' forthcoming *American Journal of Political Science*, http://papers.ssrn.com/sol3/papers.cfm?abstract_id=202206. Accessed 24 June 2016.
39. Donna Gabaccia, *Italy's Many Diasporas: Elites, Exiles and Workers of the World* (London: University College of London Press, 1998), 118.
40. James Brown Scott, 'Nationality: Jus Soli or Jus Sanguinis,' *The American Journal of International Law* 24, no. 1 (January 1930): 58–64.
41. Patrick Kury, *Über Fremde reden: Überfremdungsdiskurs und Ausgrenzung in der Schweiz 1900–1945* (Zürich: Chronos Verlag, 2003).
42. Karl-Alfred Schmidt, *Unsere Fremdenfrage* (Zurich: J. Leemann, 1900).
43. Roberto Sala, 'Vom "Fremdarbeiter" zum "Gastarbeiter": die Anwerbung italienischer Arbeitskraefte fuer deutsche Wirtschaft (1938–1973),' *Vierteljahshefte fuer Zeitgeschichte* 55, no. 1 (2007): 93–120.
44. For the text of the law, see https://www.admin.ch/opc/de/classified-compilation/19310017/200501010000/142.20.pdf. Accessed 30 August 2016.
45. English-language scholarship tends to call both groups 'guest workers', see Philip L. Martin and Mark J. Miller, 'Guestworkers: Lessons from Western Europe,' *Industrial and Labor Relations Review* 33, no. 3 (April 1980): 315–35.

46. For current use, see http://saisonniers.enligne-ch.com/index.php?lang=en Accessed 30 August 2016.
47. P. Wanner and E. Piguet, 'The Practice of naturalization in Switzerland: A statistical overview,' *Population* 57, no. 6 (2002): 917–25. Estimated naturalisation rates in Switzerland are about one-third, in the U.S. about half, and in Canada about three-quarters.
48. BV Art. 121 and Art. 121a (neu); UeBest Art. 197 Ziff. 9 (neu), https://www.admin.ch/ch/d/pore/vi/vis413.html. Accessed 31 August 2016; Winnie Agbonlahor, 'EU and Switzerland need to reach agreement "quickly" on Swiss immigration referendum, says president of European Parliament,' *Global Government Forum*, 1 July 2016, http://www.globalgovernmentforum.com/eu-and-switzerland-need-to-reach-agreement-quickly-on-swiss-immigration-referendum-says-president-of-european-parliament/. Accessed 30 August 2016.
49. Pierre Gentile and Maya Jegen 'Paradise news' in Bernd Baumgartl, Adrian Favell and Massimo La Torre, eds., *New Xenophobia in Europe* (London: Kluwer Law International 1995), 354.
50. Gabaccia, 'Nations of immigrants.'
51. Mathias Czaika and Hein de Haas, 'The globalization of migration: Has the world become more migratory?,' *International Migration Review* 48, no. 2 (Summer 2014): 283–323.
52. Data compiled from United Nations Department of Economic and Social Affairs, Population Division, *International Migration 2013*, http://www.un.org/en/development/desa/population/publications/migration/migration-report-2013.shtml. Accessed 31 July 2016.
53. Marc Morjé Howard, 'The causes and consequences of Germany's new Citizenship Law,' *German Politics* 17, no. 1 (2008): 41–62.
54. Mawuna Remarque Koutonin, 'Why are white people expats when the rest of us are immigrants?,' *The Guardian*, 13 March 2015.
55. Sunil S. Amrith, *Crossing the Bay of Bengal: The Furies of Nature and Fates of Migrants* (Cambridge, MA: Harvard University Press, 2013); Kelvin E. Y. Low, *Remembering the Samsui Women: Migration and Social Memory in Singapore and China* (Vancouver: University of British Columbia Press, 2014); and John Solomon, *A Subaltern History of the Indian Diaspora in Singapore: Gradual Disappearance of Untouchability, 1852–1965* (Milton Park: Routledge, 2016). See also the useful volume edited by Derek Heng and Syed Muhd Khairudin Aljunied, *Singapore in Global History* (Amsterdam: Amsterdam University Press, 2011).

FURTHER READING

Alba, R., and V. Nee. *Remaking the American Mainstream: Assimilation and Contemporary Immigration*. Cambridge, MA: Harvard University Press, 2003.

Amrith, S. S. 'Reconstructing the "Plural Society": Asian Migration Between Empire and Nation, 1940–1948.' *Past and Present* 210, no. 6 (2011): 237–57.

Amrith, S. S. *Crossing the Bay of Bengal: The Furies of Nature and Fates of Migrants*. Cambridge, MA: Harvard University Press, 2013.

Anand, D. *Hindu Nationalism in India and the Politics of Fear*. New York: Palgrave Macmillan, 2011.

Anderson, B. *Imagined Communities: Reflections on the Origin and Spread of Nationalism*. Rev. ed. London and New York: Verso, 2006.

Arnold, R. 'The Dynamics and Quality of Trans-Tasman Migration, 1885–1910.' *Australian Economic History Review* 26 (1986): 1–20.

Bade, K. J. *Migration in European History*. Malden and Oxford: Blackwell, 2003.

Bade, K. J., P. C. Emmer, L. Lucassen, and J. Oltmer, eds. *The Encyclopedia of Migration and Minorities in Europe. From the 17th Century to the Present*. New York: Cambridge University Press, 2011.

Ballantyne, T. 'Mobility, Empire, Colonisation.' *History Australia* 11 (2014): 7–37.

Bammer, A., and R.-E. Boetcher Joeres, eds. *The Future of Scholarly Writing: Critical Interventions*. Basingstoke: Palgrave, 2015.

Bashford, A., and J. McAdam. 'The Right to Asylum: Britain's 1905 Aliens Act and the Evolution of Refugee Law.' *Law and History Review* 32, no. 2 (2014): 309–50.

© The Editor(s) (if applicable) and The Author(s) 2019
E. Henrich and J. M. Simpson (eds.),
History, Historians and the Immigration Debate,
https://doi.org/10.1007/978-3-319-97123-0

Berridge, V. 'Public or Policy Understanding of History?' *Social History of Medicine* 16, no. 3 (2003).

Berridge, V., and J. Stewart. 'History: A Social Science Neglected by Other Social Sciences (and Why It Should Not Be).' *Contemporary Social Science: Journal of the Academy of Social Sciences* 7, no. 1 (2012).

Bishop, C. 'Women on the Move: Gender, Money-Making and Mobility in Mid-Nineteenth-Century Australasia.' *History Australia* 11 (2014): 38–59.

Bloch, M. *The Historian's Craft*, trans. Peter Putnam. Manchester: Manchester University Press, 1954.

Burrell, K., and P. Panayi, eds. *Histories and Memories: Migrants and Their History in Britain*. London and New York: Tauris Academic Studies, 2006.

Burton, A. *After the Imperial Turn: Thinking with and Through the Nation*. Durham and London: Duke University Press, 2003.

Byrnes, G. 'Nation and Migration: Postcolonial Perspectives.' *New Zealand Journal of History* 43 (2009): 123–32.

Cahill, D. *Intermarriages in International Contexts. A Study of Filipina Women Married to Australian, Japanese and Swiss Men*. Quezon City: Scalabrini Migration Centre, 1990.

Carmichael, G. A., ed. *Trans-Tasman Migration: Trends, Causes and Consequences*. Canberra: Australian Government Publishing Service, 1993.

Carpenter, L., and L. Fraser, eds. *Rushing for Gold: Life and Commerce on the Goldfields of Australia and New Zealand*. Dunedin: Otago University Press, 2016.

Castles, S., and M. J. Miller. *The Age of Migration: International Population Movements in the Modern World*. 4th ed. Basingstoke: Palgrave, 2009.

Chatterjee, P. *The Nation and Its Fragments: Colonial and Postcolonial Histories*. Princeton: Princeton University Press, 1993.

Chua, B. H. 'Culture, Multiracialism and National Identity in Singapore.' In Kuan-Hsing Chen, ed. *Trajectories: Inter-Asia Cultural Studies*, London: Routledge, 1998.

Cohen, J., M. Howard, and M. C. Nussbaum, eds. *Is Multiculturalism Bad for Women?* Princeton: Princeton University Press, 1999.

Cohen, R., ed. *The Cambridge Survey of World Migration*. Cambridge: Cambridge University Press, 1995.

Connell, J., ed. *The International Migration of Health Workers*. New York and London: Routledge, 2012.

Constable, N. 'Migrant Workers and the Many States of Protest in Hong Kong.' *Critical Asian Studies*, 41, no. 1 (2009): 143–64.

Cox, P. 'The Future Use of History.' *History Workshop Journal* 75, no. 1 (2013).

Cunneen, C., and J. Stubbs. *Gender, 'Race' and International Relations. Violence Against Women in Australia*. Sydney: Institute of Criminology Monograph Series No. 9, University of Sydney, 1997.

Delap, L., S. Szreter, and P. Warde. 'History and Policy: A Decade of Bridge-Building in the United Kingdom.' *Scandia* 80, no.1 (2014).

Donato, K., and D. Gabaccia. *Gender and International Migration: From the Slavery Era to the Global Age.* New York: Russell Sage Foundation Press, 2015.

Drakeman D. *Why We Need the Humanities: Life Science, Law and the Common Good.* Basingstoke and New York: Palgrave Macmillan, 2016.

Fisher, M. H., S. Lahiri, and S. Thandi, eds. *A South Asian History of Britain: Four Centuries of Peoples from the Indian Sub-Continent.* Oxford and Westport, CT: Greenwood World Publishing, 2007.

Foner, N. *From Ellis Island to JFK: New York's Two Great Waves of Immigration.* New Haven: Yale University Press, 2000.

Fraser, L. *Castles of Gold: A History of New Zealand's West Coast Irish.* Dunedin: Otago University Press, 2007.

Fry, J., and H. Glass. *Going Places: Migration, Economics and the Future of New Zealand.* Wellington: Bridget Williams Books, 2016.

Gabaccia, D. R., 'Nations of Immigrants: Do Words Matter?' *The Pluralist* 5, no. 3 (2010).

Gabaccia, D., and F. Ottanelli, eds. *Italian Workers of the World: Labor Migration and the Formation of Multiethnic States.* Urbana and Chicago: University of Illinois Press, 2005.

Galbally, F. *Migrant Services and Programs, Report of the Review of Post-arrival Programs and Services for Migrants.* Canberra: Australian Government Publishing Service, 1978.

Goodman, A. 'Nation of Migrants, Historians of Migration.' *Journal of American Ethnic History* 34, no. 4 (2015): 7–16.

Greeman, G., and N. Mirilovic, eds. *Handbook of Migration and Social Policy.* Cheltenham and Northampton: Edward Elgar, 2016.

Green, A. 'History as Expertise and the Influence of Political Culture on Advice for Policy Since Fulton.' *Contemporary British History* 29, no. 1 (2015).

Green, A. *History, Policy and Public Purpose: Historians and Historical Thinking in Government.* London: Palgrave, 2016.

Green, N. L. 'Americans Abroad and the Uses of Citizenship: Paris, 1914–1940.' *Journal of American Ethnic History* 31 no. 3 (2012): 5–34.

Guan, K. C., D. Heng, and T. T. Yong. *Singapore: A 700 Year History: From Early Emporium to World City.* Singapore: National Archives of Singapore, 2009.

Hamer, P. *Māori in Australia: Ngā Māori i Te Ao Moemoeā.* Wellington: Te Puni Kokiri, 2007.

Hempenstall, P. 'Overcoming Separate Histories: Historians as "Ideas Traders" in a Trans-Tasman World.' *History Australia* 4 (2007): 1–16.

Henrich, E. 'Museums, History and Migration in Australia.' *History Compass* 11, no. 10 (2013): 783–800.

Hing, B. O. *Defining America Through Immigration Policy.* Philadelphia: Temple University Press, 2004.

Hobsbawm, E. *How to Change the World: Tales of Marx and Marxism.* London: Little, Brown, 2011.

Hoerder, D. *Cultures in Contact: World Migrations in the Second Millennium.* Durham: Duke University Press, 2002.

Hoerder, D., and C. Harzig, *What Is Migration History?* Cambridge, UK: Polity Press, 2009.

Hollifield, J. *Immigrants, Markets, and States: The Political Economy of Postwar Europe.* Cambridge, MA: Harvard University Press, 1992.

Holmes, C. *John Bull's Island: Immigration and British Society 1871–1971.* Basingstoke and London: Macmillan Education, 1988.

Holt, E. 'Writing Filipina-Australian Brides: The Discourse on Filipina Brides.' *Philippine Sociological Review* 44, nos. 1–4 (1996): 58–78.

Hsia, H.-C. 'The Making of a Transnational Grassroots Migrant Movement.' *Critical Asian Studies* 41, no. 1 (2009): 113–141.

Hui, W.-T. 'Regionalization, Economic Restructuring and Labour Migration in Singapore.' *International Migration*, 35, no. 1 (1997): 109–130.

Huish, R. *Where No Doctor Has Gone Before: Cuba's Place in the Global Health Landscape.* Waterloo, ON: Wilfred Laurier University Press, 2013.

Kaur, R. 'Distinctive Citizenship: Refugees, Subjects and Post-colonial State in India's Partition.' *Cultural and Social History* 6, no. 4 (2009).

Kivistö, H.-M. 'Asylum as an Individual Right in the 1949 West German *Grundgeset.' Contributions to the History of Concepts* 9, no. 1 (2014): 60–73.

Kleinig, M., and E. Richards, eds. *On the Wing: Mobility Before and After Emigration to Australia: Visible Immigrants: Seven.* Adelaide: Anchor Books, 2012.

Kushner, T. *Remembering Refugees: Then and Now.* Manchester and New York: Manchester University Press, 2006.

Jordanova, L. *History in Practice.* London: Hodder Arnold, 2006.

Lambert, H., F. Messineo, and P. Tiedemann. 'Comparative Perspectives of Constitutional Asylum in France, Italy, and Germany: *Requiescat in Pace?' Refugee Survey Quarterly* 27, no. 3 (2008): 16–32.

Lentin, A., G. Younge, and G. Titley. *The Crises of Multiculturalism: Racism in a Neoliberal Age.* London: Zed Books, 2011.

Levitt, P. *Artifacts and Allegiances: How Museums Put the Nation and the World on Display.* Oakland: University of California Press, 2015.

Lindio-McGovern, L. *Globalization, Labor Export and Resistance: A Study of Filipino Migrant Domestic Workers in Global Cities.* London: Routledge, 2012.

Liu, J. H., and D. J. Hilton. 'How the Past Weighs on the Present: Social Representations of History and Their Role in Identity Politics.' *British Journal of Social Psychology* 44 (2005).

Low, K. E. Y. *Remembering the Samsui Women: Migration and Social Memory in Singapore and China.* Vancouver: University of British Columbia Press, 2014.

Lucassen, J., and L. Lucassen, eds. *Globalising Migration History. The Eurasian Experience (16th–21st Centuries).* Leiden and Boston: Brill, 2014.

Lucassen, J., L. Lucassen, and P. Manning, eds. *Migration History in World History: Multidisciplinary Approaches.* Leiden and Boston: Brill, 2010.

Lucassen, L. *The Immigrant Threat: The Integration of Old and New Migrants in Western Europe Since 1850.* Urbana and Chicago: University of Illinois Press, 2005.

Lyons, M. 'Writing Upwards: How the Weak Wrote to the Powerful.' *Journal of Social History* 49, no. 2 (2015): 317–30.

Macintyre, S., ed. *The Historian's Conscience: Australian Historians on the Ethics of History.* Carlton, VIC: Melbourne University Press, 2004.

Manning, P. with T. Trimmer. *Migration in World History.* 2nd ed. New York: Routledge, 2012.

Markus, A., and M. Semyonov. *Immigration and Nation Building: Australia and Israel Compared.* Cheltenham, UK: Edward Elgar, 2010.

Matthijs, K., K. Neels, C. Timmerman, and J. Haers, eds. *Beyond the Demographic Divide: Population Change in Europe, the Middle-East and North Africa.* Farnham: Ashgate, 2015.

McDowell, L. *Working Lives: Gender, Migration and Employment in Britain 1945–2007.* Chichester: Wiley-Blackwell, 2013.

McKeown, A. 'Global Migration: 1846–1940.' *Journal of World History* 15, no. 2 (June 2004): 155–89.

McKeown, A. *Melancholy Order: Asian Migration and the Globalization of Borders.* New York: Columbia University Press, 2008.

Moch, L. P. *Moving Europeans. Migration in Western Europe Since 1650.* Bloomington: Indiana University Press, 2013.

Mole, N., and C. Meredith. *Asylum and the European Convention on Human Rights.* Strasbourg: Council of Europe Publishing, 2010.

Monnais, L., and D. Wright, eds. *Doctors Beyond Borders: The Transnational Migration of Physicians in the Twentieth Century.* Toronto: University of Toronto Press, 2016.

Neocosmos, M. 'The Politics of Fear and the Fear of Politics: Reflections on Xenophobic Violence in South Africa.' *Journal of Asian and African Studies* 43, no. 6 (2008).

Neumann, K. *Across the Seas: Australia's Response to Refugees: A History.* Collingwood: Black Inc., 2015.

Neumann, K., and G. Tavan, eds. *Does History Matter? Making and Debating Citizenship, Immigration and Refugee Policy in Australia and New Zealand.* Canberra: ANU Press, 2009.

Nicholls, G. *Deported: A History of Forced Departures from Australia.* Sydney: UNSW Press, 2007.

Nicholson, F., and P. Twomey, eds. *Refugee Rights and Realities: Evolving International Concepts and Regimes.* Cambridge: Cambridge University Press, 1999.

Noiriel, G. *The French Melting Pot: Immigration, Citizenship and National Identity.* Minneapolis: University of Minnesota Press, 1996 [1988].

Olusoga, D. *Black and British: A Forgotten History.* London: Macmillan, 2016.

O'Malley, V. *Haerenga: Early Māori Journeys Across the Globe.* Wellington: Bridget Williams Books, 2015.

Ong, A. *Flexible Citizenship: The Cultural Logics of Transnationality.* London: Duke University Press, 1999.

Oswin, N., and B. S. A. Yeoh. 'Introduction: Mobile City Singapore.' *Mobilities* 5, no. 2 (2010): 167–75.

Panayi, P. *An Immigration History of Britain: Multicultural Racism Since 1800.* Harlow: Pearson, 2010.

Peberdy, S. *Selecting Immigrants: National Identity and South Africa's Immigration Policies, 1910–2005.* Johannesburg: Wits University Press, 2009.

Penovic, T., and A. Dastyari. 'Boatloads of Incongruity: The Evolution of Australia's Offshore Processing Regime.' *Australian Journal of Human Rights* 13, no. 1 (2007): 33–62.

Phillips, J., and T. Hearn. *Settlers: New Zealand Immigrants from England, Ireland and Scotland, 1800–1900.* Auckland: Auckland University Press, 2008.

Pickles, K., and C. Coleborne, eds. *New Zealand's Empire.* Manchester: Manchester University Press, 2016.

Pickles, K., L. Fraser, M. Hill, S. Murray, and G. Ryan, eds. *History Making a Difference.* Cambridge: Cambridge Scholars Publishing, 2017.

Piguet, É., A. Pécoud, and P. de Guchteneire, eds. *Migration and Climate Change.* New York: UNESCO and Cambridge University Press, 2011.

Polian, P. *Against Their Will: The History and Geography of Forced Migrations in the USSR.* Budapest: CEU Press, 2004.

Poot, J. 'Trans-Tasman Migration, Transnationalism and Economic Development in Australasia.' *Asian and Pacific Migration Journal* 19 (2010): 319–42.

Robinson, K. 'Of Mail-Order Brides and "Boys' Own" Tales: Representations of Asian-Australian Marriages. *Feminist Review* 52 (1996): 53–68.

Roszak, T., ed. *The Dissenting Academy: Essays Criticizing the Teaching of the Humanities in American Universities.* London: Pelican, 1969.

Saroca, C. 'Filipino Women, Sexual Politics, and the Gendered Discourse of the Mail Order Bride.' *JIGS (Journal of Interdisciplinary Gender Studies)* 2, no. 2 (1997): 89–103.

Saroca, C. 'Filipino Women, Migration, and Violence in Australia: Lived Reality and Media Image.' *Kasarinlan: Philippine Journal of Third World Studies* 1, no. 1 (2006): 75–110.

Sahoo, A. K., and J. G. De Kruijf, eds. *Indian Transnationalism Online: New Perspectives on Diaspora.* Oxon: Routledge, 2016.

Sanborn, J. A. 'Unsettling the Empire: Violent Migrations and Social Disaster in Russia During World War I.' *The Journal of Modern History* 77, no. 2 (2005): 290–324.

Segal, U. A., N. S. Mayadas, and D. Elliot, eds. *Immigration Worldwide: Policies, Practices and Trends.* New York: Oxford University Press, 2009.

Simmons, A. *Immigration and Canada: Global and Transnational Perspectives.* Toronto: Canadian Scholars Press, 2010.

Simpson, J. M. *Migrant Architects of the NHS: South Asian Doctors and the Reinvention of British General Practice (1940s–1980s).* Manchester: Manchester University Press, 2018.

Simpson, J. M. 'Where Are UK Trained Doctors? The Migrant Care Law and Its Implications for the NHS.' *BMJ* 361: k2336 (2018).

Sinclair, K., ed. *Tasman Relations: New Zealand and Australia, 1788–1988.* Auckland: Auckland University Press, 1987.

Solomon, J. *A Subaltern History of the Indian Diaspora in Singapore: Gradual Disappearance of Untouchability, 1852–1965.* Milton Park: Routledge, 2016.

Spickard, P., ed. *Race and Immigration in the United States: New Histories.* New York: Routledge, 2012.

Stearns, P. N. 'History and Policy Analysis: Toward Maturity.' *The Public Historian* 4, no. 3 (1982).

Teng, Y. M., G. Koh, and D. Soon, eds. *Migration and Integration in Singapore, Policies and Practice.* London: Routledge, 2015.

The Future of Multi-Ethnic Britain: Report of the Commission on the Future of Multi-Ethnic Britain (The Parekh Report). London: Profile Books, 2000.

Tigno, J. V., ed. *State, Politics and Nationalism Beyond Borders: Changing Dynamics in Filipino Overseas Migration.* Quezon City: Philippine Social Science Council, 2009.

Tosh, J. *Why History Matters.* Basingstoke: Palgrave Macmillan, 2008.

Tozzi, C. J. *Nationalizing France's Army. Foreign, Black, and Jewish Troops in the French Military, 1715–1831.* Charlottesville and London: University of Virginia Press, 2016.

Vasu, N., Y. S. Yin, and C. W. Ling, eds. *Immigration in Singapore.* Amsterdam: Amsterdam University Press, 2014.

Vertovec, S. *Diversities Old and New: Migration and Socio-Spatial Patterns in New York, Singapore and Johannesburg.* New York: Palgrave Macmillan, 2015.

Vertovec, S., and S. Wessendorf, eds. *The Multicultural Backlash: European Discourses, Policies and Practices.* Abingdon and New York: Routledge, 2010.

Wadsworth, J. *Immigration and the UK Labour Market*. London: LSE, 2015.

Whitaker, B. E. 'Playing the Immigration Card: The Politics of Exclusion in Côte d'Ivoire and Ghana.' *Commonwealth and Comparative Politics* 53, no. 3 (2015).

Wiley-Blackwell. *The Encyclopedia of Global Human Migrations*. Oxford: Wiley-Blackwell, 2013.

Winter, J., and A. Prost. *René Cassin and Human Rights: From the Great War to the Universal Declaration*. Cambridge: Cambridge University Press, 2013.

Yans-McLaughlin, V., ed. *Immigration Reconsidered: History Sociology, and Politics*. Oxford: Oxford University Press 1990.

Zamindar, V. F.-Y. *The Long Partition and the Making of Modern South Asia: Refugees, Boundaries, Histories*. Oxford: Oxford University Press, 2007.

Zhang, H. 'Labor Migration, Gender, and the Rise of Neo-Local Marriages in the Economic Boomtown of Dongguan, South China.' *Journal of Contemporary China* 18, no. 61 (2009): 639–56.

Ziaian, T. *Celebrating Our Success, Responses to Violence Against Non-English Speaking Background Women, The Report of the NESB Women and Violence Project*. South Australia: Women's Health Statewide, 1997.

Zolberg, A. R. *Nation by Design: Immigration Policy in the Fashioning of America*. Cambridge, MA: Harvard University Press, 2006.

INDEX

The letter n beside a page number indicates reference to a note